Living
in the
Tao

The Effortless Path of Self-Discovery

Mantak Chia
and William U. Wei

Destiny Books
Rochester, Vermont • Toronto, Canada

Destiny Books
One Park Street
Rochester, Vermont 05767
www.DestinyBooks.com

Destiny Books is a division of Inner Traditions International

Library of Congress Cataloging-in-Publication Data
Chia, Mantak, 1944–
  Living in the Tao : the effortless path of self-discovery / Mantak Chia and William
U. Wei.
      p. cm.
  Includes index.
  Originally published: Thailand : Universal Healing Tao Publications, 2008.
  ISBN 978-1-59477-294-8 (pbk.)
  1. Taoism. I. Wei, William U. II. Title.
  BL1920.C465 2009
  299.5'14—dc22

                                                              2009030079

Printed and bound in the United States by Lake Book Manufacturing

10 9 8 7 6 5 4 3 2 1

Text design and layout by Priscilla Baker
This book was typeset in Janson, with Futura, Present, and Sho used as display
typefaces

Contents

Putting Living in the Tao into Practice

The practices described in this book have been used successfully for thousands of years by Taoists trained by personal instruction. Readers should not undertake the practice without receiving personal transmission and training from a certified instructor of the Universal Tao, because certain of these practices, if done improperly, may cause injury or result in health problems. This book is intended to supplement individual training by the Universal Healing Tao and to serve as a reference guide for these practices. Anyone who undertakes these practices on the basis of this book alone does so entirely at his or her own risk.

The meditations, practices, and techniques described herein are *not* intended to be used as an alternative or substitute for professional medical treatment and care. If any readers are suffering from illnesses based on mental or emotional disorders, an appropriate professional health care practitioner or therapist should be consulted. Such problems should be corrected before you start training.

Neither the Universal Healing Tao nor its instructors can be responsible for the consequences of any practice or misuse of the information contained in this book. If the reader undertakes any exercise without strictly following the instructions, notes, and warnings, the responsibility must lie solely with the reader.

This book does not attempt to give any medical diagnosis, treatment, prescription, or remedial recommendation in relation to any disease, ailment, suffering, or physical condition whatsoever.

Acknowledgments

The Universal Tao Publications staff involved in the preparation and production of *Living in the Tao: The Effortless Path of Self-Discovery* extend our gratitude to the many generations of Taoist Masters who have passed on their special lineage, in the form of an unbroken oral transmission, over thousands of years. We thank Taoist Master I Yun (Yi Eng) for his openness in transmitting the formulas of Taoist Inner Alchemy.

We offer our eternal gratitude to our parents and teachers for their many gifts to us. Remembering them brings joy and satisfaction to our continued efforts in presenting the Universal Tao system. As always, their contribution has been crucial in presenting the concepts and techniques of the Universal Tao.

We wish to thank the thousands of unknown men and women of the Chinese healing arts who developed many of the methods and ideas presented in this book. We offer our gratitude to Bob Zuraw for sharing his kindness, healing techniques, and Taoist understandings.

We thank the many contributors essential to this book's final form: Juan Li for the use of his beautiful and visionary drawings, illustrating Taoist esoteric practices, the editorial and production staff at Inner Traditions/Destiny Books for their efforts to clarify the text and produce a handsome new edition of the book, and Susannah Noel for her line edit of the new edition.

We wish to thank the following people for their assistance in producing the original and revised editions of this book: Lee Holden for his editorial work and writing contributions, as well as his ideas for the cover; Otto Thamboon for his artisic contributions to the revised edition of this book; our senior instructors, Wilbert Wils and Saumya Wils, for their insightful contributions to the revised edition; and especially Charles Morris for inspiring and reorganizing the book. Without him the book would not have come to be.

A special thanks goes to our Thai production team: Raruen Keawapadung, computer graphics; Saysunee Yongyod, photographer; Udon Jandee, illustrator; and Saniem Chaisarn, production designer.

# Preface

Through the ages, we have been influenced by mythical schools, religions, governments, and now corporations. They have convinced us to give them our time and energy (essence)—for the good of others, but mostly for themselves. They promised they would take care of us or save us. When we gave everything, we had no time or energy left for ourselves, and in the end we had nothing except their promises. Other systems have taught us how to cultivate and grow our energy like a seed into a tree—but after a while, they told us they needed our energy for the good of others, and they convinced us to give them our tree for their own use. Other systems went even further, showing us how to grow flowers from our tree; and after the flowers blossomed, they had us pick them only for their beauty and sell them to others.

But the Tao teaches us not only how to plant (root) and grow our seed (energy or essence) into a tree, but also how to sexually cultivate and flower the seed to bear fruit, without losing our essence (original seed). Our tree (cultivated energy) will bear fruit by the hundreds, so we have an abundance to share with others who are sincere and deserving. Now think: in each piece of fruit that we bear, how many seeds are in it to share? So, if we cultivate our original seed in the Tao, instead of giving it away as other systems advise, we can share thousands of seeds for the good of others, and never lose our original seed (essence). In this book you will discover the way of the Tao and how to implement it in your life as you put up your feet and enjoy the ride. Remember there are no original thoughts in the universe—they are either used or misused—and whatever you are seeking in life, it is seeking you. So sit still, and when it comes, join and flow with it.

Your friend in the Tao,

William U. Wei,

Wei Tzu—The Professor—Master of Nothingness,

the Myth That Takes the Mystery out of Mysticism

Vision from Within

FEEL WITH THE MIND

When you look within, you begin to see what really is; and this is the beginning of your understanding of the Tao. That is the key factor and it takes the mystery out of mysticism.

We typically do not see what really is when we look at the world, because our entire thinking process is reversed from thinking in the Tao. In the West, we learn to think with our minds and feel with our hearts. In the Tao, we learn to think with our hearts and feel with our minds.

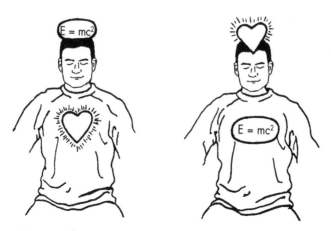

Fig 1.1. Think with your heart and feel with your mind.

In the West, what we are doing is training the mind to think or make decisions. But what we should do is let the mind do its natural function, which is to feel or observe. In the Tao, we are training the mind how to feel and observe. To use an allegory, think of the mind as an observatory tower: it observes what is. That is what the Tao is all about.

We all know what it is to think with our mind; in the West, we are trained to think things out logically. In reality, that is not what the mind is all about. The mind was made to observe. It is like driving a car. Who is driving, you or the car? The car is the mind. The car is an instrument, so the mind is an instrument. It is a tool; it does not have a mind of its own, so to speak. So it has to know where to go. It is a function; it is a retrieving machine or station. In other words, messages are sent to the body or from the body, then to the mind, and then to another part of the body. What the mind does is observe. Another word for observe is to feel or sense. This is the mind's real purpose: to feel or to observe. How it observes is through the five senses. This is the feeling process.

We do not make a judgment on something; we simply witness it.

Fig 1.2. The mind is an observatory tower.

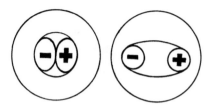

Fig 1.3. The two molecular charges separate as you slow down the mind.

We see it for what it really is and the direction on what to do comes from the heart. To do this, we must learn to think with the heart. To feel with the heart or to think with the heart we have to slow down the mind. The way to slow down the mind is through meditation. When you slow down the mind, you start to separate molecularly the two charges in the universe: the positive and the negative, the electron and the proton; and, as you slow down these two opposite forces, they separate, and as they separate there is a void. The observatory tower (the mind) then enters this void.

It is like driving a car at ninety miles an hour. When you look out the window, what do you see? Not a whole lot. But if you stop the car and start walking, now what do you see? A lot more!

The Taoists call the mind *monkey mind*. The reason they call it the monkey mind is that it always gets into a lot of mischief, because the monkey mind always has to do something. So, how do we slow down this monkey mind? Taoists can learn to observe, using the upper mind to slow down the monkey mind by tricking it. The monkey mind says, "I can do anything," but it is actually our ego saying that. We really cannot destroy the monkey mind because it is us. So what do we do? The Taoists say, "Ah, I have to figure a way to trick the monkey mind." The monkey mind needs to be active; it likes to do something all the time. So, in meditation in the Taoist system, what the Taoists actually do is ask the monkey mind to trace the thirty-two energy channels of the body.

Of course the monkey mind says, "I can do that, no problem," because it is our ego, so the monkey mind reacts to stay active; it is

Fig 1.4. The monkey mind traces the thirty-two energy channels of the body.

reacting to our request to do something because it is being challenged with its ego. It never wants *not* to do something, because that would show that it is inferior; it always wants to show that it is superior, that it can do whatever it is that you requested. This is the process of reacting, instead of thinking, "Do I really want to do this or do I not want to do this?" That is called conscious choice. But, as we go through life, we always think with the monkey mind and we always react; we do things but we never ask ourselves why we should do them, and if we really want to do them. The Taoists understand this, and they say to the monkey mind, "Can you trace the thirty-two energy channels of the body?" Of course the monkey mind says yes, because it wants the challenge, wants to be superior, using the ego. So the monkey mind says, "Okay great, what do I do?" And the Taoists say, "Oh, no problem, just sit still and focus internally. Smile down, look down within yourself, and start to feel the first channel of the body, the Functional Channel (also known as the Conception Vessel), by moving the energy down your body and then feel the energy coming up your spine, the Governor Channel (or Governing Vessel)." So the monkey mind says, "No problem, I can do this. Let's go." So, you close your eyes, and the monkey mind closes the eyes of the body, and it starts to focus within. As you do this, you feel the energy moving down the front of the body and up the spine. This is the Microcosmic Orbit, the two channels of the body. The energy moves in the Belt Channels and the Thrusting Channels, the Bridge and Regulatory Channels. The body starts to open up and you start to focus, using the upper mind to observe instead of think—to sense and feel what you are actually moving in the body.

And of course there is nothing there, because it is just energy. So, what happens when you give the monkey mind an opportunity to try something active, as the Taoists know, is that within the yang or active energy there always will come yin or nonactivity. So within the yang there is yin, and as the monkey mind is doing this activity, all of a sudden it becomes blank, no mind. It loses consciousness. In reality, what happens is that as the monkey mind starts to slow down, it enters the separation into the void; and when it enters into the void, there is nothing and everything goes blank. So for the first time, this monkey mind gets rest and peace as it enters the void into nothingness.

This is how you start to connect with the vision within, or the feeling or sense within yourself, this oneness. And so how do you actually get connected with this? Well, what takes place is that the monkey mind says, "Yes, I can do this," and it starts to focus on these channels in the body. Then after about ten minutes or so, the monkey mind says, "Hey, wait a minute, I think we've done enough of this," because the monkey mind gets bored quickly. So you say, "No problem." You open your eyes and look around and half an hour has passed. So where did the other twenty minutes go? What took place was the monkey mind entered this activity trying to trace this nothingness in the body, the molecular structure slowed down, there was a separation of the positive and negative charges in the molecular structure, and your consciousness or your observation went into this void, the nothingness, the Wu Chi (as the Taoists call it), infinity, God, or whatever you want to term it. It is as if you collected this energy and entered nothingness. As the monkey mind starts to connect with this energy, it enters nothingness, so everything goes blank.

For twenty minutes, everything just went blank. You always know when you have entered this void because there is a stillness within your body. You feel the connection with the oneness of the universe, the connection with the oneness of our infinite being. Now, the monkey mind says, "I do not know what happened, let us do it again sometime." So, you do it again, and as you slowly start to work with this you start to still this upper mind, and as you make stillness with the upper mind, you start to connect with your true consciousness, which is in the heart center. This energy will speak to you, not verbally, but it will express itself in a feeling, and this is how you learn to think with the heart. This gives you direction in your life.

Now, you are probably asking yourself, "Why do we have this monkey mind if it just gets in the way?" The reason is that we have an ego, and that is why we are here on the planet. In other words, we

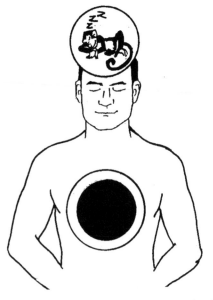

Fig 1.5. There is a stillness within the body.

think we have a better way, swimming against the river. We think we are going to develop our own ability, with a different approach to the universe. So, the Taoists say, you can swim against the river or learn to flow with the river. When you flow with the river, you actually learn how the river flows and then you can connect with the energy. A Taoist learns to flow with the river. You can swim against the river, which will cause you pain and suffering and ultimately death, which is the monkey mind, and that is like most of the egos in the world. They have an idea that they do not have to go down the river in that direction. They are reacting, thinking they can do a better job.

However, in reality, no matter what you do, going with the river or against that river, you have still got to go down that river, because that is the natural flow of the universe. No matter who you are, no matter what you do, you have to go on that river. That is the universal truth. So when you defy the river, you are defying that whole aspect of our existence. That is our ego; that is the separation.

So, why do we have this ego? Well, we have it to learn what to do and what not to do. Once we discover how to flow with the river, we no longer react against the river. So, when you make that positive realization, you start to connect with yourself on a conscious level. Without that, you would not have a conscious recognition of what is really taking place. That is true with animals: they have a consciousness, but they

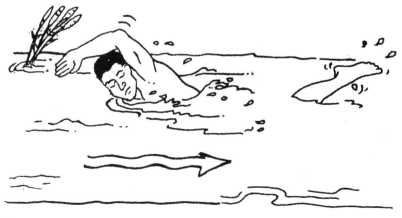

Fig 1.6. You can either swim against the river or learn to flow with the river.

flow with the river, they do not react against the river, and they do not have any free choice. They do not have consciousness of what they are doing, and if you did not have a reaction, you would not have the opportunity to make that conscious action.

THINK WITH THE HEART

As your consciousness or your monkey mind enters the void, it connects with nothingness, which is infinity, which is the Tao, or what the Taoists call the Wu Chi. It then starts to communicate back and forth ever so subtly, and eventually the inner voice will start to direct you. Now, it does not talk to you verbally; rather, it is a feeling that the mind picks up as the inner voice directs you. When you are in a situation where you are asked to make a decision and you have no idea what to do, then all of a sudden you get a feeling: I have got to do it this way. For some reason you are prone to do it this way and it turns out to be right. Then someone asks you why you did it that way, and you just say that it felt right. Well, that feeling is the direction from the inner voice.

You are probably asking yourself, "How can the physical heart actually think?" We go back to Western science and explain how the physical heart does have consciousness. Doctors have actually transplanted one person's heart into somebody else's body. In various situations, the donor's heart has carried over his or her consciousness into the receiver of the heart after the transplant. There are documented cases in which people who have had a heart transplant have picked up energies and situations of the other person. In some criminal cases, a person was killed and his or her heart was transplanted in another person, who then had consciousness of who actually killed the donor. These have been documented.

So the physical heart does have consciousness in that respect. Various religions have talked about the sacred heart or the compassionate heart. The compassionate heart or sacred heart is this consciousness, and when you start to open up the heart, you connect

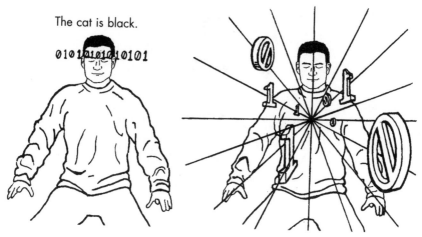

Fig 1.7. The upper mind thinks as you read, which is point to point in a sentence. The middle mind (heart center) is omniscient, thinking in all directions.

with your true self. This inner voice within will start to direct you and actually function as your thinking process. This is universal consciousness or the compassionate heart because you really cannot think with your upper mind.

The upper mind thinks like you read, which is point to point in a sentence. You start the sentence and you finish the sentence with a period. It reads from left to right in English, and right to left in Hebrew. This is how we think and it is called linear thinking. The only problem here is that the universe is not only linear or horizontal but also vertical and omniscient (three-dimensional). So the upper mind can only think of one point at a time, which means it really cannot give you the correct answer because there are too many variables. So, your superior or supreme consciousness in the heart center—which is the all-knowing consciousness of the universe—can think for you. You have got all the different angles to consider, not only horizontally, but all around. So you are going to get the correct answer to your question or situation. All you have to do is learn how to connect or tune in to that compassionate heart, the sacred heart, or that heart center in the universal consciousness.

Fig 1.8. It does not talk to you verbally, but the upper mind,
as an observatory, witnesses a feeling.

In other words, we can learn to think with the heart. Use the upper mind just to observe whatever is going on throughout your whole body, especially in the heart center. This is how you pick up this internal or inner voice. It does not talk to you verbally, but the upper mind, as an observatory, witnesses the feeling. The sensation it gives you then directs you and motivates you to do a certain correct action, as the Taoists refer to it.

Now, it can get a little confusing, because this heart center is also your emotional center. Many people pick up an emotional imbalance in the body and mistake that for their true feeling, true sense, the compassionate heart or consciousness. Basically, the emotions are an imbalance or an expression of one of the individual organs. The heart itself gives you cruelty and hatred and joy and happiness. Those are the emotions, and in the West, the emotions have been separated from the organs. In the Taoist understanding, *emotion* explains an expression of a particular organ. When you have an extreme positive or negative condition, this is what will come as an emotion through the body from the organ.

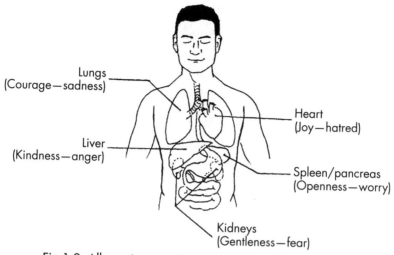

Fig 1.9. All emotions, positive or negative, are expressions of a particular organ.

In the West, the focus is primarily on the emotions, separating them from the organs and the body. In Taoism, a Taoist formula balances the organ, which balances the emotion or the expression of the organ—not too negative or not too positive. For the kidneys, it is fear. The Western expression "I was so afraid I wet my pants" points to the kidneys' feeling of fear and their positive emotion of gentleness. If somebody is afraid, you transform the fear by handling the person gently, as when a child becomes afraid and you treat that child gently, rebalancing the kidney energy.

For the liver, it is anger and aggressiveness, and the positive aspect is kindness, forgiveness, and generosity. So, when somebody is very angry with you, just use kindness, and it completely neutralizes or balances the anger that the other person is sending you or that you have within yourself. With the lungs, it is sadness, depression, and grief, and the positive emotions are courage and righteousness. Again, if people are expressing sadness, they have an imbalanced lung, so use courage to balance that energy, giving some positive energy to the lungs. For the spleen and pancreas, worry and anxiety are the negative emotions, and fairness, openness, and balance are the positive emotions.

These are the five vital organs of the body. The reason they are called vital is that you need all of them to survive. So this helps explain why many times people confuse the inner voice with an emotional imbalance. There is too much emotional energy in one of the organs and it comes through the heart center, but it is not the true feeling or the inner voice speaking out to them. So you have to be very careful. By using the Taoist formulas as a magnifying glass, you begin to focus, having the ability to transform the emotions by balancing the energy in the organs.

Fig 1.10. Using the formulas as a magnifying glass, you begin to focus and transform the organ energy.

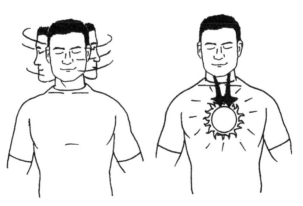

Fig 1.11. Searching outside yourself clogs your ability to focus within and pick up the inner voice or the feeling inside, which you need to do to balance the organs.

You are probably asking yourself, with all the activities in your life, "With emotions and everything else, how can I really pick up this inner voice?" This brings in another aspect you must try to consider, because you have too much attachment and unfulfilled desire. You are searching outside yourself to fulfill these desires or things that you think you need. This clogs your ability to focus within. As you become detached from your desires, they no longer draw out your emotions or create imbalances in the organs, which further clog up the heart center.

THREE MINDS INTO ONE

We have already mentioned the first two minds. The first is the upper mind or monkey mind, which you can transform into the observatory tower. The second mind we talked about is the second brain, which is called the heart center or heart mind, the conscious mind. The first mind is the observing mind; the second mind is your consciousness or your conscious mind. The Taoists also talk about a third mind, which is the lower mind. It is in the abdominal area and it is the awareness mind.

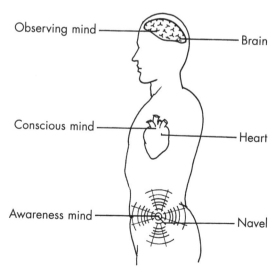

Fig. 1.12. Three minds into one

I think we have a clear idea of what we mean by the first mind, the upper mind, and a clear idea of the middle mind, the conscious mind. But what is the third mind? Again, going back to Western science, it has been proven that the abdominal area has the same nerve endings or nerve connections as the upper mind. The neural transmitters and connections in the lower abdominal area are the same as those in the brain (upper mind). Now, what do we mean by *awareness*? Awareness is expansion, like radar. It expands way out to the universe and picks up different aspects of the universe. We can use an illustration from the first U.S./Iraq war several years ago. The soldiers lived buried in the ground because of the bombing, but they had TV screens with radar. They sent out a signal and they picked up a picture of an aircraft from way out in space and transmitted that picture, the awareness from the radar, onto their TV screens.

The TV screen buried in the desert cave was the actual observer. The conscious mind was the person determining what the picture was explaining. So you have the awareness, which is like sending out radar, way out to the universe. You have your observation of the actual picture on the screen. On your forehead is a picture screen where you can visualize and observe what needs to be observed, like an internal movie picture. The conscious mind, the middle mind, is where we actually do the thinking, which is in the heart center. The Taoists say you have three minds, but we use the three minds at the same time— in other words, three minds into one mind. They call this one mind the Yi (one).

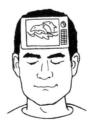

Fig. 1.13. Your forehead is a picture screen where you can visualize and observe what needs to be observed.

The abdominal area, or lower tan tien—the lower mind—is the awareness, what we in the West call our gut feeling. When we are aware of something through this awareness, we start to feel a sensation in the gut or abdominal area, which is the third mind. Interestingly, Western science tells us that if we utilize our upper mind, or monkey mind, we use 80 percent of the energy of the body just in this thinking process. When the monkey mind is activated, the rest of the body uses 20 percent.

We put far too much of our energy in the upper mind, when in reality it does not really think for us anyway. It is really crippling us because we do not have awareness if we do not activate the lower mind and we do not have consciousness if we do not activate the middle mind. So the Taoists explain that we need to activate all three minds at the same time, which forms one big mind, the Yi.

You might now be asking, "I understand what to observe is—just witnessing and feeling and sensing like a TV picture—but what is the difference between the awareness of the lower mind and the consciousness of the middle mind?" Well, as I explained before, the awareness is like radar. You just send your energy field way out from your lower tan tien. You start to pick up radar or sensitivity way out in certain points so the upper mind or observatory mind can pick it up.

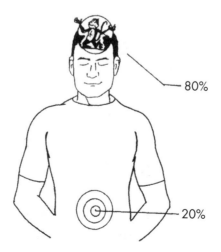

Fig. 1.14. We put far too much of our energy in the upper mind (80 percent).

Fig. 1.15. Three minds into one: observation, consciousness, and awareness

It is a conscious effort on your part to send that focal point out into space, and then you start to pick up whatever is out there. Now, once you pick up the information, you have to understand it, and this is the conscious mind—the middle mind or heart center. That conscious understanding is when you recognize what it is and you can make comparisons and then make a conscious decision, have a conscious thought, or take a conscious direction. This is where the direction and the consciousness are manifested—in the heart center. This is the complete knowing. In other words, it is deductive: you compare your experience with other aspects of knowledge and come out with a conclusion from the source of all knowledge of the Wu Chi, the nothingness.

One is radar and the other is thinking: awareness and consciousness. And you use the third, the upper mind, not as awareness or consciousness, but just to observe, just to witness what is there.

DOWN THE RIVER

The best way to explain natural flow is to consider how a river flows. A river flows in one direction. What we are doing is learning how its current flows. We are learning how to feel that inner current, that inner message. Now, you can either learn to flow with the river like a Taoist or you can swim against the river, which causes pain, hardship, disease, or death. But no matter what you do, you are always going to go down that river. Taoists say that if you are really smart you will put your feet up and enjoy the ride. What you are doing is letting go of your will and turning everything over to God's will, the natural flow of the universe. So the key to life is really just to enjoy the ride. Now how are you going to enjoy the ride going down that river? The Taoists say the key is the middle path. If you are always hitting the right and the left banks, it is a pretty rough ride. You should always try to balance yourself: not too far right and not too far left.

That is the path, the effortless path down the river, and that is how you start to connect with the flow of the universe, centering yourself and then watching the right and the left—never too far right and never too far left. You always keep your eyes open for the big rocks in the river, too. The Taoists have commented that there is only an individual path, and this is the individual path. It is a path and you are alone on it. If you look at the word *alone* and separate the *l* and the *o*, it says "all one." It is just you and your nature or you and the universe. You are all one. You are flowing down the middle path as being one with the universe.

Now, you also have some aids, or what you might call river guides. These are the other Taoists with whom you can connect in the Taoist system; there are over a thousand instructors/practitioners who can help you on your way. As instructors or practitioners, they present these magnifying glasses or formulas to help you focus and transform your energy in the internal alchemy process. These formulas help you follow that middle path. And second, and most important, instructors give you personal feedback based on their experiences. In other words, they have worked with the formulas for years and have experienced certain aspects of how they function in their own lives and they share these with you. They show you how to pick up certain energies that they have experienced and how to find your own internal guide as they have found theirs while going down that river.

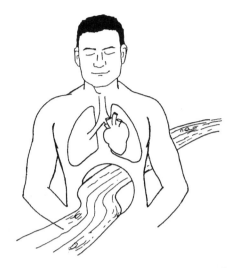

Fig. 1.16. You need to find your own guide and flow.

So in one respect you are alone, all one with the universe; but in another respect, with your river guides, you are not alone. You can connect in workshops, seminars, or just a simple email and ask for some feedback as you start to work with the formulas from the books or take individual instruction or group instruction and get this important feedback on your journey.

So it will help you when you make your own assessments and when you center yourself on that middle path. And this is how you enjoy your ride down the river.

When you get personal feedback from the instructor/practitioner, you get not only some enlightenment or understanding from his or her personal experiences, but also some encouragement. They are saying to you, "Hey, I did this and I had this happen and I did that and that happened, so do not worry about it, it is just part of the whole process." This is really a process, and that is the key.

There is not just one place to go through this spontaneous continuum. You will start working with your energy, working with the continuum, going from one place to the next; it is all a process of becoming. And in truth, there is nothing to become because you are always becoming, so there is not one "becoming." As you start to connect with this energy, you realize that other people have gone through the same process and they will share with you their experiences as they progressed with it, which will give you the incentive and encouragement to proceed with practices such as smiling down five to ten minutes every day. This will help you on your way and will help you find your middle path. You will connect with the true meaning of the Tao and begin to enjoy the ride.

THE NATURE OF THE TAO

God has never been defined as simply as the way the Tao defines it—as nature. Simply put, the Tao is nature or the way or flow of nature. As the tree grows, as the sun glows, as the river flows, as the wind blows, or how a seed becomes a rose, that is the Tao. That is God. That essence, the energy that is flowing, is the will of God, infinity, or whatever you want to call it. That same essence is inside you. Once you learn to connect with the essence inside of you, you learn to connect with the essence outside of you.

When you walk into the forest and sit down on a rock, you always feel an inner peace, an inner warming. What is happening to you? The Taoists explain in the five-element theory that you are connecting with your molecular parents and they are embracing you.

The same energy in the trees is in your liver. The same energy vibration of the heart is in the sun. The same energy vibration in the river is in the kidneys. The same energy vibration in the lungs is in the rock or the metal. The same energy vibration in the spleen and pancreas is in the earth. So that is why you feel at peace, at ease with yourself, because you are connecting with the Tao, because the Tao is connecting with you. Every aspect of nature, the five elements, is inside your body and your energy vibration. When you are born, you take that first breath. As you breathe in, you take in the energy vibration at that time and space in the universe, and in this way you get your internal

Fig. 1.17. As you take your first breath, you breathe in the energy vibration at that time and space in the universe and you receive your internal energy pattern.

energy pattern. So your liver, heart, lungs, spleen/pancreas, and kidneys are in the same energy vibration at that particular time and space as the sun, the earth, the mountains, the rivers, and the trees.

As we connect with the five elements of Earth, we also connect with the five planets. The heart connects with the energy pattern of Mars, our kidneys connect with the energy pattern of Mercury, our lungs connect with the energy pattern of Venus, our liver energy connects with the energy pattern of Jupiter, and our spleen and pancreas connect with the energy pattern of Saturn. We have these five planets connecting within ourselves, and their energy vibrations connect with our organs.

These are the five elements, but within the pakua, the eight-sided geometric vortex, is the Tai Chi symbol (yin and yang), the duality of positive and negative.

Then in the pakua are the five elements interacting in the inner structure of the eight forces. The fire and the water, Kan and Li, are below and above this postheaven pakua. Within the fire and the water, there is the positive (yang), water, and the negative (yin), fire. Then there is the earth energy, Kun, which is negative (yin) earth, and opposite is the mountain energy, Ken, which is positive (yang)

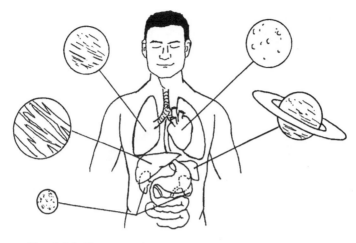

Fig. 1.18. The internal organs connect with the planets.

earth. Then we have thunder energy, Chen, which is positive (yang) wood, then above it the wind energy, Sun, which is negative (yin) wood. Opposite that is the heaven energy, Chien, which is positive (yang) metal, and above that is the lake energy, Tui, which is negative (yin) metal. So we have the five elements within the eight forces: fire, water, earth, mountain, thunder, wind, heaven, and lake.

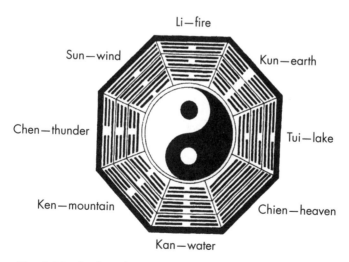

Fig. 1.19. The five elements within the eight forces: Kan, Li, Kun, Tui, Chien, Chen, Sun, and Ken

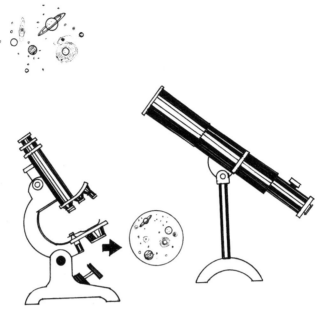

Fig. 1.20. With a telescope focused way out into the universe, you can see energy spheres. When you look through a microscope into the cell, you find the same energy spheres.

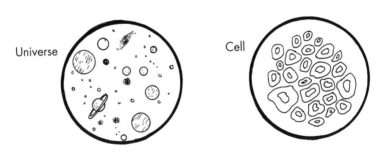

Fig. 1.21. A human cell and the center of the universe (microcosm of the macrocosm)

These are the eight forces within our universe and within our bodies. We are the microcosm of the macrocosm. When you use a telescope to look way out into the universe, you see energy spheres and energy diagrams. When you look through a microscope and see deep in the cell, again you see energy spheres. Amazingly, both pictures look exactly the same. So we are, as proven by Western science, the microcosm of the macrocosm. We are the center, because as we look way out into the universe we see the same energy patterns that we see when we look into our cells within.

Each one of us is the center of our own universe. And once we realize this, then we can find our own internal connection within the nature of the universe. This is the Taoist understanding of self-discovery: that we are the center of the universe, and as we discover ourselves, we will discover the universe.

Now, we know how to connect with the eight forces, the five elements, and the two positives and negatives, Tai Chi (duality). It all started from nothingness, what the Taoists call the Wu Chi. From there came two (yin and yang), then five (elements), and then eight (forces). As you connect in meditation with the practices in the Tao, you connect with the oneness of nothingness, with the Wu Chi and its emptiness. You connect with a moving meditation of Tai Chi Chi Kung, the moving duality of yin and yang; the Hsing I, activating the five elements of the body; and then the Pakua Palm, connecting with the eight forces in the circle movement of the universe.

The Hsing I of five elements is practiced in a straight line (linear), and the Tai Chi (yin and yang) is drawing the energy in and drawing

Fig. 1.22. Tai Chi (yin and yang): drawing the energy in and drawing the energy out as we breathe in and breathe out

the energy out as we breathe in and breathe out. These are the three internal martial arts helping us connect with ourselves by interacting and interconnecting with our whole being and the universe.

This is the Tao. This is Mother Nature. As the tree grows, as the sun glows, as the wind blows, as the river flows, and as the seed becomes the rose, it is the life force that makes these things move, grow, and become. This is what the Tao is: the life force.

LINEAR THINKING (POINT TO POINT)

There is another reason why the mind thinks rather than observes: we think in the same manner as we read. In English, we learn to read from left to right, from point to point. Therefore, we are trained to think from point to point. That is called linear thinking. It is fine, but it is not the universe that we live in. The universe is not only a horizontal reality, which is left and right, but also vertical, which is up and down, and omniscient, which is all around. There is no way for the mind to conceive what the universe is. It is beyond the thinking process of the mind. It is beyond words. It is beyond everything we can utilize with the function of this upper mind. There are too many variables to consider for the upper mind.

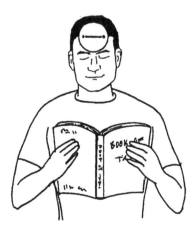

Fig. 1.23. We think from point to point, which is linear thinking.

It is as though we are living in a two-dimensional world but are trying to imagine a three-dimensional reality. This reality is beyond the mind's comprehension. There is no way we can actually think with the upper mind and obtain the correct answers or action in the universe from all directions at the same time.

We cannot make enough evaluations to make the correct conclusion in a situation. The very apparatus we use to try to make sense out of reality, the mind itself, is structurally inadequate. It is because we insist on thinking with our upper mind that we are in such a terrible mess in the West. We are functionally disoriented. That is why the Taoist approach does not use the upper mind for thinking, but uses it just to observe. We have two other minds to utilize: the lower mind, abdominal mind, tan tien mind, or awareness; and our middle brain, heart mind, or consciousness.

That is how we activate the mind—three minds into one. We breathe into the upper mind, and as we exhale we lower all the energy of the upper mind down into the lower mind, the abdominal area. As we breathe in we expand the abdominal area, emptying the upper mind (all thoughts, projections, images, and desires) into the lower mind, and as we exhale we draw that smiling energy up the spine back into the upper mind. As we breathe in and breathe out we activate the upper mind, using it as an observatory tower.

As we expand the abdominal area, we expand the awareness way out to the universe, activating the lower mind. As we breathe in and out, we feel a softening in the heart center, which activates our conscious mind by breathing in and breathing out, smiling in and smiling out, activating three minds into one: observation, consciousness, and awareness. So instead of using one mind incorrectly, we can use three minds and form three minds into one, which is the Yi.

So we are going to change the activity of the upper mind, using it not to think but to observe. We are going to utilize the middle mind of consciousness to think, activating the universal knowledge. Then we are going to utilize the third mind of awareness to become aware of everything we can. As we expand our consciousness way out to the

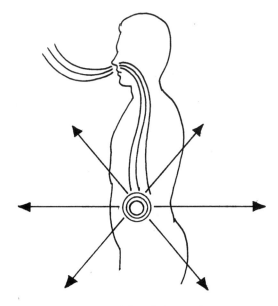

Fig. 1.24. As you expand the abdominal area, you expand
your awareness way out to the universe.

universe and utilize our awareness, the three minds form into one.

When we use the upper mind to think, we are limiting our perspective and scope. As we experience the world with linear thinking, we are living in a two-dimensional world, and it is very hard to explain

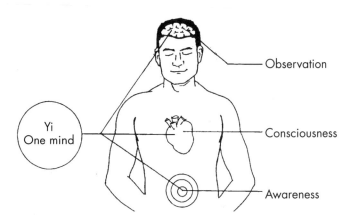

Fig. 1.25. Three minds form into one.

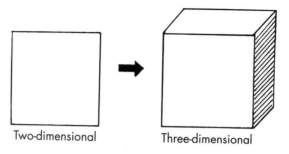

Two-dimensional   Three-dimensional

Fig. 1.26. We think in two-dimensional concepts, but we live in a three-dimensional world.

and understand the world with two-dimensional concepts because we actually live in a three-dimensional world. This creates a lot of havoc, misunderstandings, and misinterpretation.

This limits our scope and understanding of the universe, which is also vertical and omniscient. So when the monkey mind utilizes this, our ego gives the wrong impression and answers. Here is an example of how this works: How much is 150 and 50? Well, a two-dimensional mind would say, with pure logic, 200. But in this case, the answer is not 200; it is 250. Why? Well, you assumed we started with zero.

Fig. 1.27. How much is 150 and 50? A two-dimensional mind would say 200, with pure logic. Wrong. The answer is not 200, but 250. Why? We did not start with zero.

Fig. 1.28. When you assume something, if you separate the second *s* from the *u* and the *u* from the *m*, you make an *ass* out of *you* and *me*.

When you assume something, if you separate the second *s* from the *u* and the *u* from the *m*, you make an *ass* out of *you* and *me* (ass-u-me). So, because we did not start with zero, we started with 50, the answer is 250. If you have a two-dimensional view you cannot see that we do not always start with zero; sometimes we start with 50 or any number depending on the changing circumstances.

That is what happens when we do not have complete vision or complete understanding. When we limit ourselves to thinking with one mind incorrectly, we in fact have three minds to utilize: one to observe, one to be aware, and one to have consciousness. Three minds work as one to feel, think, and perceive. So, why limit ourselves incorrectly when we can expand ourselves, our true reality, utilizing and comprehending the whole universe with three minds? This is what the Taoists do. This is the way of the Tao: three minds into one.

KNOWING WITHOUT KNOWING

The only way we can think logically is with the heart (inner voice), which goes beyond time and space. To think with the heart puts us beyond time and space into true reality.

We tap into the omniscient, which is everywhere. We cannot figure this out with the upper mind. In reality, there is nothing to figure out. That is why the Tao says, "Once you connect with the inner voice, you know without knowing."

It just is. It is a feeling. It is sensing. That is basically how you learn to see in the way of the Tao. To live in the Tao, you must look at things, feel things, see things, or sense things in the Tao with no beginning (past) or ending (future)—just being (present) by living in the now, Living in the Tao.

What you are doing in reality is connecting with universal consciousness; that is really the knowing without knowing. When you connect with universal consciousness, you are drawing in all information from the universe. And believe it or not, this takes us back to Western science, which has proven that everything in the universe, all the knowledge, is in every cell of our body, in our DNA.

So when you start slowing the mind down, you start focusing and connecting with the universal consciousness in your cellular structure. You are actually learning how to tap into the DNA within yourself through meditation. So in reality what you are doing with the formulas is twofold. First, it is a monkey mind exercise that teaches you to still and quiet the mind by an active meditation. Second, the

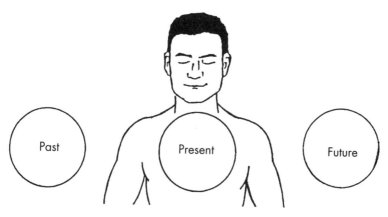

Fig. 1.29. Sense things in the Tao with no beginning (past)
or ending (future); just be (present).

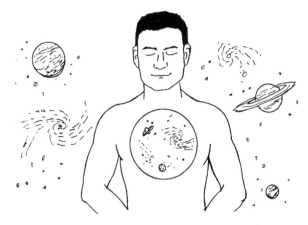

Fig. 1.30. In reality, you are connecting with universal consciousness.

actual step-by-step formula, such as the Inner Smile, activates itself as you enter the cellular structure and tap into its DNA in the internal alchemy process. The mind will become still through excessive activity because it becomes tired.

In internal alchemy, you are changing one substance into another, transforming one aspect of consciousness into another. In other

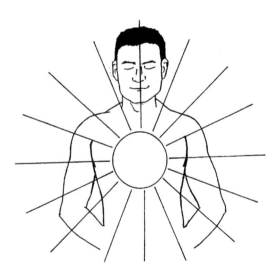

Fig. 1.31. When you connect with universal consciousness, you see things without seeing them and know things without knowing them.

words, you are taking the limited consciousness of individuality and transforming it into universal consciousness by tapping in to each cell internally. So, in essence, you are knowing without knowing. You start to develop an understanding that goes beyond time and space.

Once you feel that feeling, nobody can tell you anything different. This is what takes you into another dimension, into something you have not experienced. What you are actually discovering is everything you have already known but are just not conscious of.

That experience is taking you into this consciousness of understanding. That is the knowing without knowing. When you work with internal energy, you work with infinity, where there is no beginning or end. This is something the monkey mind cannot understand.

Every situation has no beginning and no end, so you go beyond the monkey mind by ignoring the monkey mind, by not giving it energy, either positive or negative. So it goes into a dormant state. It subsides. But the minute you give it energy, a beginning or end, it sticks its head up again. The key is just to live in the present. Just be in the now and the monkey mind remains dormant and asleep.

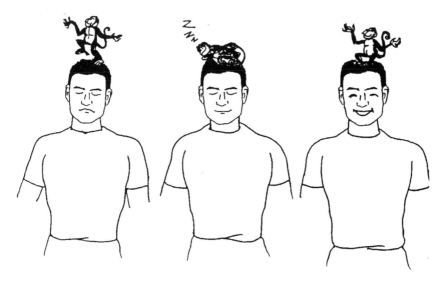

Fig. 1.32. By not giving it energy, either positive or negative,
the monkey mind goes into a dormant state.

MIND OF A CHILD

As Jesus said, "Whoever does not perceive the kingdom of God like a child shall not enter the kingdom of God" (Mark 10:15). You have to have the mind of a child to enter the kingdom of God. Children naturally think with their hearts and feel with their minds. In our Western educational institutions, we have reversed that. What we have to do is re-educate ourselves to what we were before (children) through the Taoist formulas. A mind of a child is open, honest, and sincere.

It is an innocence within ourselves. When you are a child, you are not in control of anything, so you just naturally let go and let it flow. And above all, you have a playfulness and a joy about yourself. You sing to sing—for the joy of it. You dance to dance. You play to play. You do everything for the joy of it.

To enter the kingdom within yourself, you must start to discover the child within yourself again, letting go of all the conditioning of your institutional past such as your formal education or the influence of government programs. You have been programmed by one institution to fulfill further obligations for the next. For example, school trains you to function in the institutional setting of the workplace. To connect with yourself, you must let go of all this conditioning, because you are not really in control; someone or some institution is controlling you and preventing you from thinking independently within yourself.

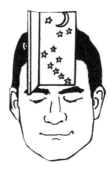

Fig. 1.33. Open mind of a child

Fig. 1.34. To enter the kingdom within yourself, you must start
to discover the child within again.

You have a choice. You can choose not to try to be in control, but to let go and to feel the energy flowing within you. You can connect and flow with it in a joyous, playful manner, like a child that plays all day and connects with the full meaning of everything. You can enjoy the ride and fill your life with joy and playfulness.

We must start trying to regain the trust we had by letting go: letting go of the worry and anxiety that we have about our responsibilities, the doing this and doing that, while in true reality there really is nothing to do.

Taoists always say: We must pay attention. Paying attention will help us on our journey, guiding us down the middle way. It will help us to watch the left and right sides of every situation so we can find the middle path.

You see, the right and left are our greatest teachers. They teach us what not to do. If we go too far right or too far left, we can always find where the middle is, if we know where the right and left are. Totally focus and connect with the middle by watching the right and left.

Fig. 1.35. In reality, there really is nothing to do.

We have to pay attention, and when we let go, we must make sure we have our eyes on the right and left. We can do simple corrective actions—not a lot, just enough to make sure we are in the middle of the flow. This is the key: to pay attention. It takes just a little effort to use that upper mind to observe instead of think.

Observing where the right and left are in our upper mind will

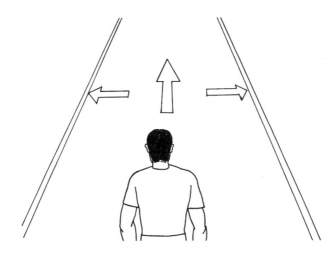

Fig. 1.36. Just watching the left and right sides of every situation helps us find the middle path.

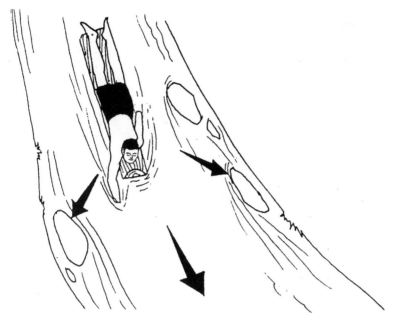

Fig. 1.37. This is the path of the Tao: connecting, paying attention, and letting go.

bring us into the middle. We need to be aware of where the left and right are, just to see where they are. This is the path of the Tao: connecting, paying attention, and letting go.

THE CARROT

When you start to think with your heart and feel with your mind, you live in the now. You observe what is there; you do what is there. An illustration of living in the now is the carrot. It is the difference between the negative, the positive, and what is really there. It is the difference between a pessimist, an optimist, and a realist (Taoist). The pessimist (negative) takes a look at a carrot and sees how narrow it is. The optimist (positive) takes a look at a carrot and sees how long it is. The realist takes a look at a carrot and—"chomp!"—eats it. The realist is the Taoist. The function of a carrot is to be eaten, not for us to see how long it is or how narrow it is. When you are thinking with the mind, you are projecting; you are seeing how narrow or long it is,

Fig. 1.38. Eating the carrot

not observing it for what it really is. When you start to use the mind for what it is intended, then you see things as they really are. You do not make judgments as to how they might be. In the West, we get into trouble because we do not see things for what they really are. We get into trouble when we use our mind not as an observatory tower, but as something to think or project with. To enter the Tao, you become aware and eat the carrot.

When we project, we send out either positive or negative projections, and we are really living in the past or future, not in the present. When we project we are sending out judgments or assessments. In our lives, utilizing the monkey mind is living the half-truth, and we project what we want people to be because we want to control them, try-

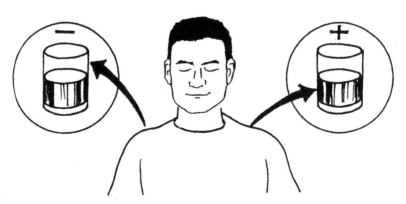

Fig. 1.39. When we project, we are sending out judgments or assessments.

ing to justify our own existence. We project on others what we want to be, either negative or positive, depending on our own circumstances.

The true reality is eating the carrot, because that is what it is for and what it truly is. As we color things good or bad, projecting the positive or negative, we lose perspective of what really is and why it is there and what its function and purpose truly are.

I, William Wei, had an interesting experience in my darkness retreat when there was no visual emotional projection (because everything was in the dark). There was no projection on any person because I could not see anyone. I did not really distinguish their voices as positive or negative; they were just there in the present. There was no visual or real contact with them on which to project anything—how they looked, where they were from, their ethnic group, their culture, their race, nothing. They were just voices in the dark.

Everyone spoke English, so there was no verbal projection, positive or negative. Living in that environment for a period of ten weeks, I connected with myself and lived in a situation with no projections. It was a very free, normal, and easy environment. I know I did not project, and nobody projected on me. It was amazing to live in an environment with no opportunity to project, one that gave a person every opportunity to live in the now, to be at one with him- or herself and everyone else. We recommend that everyone try this and see how projecting distorts the true reality of what really is.

Fig. 1.40. No visuals meant no way to project anything onto others based on how they looked, where they were from, their ethnic group, their culture, or their race.

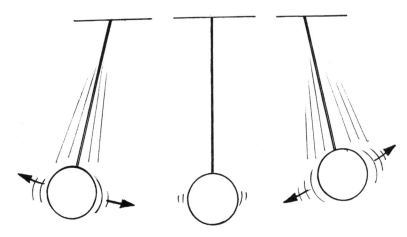

Fig. 1.41. Even if you do find yourself somehow projecting, you do not move as far left or right as you did before because you are closer to the center.

When you do your practices, something interesting happens. The direction you move on your path, with projections on the right and left, is like a pendulum moving from one direction to the other. The farther you go in one direction, the farther you are going to go in the opposite direction. With the practices, you start to project less and less, and soon you do not get too far right or left.

With enough practice, you will have no projections swinging right to left, and you will hit the center, coming out through the center line, the middle point. That is the Wu Chi. Then you move from here to another plane. Before that happens, even if you do find yourself somehow projecting, you do not move as far left or right as you did before because you are closer to the center. With this slow process, you start to connect to the center. You start just by eating the carrot.

TRANSITION INTO THE TAO

The transition in the Tao takes place through the mental, emotional, and physical bodies using concept, desire, and manifestation. It is that simple. Just think and it will be.

How do you make all these changes? How do you center yourself?

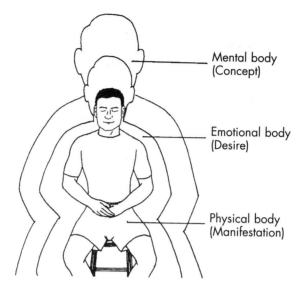

Fig. 1.42. Mental, emotional, and physical bodies using concept, desire, and manifestation

How do you do this? Of course, you are talking with the monkey mind, so just smile down. How does it really work? What is taking place in your body? How does practicing a little bit each day really work with you?

The body is made up of three bodies: the mental, emotional, and physical bodies. A strange structural situation takes place with these three bodies. The mental body controls, manages, or takes charge of the emotional body. The emotional body takes control or manages the physical body, what I like to call concept, desire, and manifestation or result.

In other words, when you start out, you need the concept behind the action because the concept or the mental body controls the emotional body. The emotional body is the desire to make it happen and the physical is the manifestation. Without the concept you will never take control of the emotional body or create the desire to make the results happen. The key is the concept—initially. This activates the emotion, which manifests the result. The mental body controls the emotional

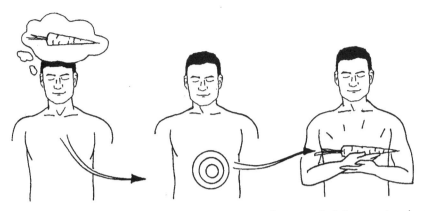

Fig. 1.43. Without the concept, you will never take control of the emotional body or create the desire to make the results happen.

body and the emotional body controls the physical body. In the area of marketing and sales, this has been brought out many times with the acknowledgment of the power of positive thinking. Once you have the concept, you generate a positive thought, which produces another positive thought or result. You have to understand how it works for you to manifest, materialize, or accomplish anything.

As Napoleon Hill once said, "What the mind can conceive and believe, the mind can achieve." The mind is the observatory tower, the conscious mind (the consciousness) and gut feeling (the awareness). When you get the concept, you have the understanding, and then you can create the desire from the concept, giving you the result. Without that pattern or process, nothing will ever be accomplished.

The manifestation can take place almost instantaneously if you are very good at conceptualizing and creating the emotional body or activating the emotional body to give you the results. The more you practice and the more you start to connect with that energy and understanding, the faster the results will be. We do it all the time; we just don't realize it because we aren't aware of what we are doing.

Anything that is made by humans was always a concept first that was then put on a blueprint, went into engineering, and put into manufacturing. All the components to build it were assembled at a factory

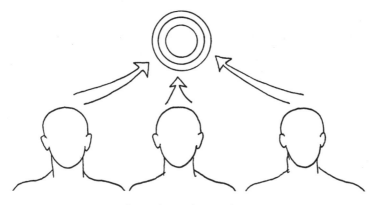

Fig. 1.44. Once you have the understanding, you can create the
desire from the concept, and that will give you the result.

where the product was built. That is how it was manifested. We do the
same thing in our daily lives. Once you have the concept—what you
want, how you are going to get it, and how it works—then it is just a
matter of time before your emotional body will actually manifest it
through your physical body into the physical plane.

This really works a lot in marketing and sales. When you want a
new car, or you want this or that, you put the image out there, and
then through time you will manifest it. It happens all the time but you
are just not conscious of it. When you become conscious of it, it will
happen quicker and quicker and quicker. So the more you practice, the
more it will start to manifest itself. You need the concept to create the

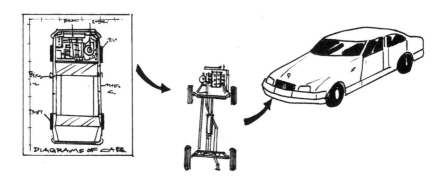

Fig. 1.45. Blueprints, components, assembly, and completion

desire, and that manifests the result. The mental body controls the emotional body, and the emotional body controls the physical body.

I, William Wei, have noted that in my life there are many examples of this taking place. The more I started to connect with it, the more I started to understand it, and the more I started selecting a particular manifestation. When I was in marketing and sales thirty years ago, I wanted to buy a Cadillac for my mother. Part of the promotional incentive for the company I worked for was a Cadillac; we could earn bonuses through sales. I got a picture of this Cadillac that I thought really looked good and put it on my desk. That was my concept. Six months went by and I did not think about the picture on my desk. It was underneath the glass desk mat. I forgot about the Cadillac and got involved in the sales of the company and kept working and working. Then after about six months, I earned enough to get the Cadillac on the sales credit. So I came to buy the Cadillac (again I forgot about that picture) and somehow bought a used Cadillac in the next town. I brought it home and gave a big surprise to my mother and she was overjoyed. Then about two weeks later I went to my desk and looked down and guess what? The Cadillac that I purchased was the one in the picture, underneath my glass mat. It was the same car, same design, and same color. I was flabbergasted.

About thirty years later I bought some land, Wu Chi Acres. It is the most beautiful property I have ever been on. I could not imagine how I had the opportunity to be a part of this land and now actually own it. One day, I brought the first revision of *Living in the Tao* onto the property. I was walking around and I happened to look at the cover of the book. I could not believe it—the actual Wu Chi Acres is on the cover! It was the same design and everything. I had designed its cover about five years before I ever saw the land. I just was not aware, but I *was* aware on one level because my mental, emotional, and physical bodies were working. I actually manifested it through my concept and created the desire to make it happen. This gives you the whole idea of manifestation and how it works. It works all the time. We just need to become aware of it and it will work even better for us.

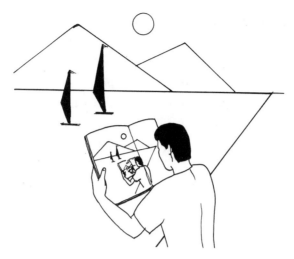

Fig. 1.46. I was walking around the property when I looked at the book cover. The picture on the cover looked the same as the property.

Once you have a concept, you can send that concept out into the universe. The universe, the empty space way, way out, is like a mirror. When you send that concept way, way out into the universe, it mirrors or reflects back to you whatever you want. It is a natural phenomenon. All we need is to practice it enough and we will be

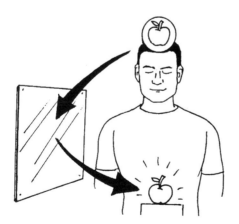

Fig. 1.47. Once you have a concept, you can send that concept out into the universe. The universe is like a mirror. When you send a concept out into the universe, it reflects back to you whatever you want.

able to create something instantaneously in our hands, like an apple or an orange. If we utilize the same amount of energy and focus as we do in many of our mundane activities like sports, business, or human relationships, we can do it. We focus, focus, focus to achieve something when in reality we can use the same mundane activity or discipline and really be able to manifest anything we want in this world just by having the concept, which creates the desire, which results in the manifestation.

This is the key: concept, desire, manifestation. All we have to do is practice. It is happening all the time in our lives, we are just not aware of it. We are just not conscious of it. Once we become conscious of it we can learn how it works and get it to work for us, effortlessly. That is the key. As the ancient Taoists said, "If we are really smart, we put our feet up and enjoy the ride" in the effortless path of the Tao.

Journey into Nothingness

NOTHING IS EVERYTHING

What is "nothingness"? Nothingness is everything. When you are in the middle of nothing you are in the presence of all things. Everything came from nothingness. In Western science, we have a sense of this with the Big Bang theory—that everything came after that explosion. It was actually a reflection. The journey into nothingness is going back to this nothingness. This nothingness is God, infinity. It is beyond words. That is what the Tao is. As Lao-tzu explained, "This Essence is beyond words. Since we do not have any words for it, I will call it the Tao." And that is exactly what he was talking about.

When you use any word to explain the nothingness—God or infinity—you create limitations, and that is why nothingness is beyond all words. When you give the Tao a word, the words limit its actual scope or magnitude. In the Lao-tzu situation, he knew the monkey mind had to give "it" a name, so he just called it the Tao. Getting back to the Big Bang theory, as a concept, this is exactly what took place in the Taoist version of the creation of the universe, with the reflection of a concept into the empty space of the universe, which was the bang.

Fig. 2.1. Everything came from nothingness.

What we did collectively was form one thought or one energy, and, having this conscious thought, we sent it out to the universe, into the nothingness, and it was reflected back like from a mirror. This is the whole manifestation process. This is how we can also manifest everything from nothing because that is how we create everything in the first place. Life is really like one spirit: we form a thought, we send it out into the universe, and like a mirror, it reflects back to us the image of our thoughts into a physical manifestation. It is amazing what we can do once we understand and master it. Think of whatever we desire in life and send it out into the universe, and by projecting it into the empty space, it will come back to us a hundredfold, or exactly as we desire.

We can do a little bit of this each day and, over time, it will manifest itself in the physical plane. It will appear to us; it will happen when we least expect it. Whatever it might be, whatever the thought, configuration, or concept, it will manifest.

The original act of the total creation of the universe we do every day as we create through thought. By thought we can manifest anything we want. When we practice and understand the concept, we

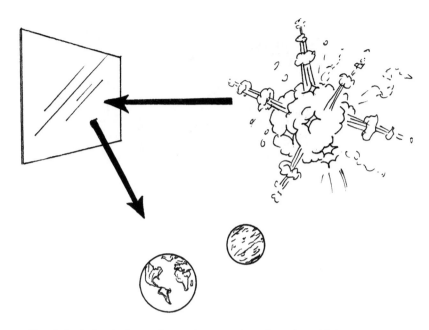

Fig. 2.2. Collectively, we formed a conscious thought, which was sent out into the nothingness and reflected back in the physical form.

create the desire and it manifests. So, with a clear understanding of what we are doing, we can focus more strongly, and as we send our thought out into the universe, it sends it back like a mirror and manifests here in the physical plane. The more we practice, the more we can do it quickly and easily. By focusing on it every day, we will start to be aware of the manifestation. But without focusing, we will never pick up what we manifested. It never appears to be what actually is because we are confused with so many distractions. We either forget to look for it or we lose sight of what it is we want.

It is very important to be careful what you think, because what you think will ultimately be reflected back to you. So choose your thoughts wisely and use very few words for it to be manifested. As you think, so you will become.

This is what happens when people pray. When they pray or petition to God, they send the energy out to the heavens and they expect their prayers to be answered. Sometimes they are, but not for the

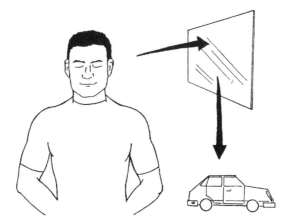

Fig. 2.3. As we send it out, it manifests here in the physical plane.

Fig. 2.4. When people pray, they send the energy out to the heavens.

reason they think. If you have the correct concept, you will be more effective in the manifestation of what you are asking for. That is basically what prayer is all about.

Prayer is asking God for something: virtues, a car, beautiful wife or handsome husband, money, or whatever it is. It is petitioning. In reality, what is taking place is that people are sending out their energy, and if they focus it properly, it is more effective.

From that empty space, everything has come. My mother once told me, "It is a great world if you do not weaken," and I (William Wei) always told her, "It is a great world if you know what you are doing." With this concept, you know exactly what you are doing and you will be more effective in your manifestation or your petitioning. You are God and you just have to utilize that ability within yourself, because you forgot who you are.

That is another interesting aspect of life: people believe that when they send their energy into God, it will happen or manifest— but it is not as effective as they like because they misunderstood the concept. When you put your energy into something, then it happens. If you do not put your energy into it or your understanding,

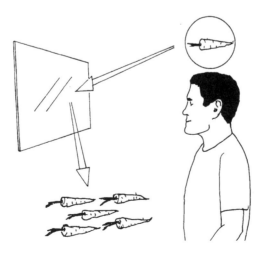

Fig. 2.5. The energy is yours and as you send it out into the nothingness, it will come back manifested and multiplied.

it will not happen. That is why people talk about magic. They feel that the magician will have an advantage over them or lead them to disaster. In reality, if you have no energy to put into it or no belief in it, it has no power at all because the power is yours. As you give power or energy to something, it has life. If you do not give it any power, as in a system or understanding, it has no power over you. It is your energy or power, and that is the key to understanding any system or concept.

So you send the energy out and it comes back to you multiplied—but it is still your energy. It is the same thing with any belief system. If you put your energy into it, then it has validity. If you do not put your energy into it, it has no validity. You are the creator and you are the one manifesting. It is *your* energy.

NOWHERE TO GO

Going back into ourselves is to rediscover what we already know. We are just not conscious of it. So all we are doing is discovering what is already there. There is nowhere to go. There is nowhere to leave. We are here now, but to discover this is a slow process.

Once you discover this nothingness, the journey into nothingness is infinite. Infinity is a continuum. What this means for us is that we are continuously becoming, like climbing a mountain. You get to the top. You look around. There is another mountain. You climb that mountain. You look around. There is another mountain. There will always be another mountain. There will always be something to become. That is the nature of infinity—no beginning and no end. So it is a continuum whichever way you go. You will always become. So, if you are always becoming, there is nowhere to go because you are already there. In a relative sense, if you are always becoming, you are always getting to the top of the mountain. When you get to the top of the mountain, you realize there is always going to be another mountain. So there is nowhere to go.

There is nowhere to go. People get caught up in this rat race,

Fig. 2.6. You get to the top. You look around. There is another mountain.
There will always be another mountain.

this monkey mind environment of ours, and they are always saying, "Oh, I just need to do this and then I will be fine or I will have time to be with my family or be with myself." They are always chasing something like a new job, to earn more money, to accomplish this or do that—but they never really spend time enjoying themselves and doing what really is. They fail to realize that they are always becoming something new.

Since they are always becoming something, they never really go

Fig. 2.7. It never catches up to you because you are chasing it;
so sit still until it catches you.

Fig. 2.8. With this inner peace you will start to become conscious of what you already know.

anywhere, and they never really move anywhere. But their minds put them in the complete rat race. The other aspect is, whatever you want in life, it is chasing you, but you are so busy chasing it, it never catches up to you, because you are chasing it. If you sit still and wait for it, and you do what you have to do to maintain yourself instead of running around chasing everything, the thing you want will catch up to you. When it catches up, you can join and flow with it.

That is the key: the less you do the better, especially with your energy and achieving things, because there really is no place to go. You are already here and everything will come to you. That is the effortless path of the Tao.

As you begin to sit still, you realize or rediscover what you already know, but you are just not conscious of it. As you still the mind, you start to see these things and you discover what it is that you forgot. This is the whole process of rediscovering.

It only happens when you sit still and find yourself at peace. With this inner peace you will start to become conscious of what you already know. That is really why there is nowhere to go and nothing to do. If you sit still, you realize that you are already there with no place to go.

FLOWING WITH THE RIVER

As one of my Taoist masters once told me, "Ah, professor, you need more suffering." In other words, if you are doing something wrong, you are going to create pain and suffering for yourself. In the West, we say, "No pain, no gain"—but there is really no gain in pain.

In the Tao, if there is pain, then you are doing something wrong. Pain is an alarm system in the body. It is telling us we are swimming against the river. When we enter the journey into nothingness, we start to focus on the flow of the river. This journey into nothingness is a slow process. With the Taoist formulas, you learn how to make the discoveries of this journey on your own. You are your best teacher; you are the only one who can feel exactly what is inside you—not me and not any instructor. Only *you* know what it feels like inside you, and from that feeling you will get your direction.

That is why when you teach yourself, you start to become energetically independent and become self-sufficient in every aspect of your life. You will know exactly what to do for you because you have the ability to feel what is inside you and to know what you need. As you start to feel what is going on inside the body, you will start to connect with emotional and mental realms and you will know exactly

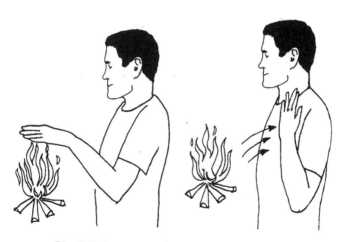

Fig. 2.9. Pain is an alarm system in the body.

Worship

Good works

Wisdom

Fig. 2.10. There are three paths to enlightenment.

what to do, when to do it, and why you are doing it. This is all in the path of the Tao.

The Taoists say that there are three paths to enlightenment. One is of prayer and worship: it can happen but you never know why, when, or how. The second is of good works: it can also happen but you never know why, when, or how. The third is the way of the Tao: this is one of self-discovery. You know exactly why, when, and how, because on the molecular level you are discovering the wisdom and knowledge of you and your universe. It is taking place on a molecular level with an alchemical transformation.

That is why in every stage of life's game—once you learn the formulas and learn how to tune into your own energy and pick up what is going on inside you—you will have all the answers that you need for yourself because you are the only one that can feel inside yourself. This will lead you to your own self-discovery, which is the Tao flowing down the river.

Look at the word *guru* and spell it out: G (gee), U (you), R (are), U (you). You are the guru, because you are the only one that can learn and teach yourself.

Fig. 2.11. The monkey mind can lead you away from yourself and your divinity.

We have mentioned the monkey mind several times. The monkey mind can lead you away from yourself. You are infinite and divine, but you have forgotten who you are, the forgotten God. Your ego (monkey mind) draws you away from yourself because it draws you into the monkey mind system of thinking. It draws you away from your path and your connection with the flow going down the river.

Once you start to work with the monkey mind, you give it things to do within the things it does. That is what is done within the meditations in the Taoist system. You learn to let the monkey mind move, and when it becomes bored, you will enter the void through this process.

Everything slows down once this meditation connects. The ego, the separation from true reality, will start to become tired as you let go of it. You do not give it any positive or negative energy as you let go and it goes into a dormant state. The minute you give the monkey mind or ego some energy (positive or negative—either resisting or going with it), you give it the power to overtake you. The key is not to give it any energy and use the monkey mind, the upper mind, just for its ability to observe, observing what you need to live your life.

The monkey mind gets you into a lot of trouble, so do not give it any energy, positive or negative. Once you understand how the monkey mind works, there is no reason to destroy it. The ego is you, too,

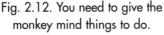
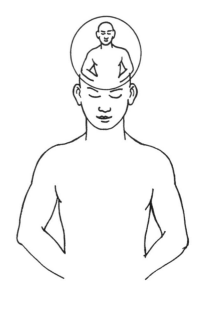

Fig. 2.12. You need to give the
monkey mind things to do.

Fig. 2.13. If you do not give the ego
any energy, then you do not give it
the power to overtake you.

and if you do not give it any energy, positive or negative, you do not
give it the power to overtake you.

Learn to work with the monkey mind, learn to become one with
it and allow it to be and have it in the inactive state. Just use the upper
mind to observe. Use the middle mind to think for you—the conscious mind, the heart center. The lower mind is the awareness center,
sending out radar from the abdomen all over the world and picking up
what you need to pick up.

The key is utilizing the three minds as one—upper mind to
observe, middle mind to think, and lower mind for awareness (the
Crown, Heart, and Tan Tien centers). Smile down and connect all
three into one. Then you can become your own teacher flowing down
that river.

YOU ARE YOUR OWN TEACHER

You are the only person who can feel and understand for yourself. No one can feel for you. And that is the beauty of the Tao. The Taoists emphasize spiritual independence. They say that you are your own guru. You are your own teacher. The formulas can simply give you guidelines. You are the only person who can actually feel what is going on inside you. I cannot. That guy cannot. Only you can discover this. Only you can sense this internal transformation going on inside you. Your journey into nothingness is your own self-discovery of who you really are.

Your uniqueness is very interesting because when you were conceived, it was a one-in-six-trillion chance that you would be you. You are totally unique; there is no one else in the universe with that particular combination.

We have neither friends nor enemies; only teachers. They teach us what we need to learn. It is our own self-discovery within and what we receive is the reflection of what we should learn from others. What is reflected from others are things we should learn about ourselves. We are the only person who can make that discovery within ourselves. Everyone around us and every situation teaches us something new about ourselves.

As the Taoists have always said, "We must pay attention." Watch the right and left sides because the right and left are always moving. To make that journey down the river you need the middle path. You can never find the middle path unless you know where the right and left are. That is why the right and left in extremes are our greatest teachers. They show us where the middle is. They are neither friends nor enemies; they are only our greatest teachers. We know where the middle path is and we know what we need to know about ourselves because we find that out in the reflection from them. The extremes show us what it is we need to know and that is why we are our own teacher.

If you give your energy over to a guru or religion, that is basically what you lose—your own energy. You discover nothing about

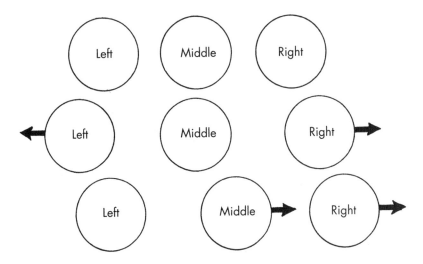

Fig. 2.14. Watch the right and left because the right and left are always moving.

Fig. 2.15. Insights learned from others contribute to your own understandings and your own discoveries.

yourself, even though you may pick up some information. When you transfer your energy and leave it to someone else to save you or take care of you, then it is up to that person to try to use your energy to take care of you. You cannot lose the energy, but you gave away the responsibility for yourself to someone else, and also your freedom.

As the Taoists say, "If you learn to take care of yourself, then there is one less person to take care of." That is how you help everyone else. In the process of learning how to take care of yourself and learning how to take responsibility for yourself, there is no reason to give your energy to anyone else. You learn to become your own internal energy manager. That is how you take control of your life and you maintain your freedom.

You can share ideas and concepts if someone is respectful, earnest, and sincere and is seeking the truth from you—but those are rare occasions. To put yourself in a position where you give your energy over to someone else, either to a teacher, a master, or a guru, you are putting yourself in jeopardy and at the mercy and judgment of others. Your fate will be determined by their limited understanding.

That is not a position to be in and it creates a whole codependent

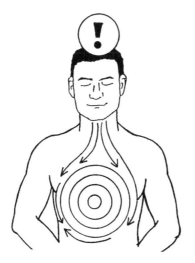

Fig. 2.16. You journey into your own self-discovery as you become your own teacher, guru, and master.

situation for you. You are dependent on others for your own understandings and your own discoveries, and they can never discover what is best for you because they will never be able to feel what is inside you and what you really need. Only you can make that discovery.

Through the Taoist formulas, you start to learn how to make that self-discovery, utilizing the formulas to develop the observation mind, the conscious mind, and the awareness mind, the three minds into one. You journey into your own self-discovery as you become your own teacher, guru, and master. You become your own parent, and who could be a better parent to you than you?

EMPTY VOID

Although the West conditions us to think of nothingness as an empty void, in reality, even contemporary cosmology tells us that nothingness is where everything came from. The Big Bang theory is a Western concept. It did not come from the East. The marriage between the West and the East is slowly coming together. Western science is discovering the reality of the East, which is the Tao.

Living in the Tao is a complete lifestyle. When you begin to look at things with your mind as an observatory tower and your heart as your thinking power, your whole life changes totally. But it happens gradually.

Fig. 2.17. As we start to slow down the mind, we start to enter into that emptiness inside ourselves.

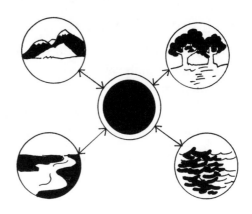

Fig. 2.18. This emptiness that we talk about is the delicate balance between everything in the universe.

Fig. 2.19. Everything came from nothing.

The emptiness is really within us. Everything we think is actually an illusion about ourselves. Western science tells us that if we deflated ourselves, removing all the emptiness, we would be compressed to the size of a grain of sand. As we start to slow the mind down, we start to enter into that emptiness inside ourselves. When we focus within ourselves, we start to discover our own essence, and we link ourselves to the rest of the universe.

This emptiness that we talk about is the delicate balance between everything in the universe. That is exactly where everything came from. The delicate balance in the emptiness became everything that gives us the shape and form of the universe. As we start to connect with ourselves, we start to see the emptiness within us and that balance within our own being.

How do we come into relationship with the rest of the universe? As we enter the void, we start to connect with everything because everything came from nothing. Within the void there is the nothingness. That is our salvation—getting back together within ourselves.

TWO LITTLE PINE TREES

When I (William Wei) was a child, my parents moved into a house with two little pine trees right next to the house. Then I went off to grade school, high school, college, and had several businesses. As I was doing all this, I would visit my parents' home periodically. I kept coming back. Finally, after thirty years, I walked up to my parents' home. I looked at those little pine trees and guess what? Both of those pine trees were bigger than the house. I could not believe it. It was like they just appeared. But they were there all the time. If you looked at them, they were not moving or visibly growing. Over a long period, the whole transformation took place. That is exactly what happens in the Tao. By practicing the formulas over time, the transformation happens in you. It is so subtle that you do not even realize it until you look at it and see those two big pine trees next to that little house.

When you do the practices, your whole life changes as you connect with yourself and make self-discoveries. But it all happens very

Fig. 2.20. Those pine trees were bigger than the house.

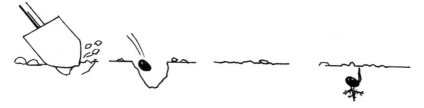

Fig. 2.21. If you plant a tree and you keep digging it up all
the time, it never grows.

subtly. You do not realize what is happening in your life with the changes that take place. Our monkey mind would get in the way if we focused on the changes. It always upsets everything because it has to be active. If you plant a tree and you keep digging it up all the time, it never grows. Nothing is accomplished. The digging up is really the monkey mind's interference with the growth process of that tree, the natural flow of the river.

This change takes place subtly. We are not really aware that it's happening until one day we wake up and look around and see the change, and we cannot believe it. The two pine trees became bigger than the house. But if you look at them, they are not doing anything. They just sit there absorbing the air, mist, and sunshine, growing with the flow of the universe.

That is what takes place in your life as you slow the mind down

Fig. 2.22. This change takes place subtly.

and connect with the inner voice inside yourself. With this empty force or void, you start to develop a communication, and more importantly you start to formulate your consciousness, just like a seed growing inside you. This is the seed of consciousness. And what happens to a seed? It grows into a tree.

When you have any questions about the Tao, just look outside into nature and the answers will come to you, because the answers are in the forest. Everything is revealed in the forest, mountains, rivers, sun, sky, and trees. As you look at the tree, a seed drops down, burrows itself into the ground, and disappears. Nothing looks like it is happening, but everything is happening. It is rooting itself in the soil—and then after six months it breaks the surface of the soil and becomes a little tree. In six months to a year, it becomes a pretty-good-sized tree. In ten to fifteen years, it becomes a big tree; then after thirty, forty, fifty years it is a huge tree; and in seventy to eighty years, it is a gigantic tree. Then a hundred years pass and it is that big oak tree out there. All we see is the big oak tree and we do not see the hundred years.

The same thing is true for us inside because we are growing that seed of consciousness. The same energy that is inside the tree is in us. What would happen if we dig up that tree before it starts to grow? Nothing. It just dies. We just let it be, we just do our practice a little

Fig. 2.23. This is the seed of consciousness growing within.

Fig. 2.24. What happens if you give it too much sun and too much water?

bit each day. A little bit of sunshine, a little bit of water, and before too long it becomes that big oak tree.

What happens if you give it too much sun and too much water? It dies. So just give it a little bit, a little bit of practice each day. That is why we say to make this transformation we just do a little practice each day, five to ten minutes. You are that little tree inside and you do not need that much sunshine or water (i.e., practice) each day.

As you grow that conscious seed inside yourself, a little practice each day, a little sunshine, a little water, you will grow into that big tree. As the seed of consciousness gets bigger inside you, you do a little bit more practice as time goes along. The key is just to do a little bit. In the first five to ten years, this transformation will take place, and you will be like the pine trees, bigger than the house.

A LITTLE SEED

This is how the internal energy works in the body. The internal energy is infinity. That same internal energy in your body is in that tree's body. When an acorn drops off a tree, it hits the ground. After six months or so, it slowly bores its way into the earth and disappears, but as it bores its way into the earth it begins to root itself. It appears

Fig. 2.25. When an acorn drops off a tree, it hits the ground. After six months or so, it slowly bores its way into the earth and disappears, but as it bores its way into the earth it begins to root itself.

as though nothing is happening. But after another six months or a year, it breaks through the earth's surface as a little tree. Two or three years pass, and it is a little bigger. Ten or fifteen years pass, and it is even a little larger. Then twenty or thirty or forty years pass, and it is a big tree. But after a hundred years pass it is that big oak tree standing there.

That is exactly how our internal energy transforms in our body. We are not aware of what is happening. As long as you practice a little bit each day, working with the formulas, giving the tree a little water and sunshine each day, gradually everything in your life will change.

The energy on this planet is here for us to learn to connect with ourselves, and that flow is within us. The same energy is in the river, which is in our kidneys; in the sun, which is in the heart; in the mountain, which is in the lungs; in the earth, which is in the spleen; and in the trees, which is in the liver. The universe is in us. As we learn to connect with that flow, we learn to flow with the universe, internally and externally. But it takes a while to make that connection and that realization, and many of us have been coming back trying to make that discovery. As the Taoists say, "You do not have to come back; you

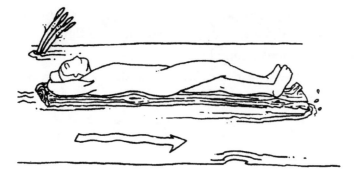

Fig. 2.26. No matter what you do, you will still float down the river.

can learn all your lessons in one lifetime." So, you can learn to flow with that river, flow with yourself, and let go of this monkey mind.

Now, how you let go of it is actually working with it; you do not really give it energy either positive or negative. This is what the Taoists call the Wu Wei. You do not give any positive energy, because it will only trick you, and you do not give any negative energy, because that will give it the energy to overtake you. By letting go, you will connect with the flow of the river. So, what do you do? Really nothing. So that is the Wu Wei, the art of doing nothing, but of accomplishing everything.

Fig. 2.27. The universe is flowing within us.

Because when you are doing nothing, you do not obstruct the flow of the Tao, the flow of that river, and the flow of the universe. So, when the monkey mind sticks its head up, you do not give it any energy, positive or negative. You try to direct it indirectly, and you start to flow with the energy to just observe and try to convince the monkey mind to just watch, listen and observe, sense and feel. The real function of the monkey mind, as we mentioned before, is as an observatory tower.

So, if you do not give it any power, you do not resist it, and then you do not give it the power to overtake you. When you do not give it any power, the monkey mind goes into a dormant state. It becomes inactive, and then you start to connect with the flow of the universe. You discover the less you do in life, the better for you and everyone else. Because you take such an active role using this monkey mind in reacting to situations, you end up swimming against that river and you obstruct the flow of the Tao or the flow of the universe. The minute you give the monkey mind some energy, it goes from a dormant state to an active state. So, in the process of the Tao, you do not destroy the monkey mind. If you destroy the monkey mind, you destroy yourself. So, you cannot destroy it, but you can let go of it, because it is just energy, positive or negative. That is the whole process of the Tao, learning to let go. Letting go of a lot of our conditioning of culture and family. You just let go and you connect with the natural flow of the universe.

If you just let go and connect with the universe, you lose your consciousness, your individual consciousness. You are not losing consciousness, because you were never totally conscious. In other words, if you do not connect with the universe, then you never have your complete consciousness or what we call superior consciousness, superconsciousness, or total consciousness, because you are limiting yourself with your own perspective. So you do not have the rest of the consciousness of the universe. By connecting with the flow, not only do you have your own consciousness, but you also have total consciousness as well.

So you are connected not only with your individual self but also with the whole universe. To do this you must learn to let go. This whole path is what the Taoists call the Wu Wei, the path of nothingness, the art of doing nothing. Doing nothing, you do a little bit of what the Taoists call correct action. In other words, you adjust a certain movement or you observe in a certain way; this is action on your part, and you receive the most for the least effort, or very little action. It is like something's coming at you really fast and all you do is turn your body slightly. You never even move your feet, you just turn the body and bend yourself a little bit, or you turn your ankle and your knee, but you never lose contact with yourself, and the other party misses you. So that is the correct action: you adjust your position or the position of your body.

As you slow the mind, the inner voice will start to direct you with correct action. It will show you what little you should do, or what correct action you should do. This will help you in your life. But this is a slow process, and as your monkey mind has taken over your life for many, many years, it is going to take a while to connect with this energy and this understanding.

The Taoists say, all you have to do is a little bit of practice each day, and as you do a little bit of practice with the meditation and Chi Kung, a conscious transformation takes place and you will start to learn to think with your heart and feel with your mind.

Fig. 2.28. It is like something's coming at you really fast and all you do is turn your body slightly and you avoid it.

Fig. 2.29. Too much water and sunshine will kill the little seed. Just a little practice each day will grow a big tree of consciousness within you.

What happens when you give the little seed too much water and sunshine? It dies. It's the same with your practice: as you grow the seed of consciousness within, if you do too much practice, it will die. The same energy in the tree is inside you. You just need a little bit of practice each day and you will grow into a big tree of consciousness within.

What happens when you keep digging up the tree? It never grows. The same is true with the Taoist practice: if you keep forcing it, it will never grow. Just do a little practice each day and let it grow. This is

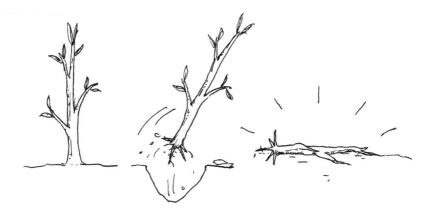

Fig. 2.30. Just like the tree will never grow if you keep digging it up, your consciousness will never grow if you keep forcing it.

Fig. 2.31. As the tree grows bigger, it needs more sunshine and rain, just as your consciousness will need more practice as it grows bigger.

the yin part of the practice, the doing nothing, allowing the energy to grow just like the tree. This is the most important part of the practice—allowing the Tao to grow the energy. The most important part of the practice is to do nothing. And the less you do the better.

One day your consciousness will grow into you and you will become conscious. This is the way of the Tao; this is the effortless path of growing the tree within.

When the seed of consciousness inside grows bigger and stronger, it needs more rain and sunshine (practice) each day to grow just like the tree in the forest. Listen to your consciousness and it will tell you when it needs more practice.

WHAT A LITTLE A LITTLE WILL DO

Just do five to ten minutes of practice each day when you start, and gradually build up as your inner tree gets bigger. It manifests itself externally in a very slow but methodical manner. And that is how you begin your journey into nothingness. As the Taoists say, "It is amazing what a little a little will do." As you enter into nothingness, you

Fig. 2.32. You have to do some correct action, which is called the Wu Wei.

enter into everything. A little of nothing means the presence of all things. As you focus on the nothingness, you become all things.

It is still important to do five to ten minutes of practice a day. Just like that little tree, if you do not give it any water or sunshine, it will die. But you have to do some correct action, which is called the Wu Wei. Correct action is just enough to allow the process to continue; not too much, just a little bit.

As a Taoist, once you start to focus on the Taoist formulas, you

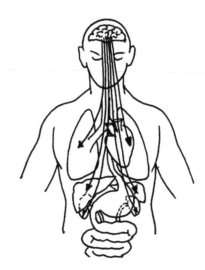

Fig 2.33. You start to concentrate and draw the energy inside and still the mind by drawing and balancing the organ energy.

start to concentrate and draw the energy inside. You start to still the mind by drawing in and balancing the organ and emotional energy, and settling it. Then it does not interfere with your focusing because it is balanced. It is not trapped because the emotions become balanced and then you start to become detached. That is the whole part of letting go—surrendering in Western psychology or forgiveness in Christian philosophy. It is actually being detached.

The Taoists have an interesting concept of how you totally become detached through becoming satiated. How you become satiated is like filling up a cup until you cannot put any more in it and that is when you became satiated. When you become satiated, you become detached from that particular desire or that particular imbalance. It is like when you were a kid and you loved to eat candy. You ate so much candy, and after you ate it and ate it, one day you just could not eat any more. You had had enough. You might have had a little piece occasionally but you never ate it like you did when you were a kid.

It is the same way with all your desires: you need to fill the cup or become satiated. It could be with owning cars, having relationships or sex, having power in business or manipulating people—whatever it is, once you satisfy those desires or become satiated, you do not have to glut yourself or hurt anybody. It is just a matter of drawing in as much as you can until you fill up that cup, and when you fill up that cup and become satiated, then you have entered full detachment.

Fig 2.34. You become satiated, like filling up a cup until you cannot put any more in it.

Instead of resisting these desires, you let them unfold in yourself. Sometimes we tell ourselves, "If I do that I will hurt myself or hurt somebody else." But this overlooks one factor. When you do the practices, a little practice each day will start to balance your energy, by making the monkey mind run through the various energy channels of the body in meditation. Focusing on these areas will start to lessen your attachments and your desires by balancing the imbalances in your body.

As you become balanced, you can start to feel the satiation, and the cup will get filled quicker. Then there will not be as many attachments and the desires will start to fall away more quickly because of your internal practice. You are still becoming satiated, but you are also working indirectly to fill that cup by lessening the desires and lessening the compulsion to satiate yourself. So it is a kind of balance here, it is an interesting process that takes place. All you have to do is smile down, which is the first formula in the Tao. Just five to ten minutes a day. That is all.

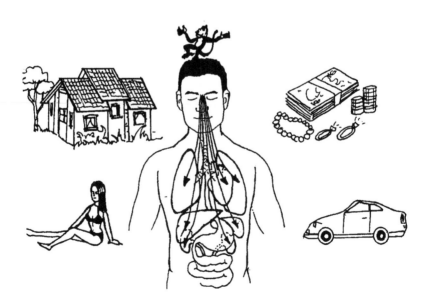

Fig 2.35. Monkey mind runs through the channels and this lessens your attachments.

CONTINUUM

In the Tao, if you became the ultimate, you would be immortal. You would go beyond time and space and beyond reincarnation or karma. There is another immortal and another and another. So it does not really matter where you are. The key is to enjoy the process, to relax and enjoy the ride. You are actually journeying yourself into nowhere. It is a continual process of becoming. You do not have a choice whether or not to climb the mountain. Because you have an essence, you are part of infinity. If you are part of infinity, you are part of the continuum. There is no choice.

The only choice you really have is how you enjoy the ride. You either learn to flow with the river, which can be quite effortless, or you can swim against it, causing suffering.

If you are doing something wrong, you are going to create pain and suffering for yourself. When you are in pain and suffering then you are really doing something wrong and you need to change what you are doing or you will continue to suffer.

To use effort or to be effortless: that is the real choice you have. It is pain or balance and gain or harmony. When you have pain, it is because you are slowly giving back and counterproducing what you really need to achieve.

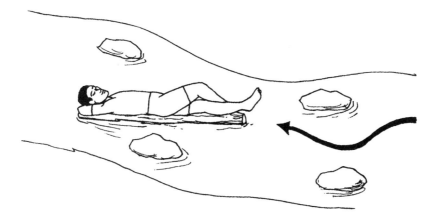

Fig. 2.36. The key is to enjoy the process, to relax and enjoy the ride.

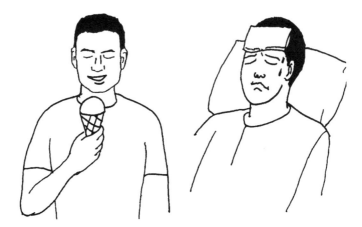

Fig. 2.37. When you are in pain and you are suffering, you are really doing something wrong and you need to change what you are doing.

Life is actually a continuum, even as you go into the next realm. People always think that there is a place to go, heaven or hell—but there is no place. Heaven is really beyond time and space, and if it is beyond time and space then there is no place to go. The only thing that makes any sense is a continuum. You are continually becoming because there is no place to go. There is nowhere to go because you are already there.

Fig. 2.38. Life is a continuum and we are always becoming.

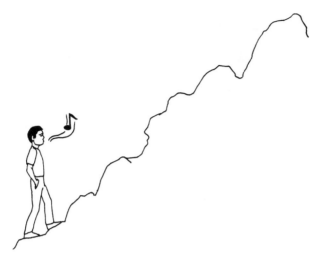

Fig. 2.39. You must learn to enjoy the ride within the
whole evolution of becoming.

You are just working through your own self-discovery, becoming everything you can become. The more you understand that, the more you will start to enjoy the effortless path.

Once you become something, there is something else to become, so the only real enjoyment is in the process of becoming. This is the key: to enjoy the ride of becoming. You are always going to become something. That is what the continuum means: you are continually becoming. You are going from mountain to mountain and always coming to the top and seeing another mountain to climb.

SELF-DISCOVERY

In the Tao, if there is pain, then you are doing something wrong. Pain is an alarm system in the body. It is telling us we are swimming against the river. When we enter the journey into nothingness, we start to focus on the flow of the river. This journey into nothingness is a slow process. With the Taoist formulas, you learn how to make the discoveries of this journey on your own.

This is a process, and once you connect with the process you start

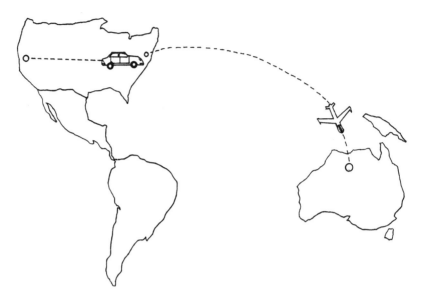

Fig. 2.40. You get into a car and the next thing you know you are on the other side of the country. You get on a plane and the next thing you know you are on the other side of the planet.

to understand that we are being conditioned for instant gratification. You press a button and you get entertainment. You get into a car and the next thing you know you are on the other side of the country. You get on a plane and the next thing you know you are on the other side of the planet.

Everything happens very fast and quickly. When you want music you press another button, or when you want to watch television you just turn it on. You forget the fact that it took fifty years to develop television. You can watch a movie in one and half or two hours and you get the whole life of a person and what transpired in that person's life. It takes many years and we cannot imagine how anybody could live through all of that, but they could not in an hour and a half. It was a whole lifetime, fifty to sixty years in which this life transpired, not half an hour.

The filmmakers take little pieces, but they do not give you the gaps, the emptiness between each piece, which make it whole. It is all

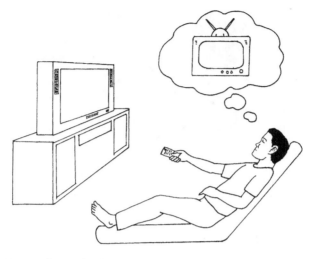

Fig. 2.41. You forget the fact that it took fifty years to develop television.

jammed and condensed together; no one could withstand the pressure of it in real life.

That is a misconception, which is how our monkey mind perceives things. It gives only one perspective and misguides us because it only uses linear or one-dimensional thinking. It does not realize that the events of this life took place over a long period—forty, fifty, sixty years.

This is how our monkey mind deceives us, and the way we think with it. We need to look at things in reality—and the reality is that it is a whole process of becoming. This process is what we should connect with and this is the joy of becoming. We should sing to sing, dance to dance, run to run, read to read, just for the joy of it. That is the key and the Tao.

The whole joy of life is the process of becoming—not the becoming, but the process of it. That is the Tao and that is your key to your own self-discovery. As you discover this, you start to understand your own being and its relationship to the universe.

In the Tao, anytime you have a question, just look outside and all the answers to your questions are in nature. When you look into a

Fig. 2.42. Our monkey mind perceives things using linear thinking, giving us only one dimension of what is happening.

pond and it is perfectly still, you will see a reflection of yourself. And when the pond is disturbed, your reflection will disappear. It is the same in higher-level meditations. When your mind becomes perfectly still through the meditations, you see the light, which is a reflection of yourself. The light, you see, is your true self. You are a light body and that is a reflection of what you see when you still the mind.

This is a part of self-discovery, discovering who you are. You are the light. You are a light body and that light is connected to everything.

This is all a process of self-discovery and it is the discovery of who you are. Once you discover who you are, you will discover where you are going and how you are going to get there. And this is the journey into nothingness.

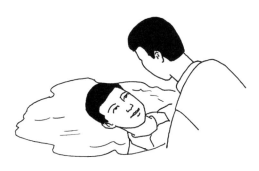

Fig. 2.43. In the reflection of a stilled pond, you see your self, and when you still the mind, you see the light, which is a reflection of your real self.

Fig. 2.44. When you are present, you are there, everywhere, and nowhere.

One of the most important discoveries in this journey is presence. When you are present, you discover who you are. When you are present, you are there, everywhere, and nowhere—all at the same time, in a space with no time. There is no past or future. There is just presence and you are present.

You just need to focus, being totally present in whatever you are doing or not doing. When you are not distracted, you are present, and that presence is the Tao. That is how you become one with your self and the Tao.

The Rock and the Drop of Water

ONE DROP AT A TIME

The "rock and the drop" is about how the mind works and how we change ourselves internally as we live in the Tao. You have a rock and a pitcher of water. You take the pitcher of water and you pour it over the rock and it makes a big splash as all of the water falls on the rock. Nothing happens except the rock is cleaner. You take the same pitcher of water and tip it just a little bit, so that only a drop hits the same spot on the rock—one drop at a time. Before all of the water is out of the pitcher, it will split the rock. The rock is your own self-realization,

Fig. 3.1. Before all of the water is out of the pitcher, it will split the rock.

Fig. 3.2. If you practice really hard, two hours per day for six months, nothing will happen if you stop your practices except a big splash.

Fig. 3.3. After ten years of practice, five to ten minutes each day, your whole life will change because you will split that rock.

your enlightenment. The pitcher of water is your energy. So what you are doing is spaced repetition, a little practice each day—not a lot, but a little. Gradually, over time, as the water falls out drop by drop onto the rock, you will change your whole life.

Let me explain that a little further: when you turn the pitcher of water onto the rock, you just get a big splash. The rock is a little cleaner, but nothing has really changed. It is how you do your practices in the Tao. If you practice really hard, two hours per day for six months, then nothing will happen if you stop your practices, even though you did a lot of practice. We would rather see you working with the Taoist system, doing your practice a little bit each day for ten years, and then everything will change in your life.

In other words, practice five to ten minutes each day. After ten years of practice, five to ten minutes each day, your whole life will change, because you will split that rock. That rock is your own self-realization.

Your realization in the Tao will change your whole life. It will happen with spaced repetition, doing a little practice each day of your Inner Smile, Six Healing Sounds, Chi Self-Massage, Microcosmic

Orbit, Iron Shirt, and Healing Love practices.* Just a little bit each day, and then your whole world will change.

It is a subtle change; you do not even realize it is happening. All you do is just a little bit of practice each day and everything will take care of itself. That is how you circumvent the monkey mind. The monkey mind rules your life, so you approach it indirectly. That is the key. That is how you work with the monkey mind.

As we've said, another example of this is how a tree grows. You take a look at a tree and a seed drops and hits the ground. It takes a long time to burrow into the earth, but it is rooting itself. Then it becomes a little tree as it sprouts from the surface of the soil, and it takes a little bit of sunshine and a little bit of water each day. Pretty soon, over time, it grows up into a big tree, and a bigger tree, and even a huge tree after ten, twenty, thirty, forty, fifty, a hundred years. What happens if you give that little tree, as it starts out, too much sunshine or too much water? It dies. The same thing is true with you, with your internal seed of consciousness. If you give it too much practice, it will die as well. You can only give it a little bit of sunshine and water to nurture it, to make it stronger and bigger.

As your consciousness gets bigger in yourself, then it can take in more sunshine and more water. Then your practices become a little bigger because your body hungers for them and needs to be nourished. The seed you are growing inside yourself needs to be nourished as well—as it gets stronger and bigger like a tree.

It absorbs the rain and the sun as much as it can and becomes bigger and bigger, year after year. It starts out with a little drop, one drop at a time, and as that drop hits the rock, space repetition, a little change happens a little bit each day. That is the key in the

---

*For more information on these practices, please see the following books by Mantak Chia: *The Inner Smile* (Rochester, Vt.: Destiny Books, 2008), *The Six Healing Sounds* (Rochester, Vt.: Destiny Books, 2009), *Chi Self-Massage* (Rochester, Vt.: Destiny Books, 2006), *Taoist Cosmic Healing* (Rochester, Vt.: Destiny Books, 2003), *Iron Shirt Chi Kung* (Rochester, Vt.: Destiny Books, 2006), *Healing Love through the Tao* (Rochester, Vt.: Destiny Books, 2005).

Fig. 3.4. All you do is just a little bit of practice each day and everything will take care of itself. That is how you circumvent the monkey mind.

Tao, just a little bit. As the Taoists say, "It is amazing what a little a little will do."

It starts with your intention, that is the key. Once you have the intention, why you are doing it, what it is about or what you are trying to achieve, then you can make it happen. Just having that intention once a day will help you. By just getting the thought out, it will refocus each day. Just like that tree starting out. It starts with the first bit of sunshine, and the first bit of water; one drop at a time.

Fig. 3.5. Then your practices become a little bigger because your body hungers for them and it needs to be nourished like a tree.

Even if you do not really do the physical practice, just thinking about it a little bit each day will do amazing things. Gradually you will be moved to do a little more each day by smiling down. It only takes a few seconds just to smile down and then start to move the energy in the Microcosmic Orbit, point by point.

You will feel the energy moving up your spine and down the front of the body. Then you stand in the Iron Shirt posture, feeling your roots going into the earth. You will feel the connection within your body. Then you start a little bit of packing, breathing into certain areas in the body, just standing and absorbing the energy. That is the key.

You can do either the Testicle or Ovarian Breathing, standing or sitting during any part of the day. You will just feel the connection of the energy, the cosmic or the orgasmic energy moving up the spine into your brain. You will feel that heavenly bliss. Then you will find yourself doing the Six Healing Sounds, just cooling off the body, one

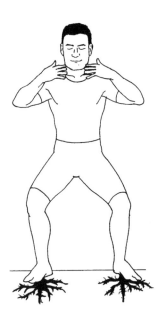

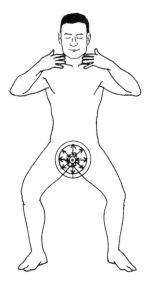

Fig. 3.6. Standing in the Iron Shirt posture, feeling the roots going into the earth, you will feel that connection within your body.

Fig. 3.7. You can do either the Testicle or Ovarian Breathing standing or sitting during any part of the day.

Fig. 3.8. "It is amazing what a little a little will do; just one drop at a time."

or two sounds or all six sounds. You are concentrating on each organ and feeling the energy being released from any pressure. You feel the body cooling down. That is all you have to do for just a little bit each day.

THE MONKEY MIND

In the West, we want everything now. Our mind gets us into a lot of trouble when we start using it to think instead of just observe—in other words, using the monkey mind. The monkey mind gets us into trouble because it always has to be doing something, usually getting us involved with a lot of things we do not need to be involved with, but we do because of our ego.

We cannot destroy the monkey mind because it is us. So what are we going to do with it? There are many different aspects to work with the monkey mind. In this section, we would like to refer to how we are tricking the monkey mind into doing what we want it to do. If we could slow it down somehow by tricking it—by making it do many things because that is what it really likes to do—it would do what we wanted it to do.

It can get us into a lot of monkey business or mischief. So the Taoists said, "Ah, monkey mind, maybe you could try to do a medita-

Fig. 3.9. To satisfy our ego, the monkey mind gets us into a lot of things we do not necessarily need to get involved with.

tion." Instead of doing a meditation and trying to empty the mind like many other systems try to do, the Taoists decided, after many years of trial and error, to have the monkey mind do an active meditation.

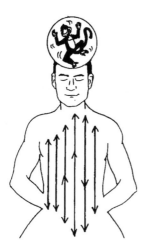

Fig. 3.10. We can slow down the monkey mind by tricking it, by making it do many things. That is what it really likes to do—many things.

Fig. 3.11. The monkey mind would get lost within itself doing all these things.

By getting the monkey mind to do many things at the same time, we cause it to lose itself. In the yang (activity), you will find the yin, the emptiness, the connection to the Wu Chi. This is how the Taoists work with the monkey mind. Slow it down indirectly with activity so it can connect with that energy inside, that void inside, the emptiness.

If you give the monkey mind direction, you will start to learn to think with the heart. It is like driving a car ninety miles per hour; you look outside and what do you see? Not a whole lot. But if you stop the car and start walking, now what do you see? This is what meditation is about. Somehow the Taoists had to work with the monkey mind to slow it down so it could start to observe what was really there instead of racing around, reacting in life and never really accomplishing what you want in your life to fulfill your intention.

The interesting thing about the monkey mind is that it tricks itself—and this is why you fall into this trap all the time. As the Taoists like to explain, "To catch a monkey, just stick a banana in a jar and the monkey will run over and try to get the banana." The monkey mind will do the same thing: it will stick its hand in the jar and grab the banana. It can easily pull its hand out, but it won't because it will not let go of the banana, and it traps itself. The monkey mind or ego would never let go of the banana, even for its own freedom.

Fig. 3.12. As the Taoists like to explain, "To catch a monkey, just stick a banana in a jar and have the monkey run over and try to get the banana."

This is how you trap the monkey mind. You get it into its own activity and it forgets what it is doing or forgets where it is, and finally it forgets what it wants. In that process, you have tricked the monkey mind and it forgets itself. It becomes dormant.

This is exactly what the Taoists do when they do the meditations. What they do is have the monkey mind do what it naturally loves to do: activity. Within that activity, they trap the mind in one area. Gradually, with enough activity, the monkey mind loses consciousness of what it is doing.

This activity is an unconscious act of trying to trace the thirty-two energy channels in the body. The energy channels are not really distinguishable because they do not really exist in the sense of "existence" within the monkey mind. As it starts the pattern, it moves through the existence of the emptiness, and then the energy is dispensed and the monkey mind gets lost in its own activity. That is exactly what happens with the active meditations in the Taoist system.

So through the Taoist practices, this is what you achieve. As you start tracing and opening up the energy channels, the monkey mind gradually loses itself in these channels and enters the void. This is how

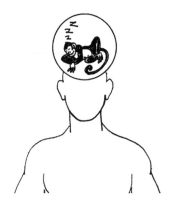

Fig. 3.13. This is how you trap the monkey mind: you get it into its own activity and it forgets what it is doing or forgets where it is and finally forgets what it wants.

Fig. 3.14. So smile down and enjoy the monkey mind and its many activities as it leads you into the Tao.

you make the connection and start to observe the nothingness and start communicating with the void, the Wu Chi.

With this observation and relationship connection, you start to communicate and connect with the inner voice, which will give you direction in your life. Basically, this is how the Taoists work with the monkey mind. So smile down and enjoy the monkey mind and its many activities as it leads you into the Tao.

THE WAY OF THE TAO

To have everything now is not how the universe works, or the way of God, or God's will. The way of God is the way the tree grows, the way the river flows, the way the sun glows, the way the wind blows, and the way the seed becomes a rose.

It is the natural movement of the universe, the harmony of the universe. The Tao is the life force. The Tao is in everything that we touch, see, smell, hear, and taste. The Tao is in the air that we breathe, it is in every breath that gives us life. The Tao is the life force within us and in everything around us. We cannot describe it or define it; we can only experience and feel it. This is the Tao and that is the way that we are studying and practicing it.

The way we are living now in the monkey mind world is reactive, running around like a chicken without its head, not having any idea what we are doing and only responding to commands that are around us. How can we change that movement into a different movement, one that is in the flow of harmony and universal movement, that is, the Tao?

This is the task in front of us. This is why the Taoists use spaced repetition to make this transition, and this is what the drop is all about. This is how the Taoists made the transformation from external expression to internal direction, and made that connection within, which is the life force, the Tao.

The inner direction is definitely different from the external direction. We have been programmed to do this for our survival in our

Fig. 3.15. The way we are living now in the monkey mind world is reactive, running around like a chicken without its head.

society. It happens first through institutionalized education, and then continues in our work and job situation. What we have done with this process is lose the key direction from within, finding that internal bliss and oneness with the universe.

We have lost the understanding and the experience of the joy of life—that is, to laugh and laugh, to dance and dance, doing it for the joy of it. We are starting to go back to that when we practice the Tao.

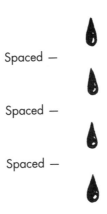

Spaced —

Spaced —

Spaced —

Fig. 3.16. This is why the Taoists used spaced repetition to make this transition and this is what the drop is all about.

In the Inner Smile, we are looking down within ourselves and reconnecting with our organs, feeling the joy, love, and happiness connecting with each vital organ: the heart, the lungs, the liver, the spleen, and the kidneys. We start sending that joy within, generating and developing the relationship with our vital organs and ourselves.

As you start to make these practices meaningful in your life, you will start to experience in your ordinary life a new joy of life, a new joy of being. This rekindles the connection with yourself and everything around you.

Through the Taoist meditations you will develop the unbelievable ability to focus. This is achieved indirectly by the passive but active Taoist meditations. It is like a magnifying glass when you place it under the sun. The magnifying glass does nothing (passive nonactivity) but the sun shines through the glass and its rays focus into a point on the ground or an object. This focusing of rays (fusing) creates heat and then fire, if the object can support a fire. With this fire you can warm yourself or cook your food; and you passively activate the fire by placing the magnifying glass in the proper position (alignment) with the sun. The magnifying glasses that you use are the Taoist formulas that transform one substance into another, which is the inner alchemy

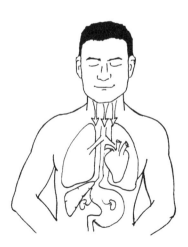

Fig. 3.17. We start sending that joy within, generating and developing the relationship with our vital organs and ourselves.

of the Tao. All you do is learn how to form and position the magnifying glasses in your body, which indirectly gives you the ability to focus, placing drop after drop after drop at the correct spot every time it hits the rock, your objective. This is spaced repetition and the ability to focus utilizing the Taoist formulas.

THE INNER VOICE

The Tao has its own time pattern. In fact, it has no time. It just is. We have created this illusion of time to get things done, or the things "we" want done. In reality, that is not the way things are. That is the way we project them to be. That is why we get into so much mischief. The thing we have to learn is to let go of the mind and let go of these concepts. Allow the mind to slow down, to connect with the inner voice. As we slow it down and connect with the inner voice, we start to connect with this process. You really cannot do it directly. You have to do it indirectly. The Taoists would say, "To resist something is to give it the power to overtake you." The effort you give to the negative energy will be used against you. In the Tao, everything is energy. Whether positive or negative, it is still energy. And being energy, it can start to absorb whatever energy there is—and there is always positive or negative energy.

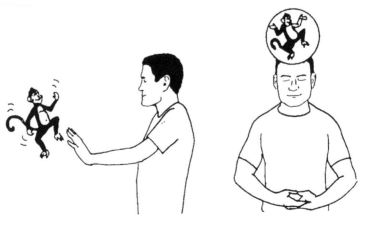

Fig. 3.18. "To resist something is to give it the power to overtake you."

As we slow down the mind, we slow down the molecular structure in the body. Within every molecule, there is a positive and negative charge. When we slow the mind down through this process of meditation, we enter the void between the positive and negative charge consciously, and this is where we connect with the Wu Chi, the void, the nothingness.

This inner voice will speak to us, not verbally, but as a feeling, allowing us to feel it. We will then be able to feel something taking place within ourselves, and it will help us decide what to do. This is how you learn to think with the heart, and you connect with the inner voice. It is a voice that does not verbally talk to you, but expresses itself through a feeling.

Think about when you're in a situation and you have to make a decision one way or the other and you have no idea what to do. All of a sudden you decide to do it a certain way and it turns out to be correct. Later someone asks you why you decided to do it that way and you say, "It just felt right." That "feeling right" is the inner voice communicating with you. You initiated and started to communicate with it with a little practice each day, activating that drop, one drop at a time.

Fig. 3.19. This is how you learn to think with the heart: you connect with the inner voice. It is a voice that does not verbally talk to you, but expresses itself through a feeling.

Spaced repetition will help you develop this relationship between your self and your inner being, the Wu Chi, the emptiness, the nothingness, infinity. Whatever you want to call it, it is your inner voice, and it gives you direction throughout your life, if you can just slow the mind down to pick it up. That monkey mind should be used just to observe. Instead of going ninety miles per hour, you just get out of the car and start walking, start making the inner connection with that inner voice as you slow down the mind. That is the key.

As you make the connection with the inner voice, it will direct you in your life, not verbally, but with a feeling, and that feeling is the way you should go. This is the way to go, being directed by that inner voice. It will take you wherever it is supposed to take you and that is your path and that is the path of the Tao.

You see the monkey mind really cannot direct you in your life because it really thinks in the same way that we read, which is point to point—like a sentence, when you start with the first word and end with a period. That is called linear thinking, which is fine if you are reading, but the universe or the world is not like that because it is not only linear or horizontal, it is also vertical, up and down, and omniscient, in all directions. So the monkey mind can only look at one point; it cannot see all the other variables to make the correct decision in life in any situation. So you must connect with a different mind.

That is the middle mind, the heart or conscious mind. That is the inner voice that gives you direction because this mind thinks in all

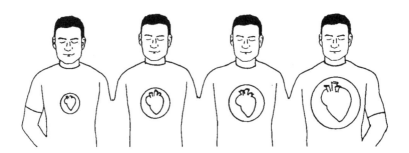

Fig. 3.20. Spaced repetition will develop this relationship with your inner being, the Wu Chi, the emptiness, the nothingness, infinity.

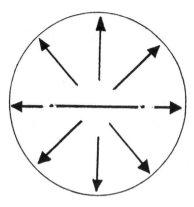

Fig. 3.21. The world is not only linear or horizontal, but also vertical, up and down, and omniscient, in all directions.

directions, horizontal, vertical, and omniscient, from every point. It sees them all at the same time and gives you the correct direction or decision to make. This will happen by practicing a little bit each day. That is why the meditations are so important, one drop at a time.

WU WEI

The ego is another word for the monkey mind. It wants to do things its way. In reality, what it wants is for you not to discover who you really are; because if you do discover who you really are, you are going to let go of the monkey mind. And the monkey mind will no longer have the same existence that it normally has, taking control of you. So, how are you going to confront this? With a little spaced repetition each day, indirectly, just concentrating on your formulas. As this process goes through you start to let go of the monkey mind (or the ego). You cannot resist the ego or you give it the power to overtake you. You cannot go with it because then it will overtake you. So what do you do? You let go. The Tao calls it Wu Wei. You do nothing.

Now people say, "Do nothing?" That's right, you do absolutely nothing—or you do something just a little; you make a small internal adjustment, which is called correct action. That is the Wu Wei. The art of doing nothing allows the universe to work through a situation without you interfering so that it can do its job. It is similar to when you are in a situation where somebody or something is coming really hard at you and you do not want to lose your position so you turn your hips slightly and it misses you.

You have to pay attention to how it is moving and you move just a little bit, but you never lose your feet or root. You just maneuver your body slightly and that is the correct action. You have not moved your position, but you have adjusted your structure so you do not collide with that incoming object. That is the Wu Wei. It is a little bit of action, correct action, but you do not give it any outward action.

The same is done when dealing with the monkey mind: you allow the monkey mind to run its course and you do not give it any positive or negative energy. Then you do not give it the power to overtake you. You just observe and gradually the monkey mind will become the observatory mind and you will start to just observe things. You do not project positive or negative as the monkey mind does. You just observe what is and you do not give it any power, positive or negative.

As you practice the Wu Wei, the art of doing nothing, you allow yourself the time or the stillness for the inner voice to come forth

Fig. 3.22. You have not moved your position, but you have adjusted your structure so you do not collide with that oncoming object.

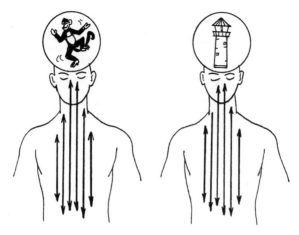

Fig. 3.23. You just observe and gradually the monkey mind will become the observatory mind.

spontaneously to give you your correct direction in life. This is the other aspect of the Wu Wei.

The less you do, the better, which allows time for the Tao to move within you, unobtrusively. The more activity you have, especially

Fig. 3.24. The less you do, the better, which allows time for the Tao to move within you, unobtrusively.

with the monkey mind, the less connected you become with yourself and your inner voice. This is the way of Wu Wei.

This allows you the opportunity to connect with the Tao by doing absolutely nothing. Correct action is paying attention to this inner voice to give you the direction you need to take spontaneously. This is the way of the Tao, spontaneously living and flowing with the universe.

ENTERING THE VOID

In reality, the ego acts just like a parasite. The only power it possesses is the power you give it, either positive or negative. It is just energy, but it is also you. You cannot destroy the ego, because if you destroy it, you destroy yourself. What you have to do is just witness it. See it for what it is and go about your business. Do not give it any energy— positive or negative. That is basically how you overcome your ego.

It takes a long time to slow the mind down and witness the ego when it is trying to manipulate what you are doing. You really cannot attack it directly because your consciousness is part of this ego. You really have to do it all indirectly. That is where the Taoists trick the mind. When you slow the mind down through Taoist meditations, the monkey mind is tricked. You are not giving it any energy so you have to redirect it. We say, "Okay, monkey mind, I will give you something to do. Let us see if you can trace the thirty-two energy channels in the body." And the monkey mind says, "Of course, I can do this, no problem. What should I do?" "Well, let us sit here and close our eyes and mouth. Just sit in silence and start moving the energy internally in the body. See if you can trace this energy." So the monkey mind says, "No problem, I can do this." After ten minutes the monkey mind says, "This is great, but I am kind of bored now." So you say, "All right [remember we do not resist the mind], go wherever you want to go." You open your eyes. You look around. You look at the clock and a half hour has passed. Now where did the other twenty minutes go?

Well, when you started to slow the mind down, you slowed every-

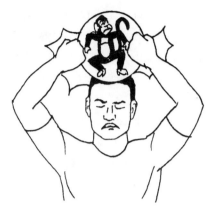

Fig. 3.25. You really cannot attack it directly because your consciousness is part of this ego.

thing down at the molecular level, which is the positive and negative charge. These two charges start to separate. As they separate, you enter the void (no time or space). You start to communicate with nothingness. You start to let go of the mind because you are not caught up in the positive and the negative now. You enter the void or the middle path. As you enter this middle path, you start to connect with infinity and communicate with God. And that is the flow of nature. As you develop this communication, a voice will start to direct you. This is the inner voice.

Fig. 3.26. You open your eyes. You look around. You look at the clock and a half hour has passed. Now where did the other twenty minutes go?

What you have done is to let go of the monkey mind indirectly by telling the mind to trace the thirty-two energy channels of the body, which, for all practical purposes, are beyond time and space. They are really the nothingness because they are just energy paths in the body.

So the mind, working with this nothingness, pretty soon forgets itself and enters the void, or your consciousness goes into the void. You begin to connect with this inner essence. This inner essence then starts to direct your life. It will happen automatically, but when you get into a situation where you do not know quite what to do, all of a sudden it will start to communicate with you. You will start to separate the positive from the negative and just observe. This voice will start to speak, not verbally, but it will speak feeling-wise into your whole essence. As you develop this, you will start to direct your life by the inner voice (infinity), with that communication. So, slowly, through the Taoist formulas, you are starting to transform your life. But you have to do it indirectly because you cannot attack the mind or the ego directly—positive or negative. You have to do it indirectly. And this indirect process is, again, what the Taoists call Wu Wei (nondoing). You are doing but not of your own will. You are being directed by the inner voice.

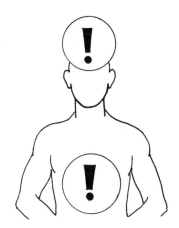

Fig. 3.27. This voice will start to speak, not verbally, but feeling-wise into your whole essence.

This is how you enter the void, the path of nothingness. After enough spaced repetition, a little practice each day, a strange thing starts to occur in your life. When you do the meditation and do the connection, you start to feel the stillness within your body connecting to the universe at the same time. That is the oneness that you feel in the meditation.

After a period of doing this practice a little bit each day, you will start to feel a spontaneous connection in your daily life. All of a sudden you will feel your body totally connected to everything around it. This just happens automatically. You are totally at one with the universe in your daily activities.

This could last for maybe five, ten, twenty minutes, and it will happen periodically over time, maybe three or four months in between, or four to five days.

After many, many years of practice, this strange occurrence happens twenty-four hours a day—and that is exactly how a sage or saint feels, totally connected to the universe.

Fig. 3.28. Twenty-four hours a day you will feel exactly how a sage or saint feels, totally connected to the universe.

LETTING GO AND CONNECTING WITH THE FLOW

This process of letting go and connecting with the flow is called forgiveness in Christianity and surrender in Western psychology. In the Tao we call it being detached. To illustrate this concept, take your hands and squeeze them to make a fist. Making a fist is our will, not the will of the flow of nature. It is by our direction. When we do this we cut off the flow of nature in between the fingers. As we cut off the flow, we cut off our connection to God (infinity). In using our own will (ego), we are resisting. It is our monkey mind at work.

So, in the West, we start to surrender from our will and begin to connect with the inner flow. In Christianity, we forgive others. We forgive ourselves. In the Tao we become detached. As we become detached, letting go of the fist, gradually our fingers open up; and the flow will loosen the fingers. As we become more and more confident in letting go of our own will (fist), allowing the natural flow to go through us, a strange thing happens: we flow with it. After many, many years of practicing the Taoist formulas, indirectly, we start

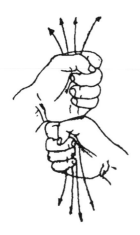

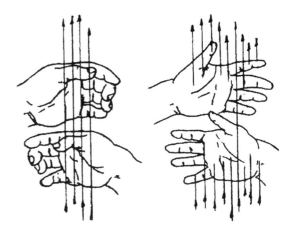

Fig. 3.29. You hold on and do not let go.

Fig. 3.30. As we become more and more confident in letting go of our own will (fist), allowing the natural flow to go through us, a strange thing happens: we flow with it.

to connect with that inner flow, learning to flow with it. Our life becomes effortless, becoming one with God, infinity, or nature. We are experiencing the letting go in our practices, and realizing it in our everyday lives.

With a little bit of practice each day, a little bit with the rock and drop, we start to make our inner connections with ourselves and the universe. This leads us to the Taoist concept of the five-element theory. Let's say you go into the woods. You sit down on a rock. It's just you and the woods, or you and nature. How do you feel? You feel at peace.

We are directly connected to the flow of the universe. You start to experience the effortlessness of life by letting go and becoming detached. This is the way of the Tao.

As you start to make this inner connection with the void, once you get that feeling of stillness and oneness in your body, then you will start to connect with the flow, the natural flow of the universe, the natural flow of this void. Then you will start to see the obstacles that obstruct you and your flow, and you learn to move around them. You learn to forgive or let go of these attachments. As these obstacles get in your way of your natural flow, you will start to let go, because the more you connect with them, the more you obstruct your flow.

As you let go or forgive yourself, you let go of a lot of people's grievances about you or obstacles they have put in your way: unfairness, lack of care, and unkindness. You start to let go and forgive them

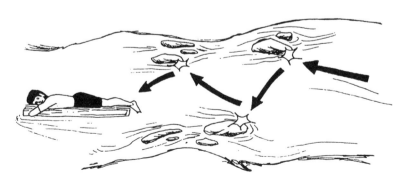

Fig. 3.31. The more you connect with life's obstacles,
the more you obstruct your flow.

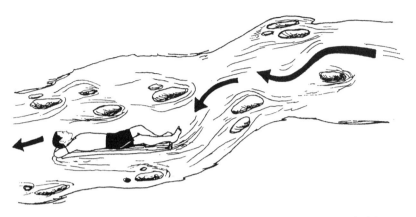

Fig. 3.32. You do not get connected to these obstructions that hold
you up in your natural flow into the void.

and yourself, because the more you let go, the more you connect with
that flow. Your life will become more and more effortless without the
obstructions blocking your way. You will start obtaining the natural
flow.

This is the whole art of becoming detached. You do not get connected to these obstructions that hold you up in your natural flow into
the void. This is the way of the Tao.

ARTIFICIAL ENVIRONMENTS

Why do you feel peace and stillness that way in the forest? Well, the
energy that you see in the sun is the same energy that is in your heart,
your heart energy. The energy that is in the tree, the wood energy, is
the same energy as in your liver, your liver energy. The energy in the
rock on which you are sitting, the metal energy, is the same as in your
lungs, your lung energy. The energy in your spleen, pancreas, and
stomach is the same energy that is in the ground (earth). The energy in
the river or stream is the same energy that is in your kidneys. So on a
molecular level, you are coming back to your molecular parents, sitting
in the woods. You are actually going back to your real home because the
energies interact and nurture one another like parents and their child.

In the West we are born and live in artificial environments. We are totally separated from God or nature. We are born in a hospital where the wood is artificial. The light is artificial. The water is artificial. The metal is artificial. It is processed and manmade. The ground we stand on is a floor (artificial ground). We are not touching the earth. So we are totally disconnected from God on a very physical, molecular level.

We are really living in artificial environments, which is fine except the energy inside us is the same energy as the tree, the river, the sun, the mountain, and the earth. In nature it is the only place we will feel at peace, because our inner being is connected to the five elements of the universe.

With artificial furniture and the artificial environment, we are slowly strangling and disconnecting ourselves from our own natural being. It is not the way of the natural flow of the Tao. Eventually, as you connect with the practice more and more, you will remove yourself from the artificial environments and connect yourself to the natural flow of the universe, where you originated. In the artificial world, you are not getting the proper support you need for your internal being, so you need to learn through the practices of the Taoist system

Fig. 3.33. Gradually you will find yourself working and connecting with this natural energy, supporting yourself with your internal energy.

Fig. 3.34. We are completely lost, disconnected from nature.

to cultivate the chi or energy within your body to flow naturally with the currents of the universe.

Gradually you will find yourself working and connecting with this natural energy, supporting yourself with your internal energy. You will start to flow and connect with that nature again. This is the path of the Tao.

The indigenous people have always let the flow of nature guide them throughout their existence. This is really where our direction will be taking us in the future as we start to connect with this natural flow and further distance ourselves from the artificial environments that do not support the natural flow of energy inside ourselves.

We live completely in artificial environments cut off from ourselves and our true nature. The more we live in these environments, the more we lose touch with ourselves and the Tao, until one day we are completely lost, disconnected from nature and our own essence.

And this is what we have created with our cultures, cities, and societies. We are totally outside ourselves, causing stress, conflict, and disease. The further we connect with nature, the further we connect back to ourselves and the Tao.

As we let go of these artificial environments that slowly destroy us, we will again slowly discover ourselves and the Tao. Through the Taoist practices, we will slowly connect back to ourselves and let go of these artificial environments, finding ourselves back in the Tao.

ANSWERS ARE IN NATURE

This is why the Tao is so beautiful, because if you ever have a question about the Tao, all you have to do is to look outside; all the answers are there in nature (in the woods) with every explanation you need. So if you want to get back to God, walk into the woods. And you will feel God's essence in every leaf, every ray of sunshine, every crystal of stone, every moist handful of earth, and every trickle of water. That is the life essence. And that is what you feel when you walk into the woods. You feel your own internal essence.

The answers are in the woods, in nature, about how to live and what to do to live. Just watch how the tree grows or how the wind blows, how the sun glows, how the river flows—and this will give you the answers for your life. You just learn to connect with nature and flow with its natural flow.

You will see how to stand upright like the tree and how to flow effortlessly through your life like the river, avoiding all the obstructions by being detached. How to surround yourself with nature and

Fig. 3.35. All the answers are there in nature.

Fig. 3.36. Root yourself in the earth to have the strength of the
mountain and the joy of the sun.

root yourself into the earth; how to have the strength of the mountain; and how to have the brightness and joy of the sun. These are the
keys of what to do in your life.

You will discover this just by studying the woods and the various
animals. You will see how they move and stretch their bodies and you
will learn this with your body using all the Taoist formulas, just like
the animals do. You will open up the internal channels of the body, in
the arms, the hips, and the spine. You will connect and become one
with nature and the energy channels in the body. This is the natural
flow of the Tao.

To observe the Tao, just walk out into the woods and watch everything in it. Do you see how little the movement is and how little you
have to move, once you find your root, just like a tree with its great
root? Just take a walk in the woods and you will feel the energy, and
the answers will be there in the woods as you smile down and connect
with the energy. As you smile down, you will start to feel the answers
come to you from within.

Fig. 3.37. You see how little the movement is and how little you have to move, once you find your root, just like a tree with its great root.

The Tao (nature) teaches you how to do everything in your life: how to talk, how to eat, how to defecate, how to have sex, and how to purify and recycle everything in your life. In nature we see this in the leaves falling to the ground composting back into dirt and thus growing everything again, which is the same process as your internal energy. The key is found in the forest.

All the answers you are looking for are within you. Just look out into the forest and you can start to see them much more clearly. You are the microcosm of the macrocosm. The macrocosm is the woods and the universe and your internal organs are the microcosm of the universe within.

Why do you feel so at peace when you sit in the woods? You are embracing your molecular parents. The same energy in the sun is in your heart. The same energy in the rivers and lakes is in our kidneys. The same energy in the mountains and rocks is in our lungs. The same energy in the earth is in our spleen. The same energy in the trees is in our liver and gallbladder.

When we are born, the first breath we take has these energy vibrations in it. The five elements of the earth connect with the five

Fig. 3.38. Our molecular parents are in the woods.

elements of the body in the five vital organs at that point in time and space. This is our internal energy pattern for our life. When we are born, we are empty, and with our first breath we fill ourselves with that energy pattern.

Once we know this from Taoist five-element astrology, we can balance our energy with a particular food or exercise. We can strengthen our weak organs (energy) and try to lessen our strong organs (energy). These answers for our own internal balance come from nature.

ONE WITH NATURE

Again, through practice with the Taoist formulas, working indirectly with your ego, one drop at a time you gradually come into this awareness. The ancient sage eventually goes into the mountain to be one with God.

This is the key to your own understanding. You will start to make your way through the letting-go process of unlearning what you have already learned through our institutions by using the technique of spaced repetition, one drop at a time. You will start to move slowly with your practice, a little bit each day, starting to remove the connection and attachments to the obstacles that block your way through the natural flow of the Tao, the oneness of the universe, the oneness with nature.

Fig. 3.39. The ancient sage eventually goes into the mountain to be one with God.

As you move your way past the obstacles, you connect with the flow by letting go, not holding on to all your programming and all your understandings and concepts that really obstruct you from the natural flow of your own essence, your own divinity. This is the natural flow of the Tao becoming one with nature.

As you become one with nature you will discover your own essence, your own bliss. As the Taoists say, "Once you become one with your own nature, you become one with nature. Join and flow with it and allow it to take you wherever it is going to take you."

You could discover an occupation that gives you great joy, and this is what you should do in your life. Whether it is a fisherman, a sailor,

Fig. 3.40. You will become one with your own essence through the letting-go process of unlearning, using the technique of spaced repetition, one drop at a time.

Fig. 3.41. You discover your own bliss, what makes you happy in your life, your own joy.

Fig. 3.42. The Tao is as simple as a flower blooming or the sun rising.

a baker, a craftsman, a woodchip man—whatever it might be, the thing that makes you most happy and at peace with yourself is what you should do. People will give you a fortune for doing what comes naturally and effortlessly to you because it is a great joy.

That is really the natural flow of the Tao, the natural flow inside you. The Tao teaches you through the practices how to eat, sleep, drive, dance, and everything that flows within yourself aligned with the Tao. You will discover who you are, as well as your purpose for being here on the earth plane.

How you obtain that flow of the Tao is through your presence. It is your being present in whatever you do that brings you in the flow of the Tao. Your total focus brings you the joy of the Tao. As you become present, you become the Tao.

Presence is the key in the Tao and anything that you do in life. Just be present and it will connect you to the Tao and its effortless path. Being present is as easy as watching a flower bloom or the sunset in the evening. It is that simple but that profound. Just being fully there is all it takes to fully experience the Tao.

What Not to Do

WISDOM

At the heart of the Tao is wisdom. To achieve wisdom, you have to learn how to define it. Wisdom is the accumulation of knowledge and the accumulation of experiences. To accumulate this knowledge takes approximately twenty years. Once you accumulate this knowledge, you have to put it to practical use and see how it works for you. This application of knowledge in your life is what is called experience. You need a long time to experience something. Let us say it takes you

Fig. 4.1. Wisdom is the accumulation of knowledge and the accumulation of experiences.

twenty years. Twenty and twenty equals forty. And the old saying is, "You do not know anything until you are forty." Around age forty, then, you begin to become wise. To be wise, according to the Taoists, is to know when to be soft and when to be hard. What you want to try to do is discover what you do not have to do to exist in this world.

Through the Taoist practices, you learn the basic ideas of living, eating, sleeping, understanding sexual relationships, balancing your emotions, centering yourself, and finding your own center.

Through these practices, you learn what you really need to do to exist in this world and survive without excess or going into extremes. You develop your own wisdom for your own life. You learn how to balance and maintain yourself, and how little effort it actually takes on your part to find what you need in life to maintain your center for shelter, travel, and eating.

Basically, when you sit down and still the mind, you realize how little it takes for you to maintain yourself and how little it takes for you to exist. All excesses are just taking energy away from you. In yourself, you will find exactly what you need, through gaining knowledge and experiences.

By implementing the practices of the Tao and in gaining the expe-

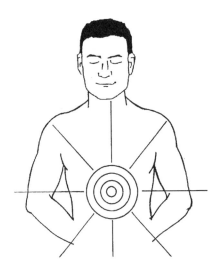

Fig. 4.2. Centering yourself and finding your own center

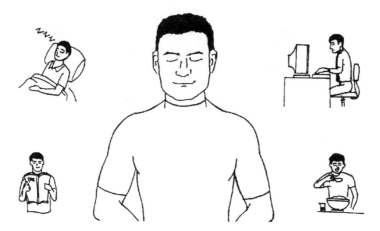

Fig. 4.3. When you sit down and still the mind, you realize how little it takes for you to maintain yourself and how little it takes for you to exist.

riences, you start to develop the wisdom for yourself to live in this world. This helps you maintain balance and oneness within yourself, finding your center and connection with the rest of the universe.

To maintain this center you discover what it takes to either yield and be soft or to be forceful when you need to be hard. The power really is in the yielding process to maintain your center, but every now and then you need to have power and concentration to become hard, strong, or forceful. As in the universe, you need the delicate balance within yourself and the Tao of the yin and the yang. You will learn when to yield and when to be forceful.

This is the key for our lives and is the basic balance within ourselves as we learn to follow the Tao. It is the balance between the yin and the yang, the middle path. As we work with the middle path, we discover our own center, and we work within ourselves to maintain our wisdom in this world and the balance with joy and happiness.

In using this application, you learn through your experiences and gain the knowledge of when to yield to the energy and when to use force with the energy. You also learn what to do when you encounter it and whatever it is when you encounter it. This is the path of following the Tao.

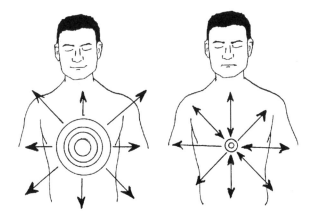

Fig. 4.4. To maintain this center, you discover what it takes to either yield and be soft or to be forceful when you need to be hard.

In many cases you learn to just yield to the energy that comes at you without losing your center. That is your middle point. In some cases, you need to know when to use force and when not to. You discover this on your journey as you flow with the current through the universe following the Tao.

Fig. 4.5. You learn when to use force with the energy when you encounter it.

REACTING

I, William Wei, grew up like many people, caught up in the Western monkey mind way of thinking. I would gather a little bit of knowledge and react to it without ever asking myself, "Is this what I really want for me? Is this really good for me?" I never stopped and thought about that. I just reacted instead of acting. People would say, "Can you do this?" And I would say, "I can do this. I can do that." But I never said to myself, "Is this good for me? Is this what I really want in life? Is this really what life is all about?"

So after about ten or fifteen years of reacting instead of acting, one day you wake up and realize you are on Mars or someplace you do not know. You say to yourself, "What am I doing here? Who are these people?" You can be in a business situation or in a committed relationship, with children or whatever. And you have no idea why you are there except that you were reacting. You never asked yourself, "Is this really good for me? Is this what I want out of it? Is this what makes me happy?"

The difficult part is getting back where you want to be. In my situation it took me about five years. Some situations might take you a lifetime. You might end up dying in that situation and you are miserable. You never took the time to ask yourself, "Is this what my life is

Fig. 4.6. One day you wake up and realize you are on Mars. You say to yourself, "What am I doing here? Who are these people?"

about? Is this really good for me? Is this what I really want? What will happen ten or fifteen years from now if I do this and this and this?" That is how you develop wisdom. The only way you develop wisdom is to experience the knowledge you have gained. You are actually going through what not to do.

Working through situations and discovering what it is you want to do is the key. Here is an example: You walk down the path and see a fire. You say to yourself, "Should I put my hand in the fire? Will it burn? I do not think it will burn, maybe it will not burn." You stick your hand in the fire and guess what? Your hand burns and starts to smell and it hurts! You pull your hand out and then you heal the hand and continue walking down the path. You see another fire and you say to yourself, "Will that hurt? Nah, it will not hurt. It hurt last time, but it probably will not hurt this time." You put your hand in again and it starts smelling and burning again and hurting. You say, "Ow, it hurt again!" You pull it out and heal the hand up again and then you keep walking down the path. You see another fire. You say, "Is this going to burn? No, it hurt two times, it cannot hurt again, that just cannot happen." Sure enough, you stick your hand in the fire and it burns again. This is an example of what really happens in life.

As you journey through life, certain situations happen and you

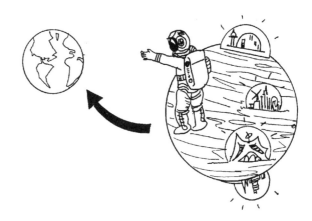

Fig. 4.7. The difficult part is getting back where you want to be. In my situation it took me about five years. Some situations might take you a lifetime.

apply yourself and then you get the result. Then it repeats itself until you learn your lesson, not to stick your hand into that particular type of fire. It could be a physical, emotional, psychological, or spiritual situation that you find yourself in, until you actually learn your lesson. Everyone has their own fire.

This is how you can gain the wisdom of what to do and what not to do. As the Taoist master once said to me, "Ah, professor, you need more suffering." What he was saying was that I needed more suffering to wake up and realize that when I stick my hand in the fire it will burn. No matter what you think it might do, it will burn. There are certain basic aspects of reality that we have to deal with on this earth plane.

We have to learn to apply ourselves and to recognize that what happened before will happen again. When we see that situation we have a conscious choice to either stick our hand in that particular fire situation or not. Every time we stick our hand in, it will eventually burn. If we need to have more suffering, we will repeat this until we do it correctly in the end or it will just keep burning us. It is really up to us, and as we learn to slowly move away from reacting and start acting with conscious choices, then we will start to develop the wisdom in our lives to make the right choices.

Fig. 4.8. By putting your hand in the fire, you can gain the wisdom of what to do and what not to do.

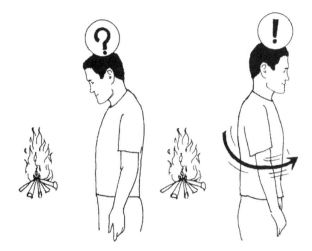

Fig. 4.9. You learn within yourself to connect with the inner voice that will give you direction, to either stick your hand in the fire or walk away.

The journey is one of understandings and knowledge we have gained through experiences to learn what to do in a particular situation and when we have to do it. This is how we learn within ourselves to connect with the inner voice to give us direction when we have no idea what to do. The more confidence we have with the inner voice,

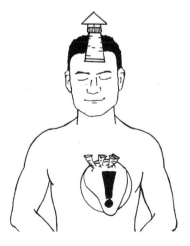

Fig. 4.10. Using the mind to observe and the heart to give you conscious choices

the more we will start to develop the inner relationship that will give us direction in our life. We will start to develop the ability to think with the heart and feel with the mind.

Using the mind to observe and the heart, with its ability to look at things from all different directions, to give you conscious choices will give you the correct answer. This is the development of your own wisdom and understanding within yourself to apply on your journey within the Tao.

The Tao is a journey of knowledge and wisdom. The Taoists say there are three ways to become an immortal or enlightened: the first way is one of worship and prayer—it can happen, but you never know why, when, or how; the second way is one of good service—again it can happen, but you never know when, why, and how; and the third way is the way of the Tao, which is one of knowledge and wisdom. The way of the Tao teaches you the right thing to do at the right time and gives you the information you need to do what needs to be done, which on a molecular level is an alchemical transformation.

Fig. 4.11. On each level, you will receive the knowledge and wisdom needed to complete that level; this is the way of the Tao.

On each level you will receive the knowledge and wisdom needed to complete that level; this is the way of the Tao. This is the way you have chosen to take or you would not be reading this book. You will receive spurts of information over a long period as you make your way through your path.

TRUE NATURE

I, William Wei, can offer my own life as an example of how you can grow through life's mistakes. In my childhood I made many discoveries of what not to do. But I was in a more controlled environment. I was fortunate because I had two parents at home, a mother and a father. So I did not get too far out of my controlled environment and I did not cause too much damage—nothing that would hinder me for the rest of my life. And that is pretty much true if you have an environment that protects you.

A lot of people do not have those environments, and they do not have the ability or the years of experience to make informed decisions that will affect them for many, many years. That is why you ideally need to be brought up by a mother and a father. You need the positive yang and the negative yin with experience to create a balance. You need the balance to protect yourself, so you can have an opportunity to grow when you are young and cannot protect yourself.

Fig. 4.12. You start to learn the difference between the yin (bucket of ice) and the yang (campfire).

Fig. 4.13. You start to learn what to do and what not to do.

When you are sheltered in a protective environment by your parents or other responsible guardians, you can start to develop a basic knowledge of how to exist. You start to learn the difference between the yin and the yang, the positive and the negative. As you develop this knowledge you will look for symbols or guidelines that support your understanding of the idea of positive and negative.

Your true nature is the nature of how your energy moves and how it connects with everything around you and also how it moves and interacts with others. You become familiar with it and how it interacts in a controlled environment.

Usually, it takes many years to find your true nature and you must go through a great many experiences in your whole process of self-discovery, gaining experience and knowledge about yourself.

ASS-U-ME

Even though I did not get too far out of balance in my childhood, I still had learning experiences of what not to do. For example, when I was around six years old I was on a haystack firing arrows with my

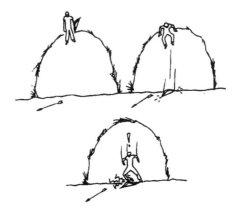

Fig. 4.14. So I threw down my bow and jumped down to show my friend the arrow. I should not have thrown down my bow, because when I jumped, I landed on it and broke my leg.

friend. There was a six-foot drop off the haystack. I shot the arrow and my friend did not know where it was. I pointed and said, "It is right there!" He still could not find it. I said, "I will show it to you." So I threw my bow down and jumped down to show him the arrow. I should not have thrown down my bow, because when I jumped, I landed on it and broke my leg. I should have set it aside and then jumped. Then I would not have broken my leg. It got me into a lot of trouble. It was a bad move on my part. I was not thinking. In retrospect, I could have saved a lot of grief by taking precautions instead of jumping into something. I reacted rather than acting with conscious choice.

Another case in which I made a big mistake when I was young: I was playing on the playground. Boys were chasing me around, which they normally did. They grabbed my hat and I ran after them. I do not remember any of this, because apparently I fell, hit my head on a rock, received a concussion, and suffered a loss of memory. I was groggy and remembered nothing of the incident.

My father became quite upset and thought that someone had done great damage to his son. He wanted to find out the truth of what happened. Unfortunately, I could not remember. But my father was so

Fig. 4.15. They grabbed my hat and I ran after them. I hit my head on a rock.

persistent in finding out that he finally quizzed some children. They gave him a story about me tripping during a game. I could not remember. It sounded like it might have happened. I thought these kids were honest. I assumed they were honest. Of course, when you assume, as the saying goes, you make an ass out of you and me (ass-u-me). You get into a lot of trouble assuming. I did. When my dad found out two weeks later that I'd been chasing the other kids because they took my hat, I was punished severely. He interpreted the disagreement over the hat as "fighting" and blamed me for hurting myself because the fight kept me from paying attention and taking care of myself. From his point of view, I shouldn't have engaged in the fight to begin with. At the time, I could not watch television for six months and I missed my birthday and Christmas. I learned the hard way. When you learn "what not to do" you remember these lessons. And that is part of gaining the knowledge and gaining the experience.

It got very dramatic for me when I got out of my parents' protection at about age eighteen. That is why strong parental figures are so important in the upbringing of a child. When kids are in their late teens and early twenties, they can make some biggies of "what not to do."

We have all our own lessons from our childhood of what not to

Fig. 4.16. At the time, I could not watch television for six months and I missed my birthday and Christmas.

do, and a lot of times we have no idea what to do, so we just do things. But we can get ourselves in trouble. We have to take some caution about ourselves and look through life and all its circumstances to have the joy of life. The child learns to play with anything it comes in contact with. The real joy of life is connecting with yourself internally and doing what really makes you happy, just as a child enjoying the simple things of life.

So, when you assume, you base a lot of the assumptions on someone else's reality and what someone else said to you. But your life might not apply to others and what applies to others probably does not apply to you. Once you learn to discover yourself and what really applies to you, you will start to know what not to do.

THIEVES

As I got into my teens, I did not have a whole lot in my life, at least of what I thought was important at the time. I did not have enough knowledge or experience to understand certain facets of life. I wanted to become a multimillionaire. I would do anything within the ethical limits given by my upbringing to put forth the effort to reach that goal. I began when I was twenty-one, with another friend of mine. We went into the insurance business. We started an insurance agency.

I had no background in it whatsoever. I was still in college. I took a leave of absence eventually to set up this business. For the next fifteen years, I started six or seven different businesses. I eventually ended up in industrial sales. I accumulated over $2,500,000 through my efforts in sales. But then I discovered, through the accumulation of this money, that the only thing wealth ever brought me was thieves. They are more clever and smarter than you or I, and they will get every dime. They also come in both genders.

So I discovered many things about what not to do. I discovered how to make money through sales. I also discovered that it was no more effort to sell 100,000 items than it was to sell one item.

So I went into industrial sales because I could sell more. When you accumulate this kind of money, and you are very young, even though you worked for it and you had respect for it, you lose it and you really feel bad.

You feel so bad, in fact, that you wish you had never earned it. You

Fig. 4.17. I accumulated over $2,500,000 through my efforts in sales.

end up where you started out, except that you have had all of these frustrations—first in obtaining the wealth, and second in losing it. I would have been better off if I had not made it. You discover that wealth does not give you happiness, even though in the West that is what they say will bring you happiness. This is a falsehood. My Taoist practices of the living Tao brought me to that understanding.

Once you struggle to make money and you finally make it, you discover the thieves. Now, the thieves will leave you alone if you do not have any money. They have no interest in you. If you have money, they will find you. And they will take it. So there are some guidelines you need to follow if you are going to learn from your experiences in life.

Money is another form of energy, and when you start to accumulate your energy, you start to manifest it as money. Money is just an equivalent of the time and effort you put into doing something in a monetary unit. It takes all your time and focus on one area, and you start to generate a multitude of energy in the form of money. In the Taoist perspective, instead of trying to formulate energy into money, what you should try to do is to internalize it into your own energy

Fig. 4.18. Now, the thieves will leave you alone if you do not have any money. They have no interest in you. If you have money they will find you. And they will take it.

within yourself, to center and ground yourself, to fortify the energy. It is more permanent.

Instead of sending the energy out in units of money so it can be stolen by greed from other people, be aware of it. It is externalized from you and you need to learn to internalize. Build up these energy units within yourself and live a long and prosperous life of joy and simplicity as opposed to running around in the rat race accumulating all these things that you do not end up enjoying. When you send the energy out as units of money, you need to protect that money or you need to manage that money and get it to work for you.

That is when the thieves come in and volunteer to manage and control it for you and in the end they only steal all of it or squander it. All you know is that you have lost that energy, lost that money. What you need to do is continue that same work process, but in a different way—to internalize the energy to recharge and guard that energy within your body. This conserves the energy and does not let it leave your body. This is accomplished by doing the Taoist practices within the Taoist system. You generate a huge bank of money or energy inside yourself and you can spend it wisely as you work through more of your soul's journey and your self-discovery of what to do in life and what not to do.

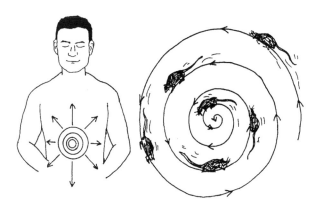

Fig. 4.19. Build up these energy units within yourself and live a long and prosperous life of joy and simplicity as opposed to running around in the rat race.

The Tao teaches you not to lose that energy through its practices. When you put it in units of money, you have that opportunity to lose it. If you put it in units of energy and internalize them within yourself as stored energy, then you do not have to waste it and you learn to live externally on very little, and then you do not squander anything that you saved up inside yourself.

This is the path of the Tao and the lesson that I learned in accumulating all the units of energy externalized as money, which was soon squandered over many years. I learned the path to internalizing the energy, which will last for many, many years to come. I am learning to listen to that inner voice, which is becoming more audible. That is the lesson of the Tao of what not to do with your energy. What you do is invest in yourself instead of investing in the stock market and other businesses.

You invest in your own internal energy and your own life by recharging and conserving your own internal energy and how to evolve this energy internally inside yourself by generating and storing it within your energy. You then become a being of light and you live

Fig. 4.20. If you put your internal energy in units and internalize them within yourself as stored energy, then you do not have to waste it and you will learn to live externally on very little. Then you do not squander anything that you saved up inside yourself.

within yourself on that light and you need very little external aspects to sustain yourself. You have learned to be self-sufficient within your own being, and that is the key to the Tao.

Thieves cannot steal what they do not understand and cannot see. The thief is only interested in stealing everything externally and has no idea what you are doing internally. The Taoists always say: "Speak without emphasizing your words, for the minds of others are slow, which allows you to make your escape in time." So move through life effortlessly and achieve what you need to achieve by living through the Tao. Be very unassuming and very simple. As the Taoists always say, "Become a blade of grass in a field of grass and you will live a very full life." You will find your own spiritual essence and your own individual being and advance yourself, just by playing a simple role in a simple life.

CONSCIOUS CHOICES

First, you really have to know yourself. What makes you happy, how you function, and how you work—your whole makeup. Life is the discovery of who you are. It is your own personal journey. No one really knows you except you. To discover who you are takes many, many years of studying yourself. The key is to ask yourself questions: 1) Who am I? 2) What do I enjoy? and 3) Where do I want to go? Until these questions are answered, you are really floundering along with no direction, no idea where you are or where you are going; and that is how you end up reacting instead of acting.

In the West, people have so many options, so many choices, that we essentially have no choice. We do not know who we are. I, William Wei, was the same way. I got the concept from the West that if you do this and this and this, then this and this and this will happen. Well, I did this and this and this. And something else happened. I discovered it did not bring me the peace that I was looking for. There were, in my case, some hilarious incidents on the journey.

Fig. 4.21. The key is to ask yourself the following questions:
1. Who am I?
2. What do I enjoy?
3. Where do I want to go?
Until these are answered, you are really floundering along with no direction.

The key to conscious choice is to slow the mind down. To make a conscious choice you need to slow everything down, to give yourself the opportunity to see things for what they really are. As I mentioned before, you need to know who you are, you need to know what you enjoy, and you need to know where you are going.

This takes a journey to discover and you will make little discoveries on the way of what you do not want, who you are not, what you do

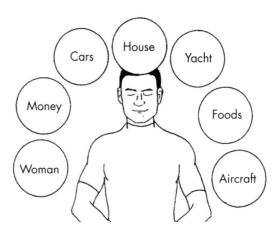

Fig. 4.22. In the West, people have so many options, so many choices, that they essentially have no choice.

not like to do, or where you do not like to go. Slowly, with enough of these discoveries, you will discover who you are, what you enjoy, and where you are going.

The journey starts out slowly. As the Taoists say, "A thousand-mile journey starts with the first step." As the professor says, "A thousand-mile journey ends with the last step." In other words, it takes one step at a time.

Give yourself enough time to enjoy the ride and take one step at a time. Discover initially who you are not, what you do not enjoy, and where you do not want to go. Then you do not go in those places and you do not assume you are somebody you are not. You really sit back and find it within yourself what you truly enjoy, and then your life will become simple and your choices will become conscious.

You first must start and then you can begin to enjoy the ride. If you are not enjoying yourself, then stop whatever you are doing. You could be in a crazy situation with a lot of crazy different people and hilarious incidents, but deep down, you can feel if you are happy or not. If you are not happy, get out of there. If it's a certain place that's making you unhappy, get out of there and do not ever go back.

Then you will discover who you are and who you are not. In many

Fig. 4.23. A thousand-mile journey ends with the last step.

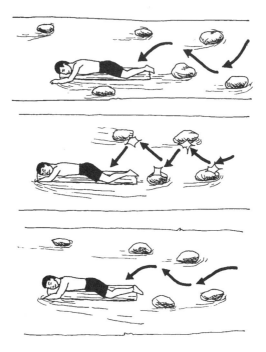

Fig. 4.24. You first must start and then you can begin to enjoy the ride.
If you are not enjoying yourself, then stop whatever you are
doing and do something else.

situations in my own life I am in a group of people and I say, "Who are these people? I do not know how I got here." So you must start making conscious choices right away and take responsibility for yourself.

Through the Taoist practices in the Taoist system, you learn to slow the mind down so you can see what is really going on and make a conscious choice. When you are moving so fast, especially in the monkey mind world, the rat race, there is no way you can slow down long enough to really ask yourself the key questions: What is my life about, where am I going, and who do I want to be? You cannot make those conscious choices.

The first step is to develop a daily practice. A little bit of sunshine, a little bit of water each day to grow that consciousness inside yourself. The only way to do that is to take the time, five to ten minutes every morning, and just smile down. This will work the energy a little bit

Fig. 4.25. When you are moving so fast, in the rat race, you never ask yourself, "What is my life about, where am I going, and who do I want to be?"

in your body and you will start to develop that consciousness within yourself. You will discover who you are, what you enjoy, and where you are going. Gradually, over time—five, ten, fifteen years—you will have a very clear picture of who you are, where you are going, and what you enjoy. That is the key: to take the time and the effort to structure yourself in a pattern where you can start to make some conscious choices with your life. It is your journey and no one else's.

Nobody else can feel what you feel inside. Only you can. You are your own guru, your own teacher, your own master—no one else but you. All the Tao teaches you are some simple guidelines, formulas, or practices to help you discover yourself. It is your discovery because you are the only one that can discover you. As you discover yourself, you will discover the Tao.

There is no hurry on this journey. Just remember that there is no place to go and you have all the time in the world to get there. Wherever you are, you are already there. In the Tao you live in the now—there is no future and there is no past. There is just the next step. It is a continuum of becoming because you will always be faced with another hill

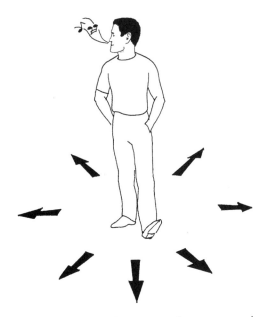

Fig. 4.26. Just remember that there is no place to go and you have
all the time in the world to get there.

to climb. It does not matter where you are, where you come from, or
where you are going; there is always another step to take. The key is to
enjoy the ride and take your time. The problem when you are young is
that you are in a hurry to die, and when you get older you realize that
you are almost dead, so you are in no hurry to die.

Youth is wasted on the youth because you just need to slow down
a little bit and make some conscious choices, which will save you a lot
of pain, anxiety, and frustration. Just learn to smile down and slow
everything down to make some conscious choices—like deciding
where you really want to go. That is the key: just smile down and the
rest of the world will smile with you. When you work the Inner Smile,
you smile down to your organs and they smile back. You become that
beam of light within and that shining energy inside will attract the
people who are smiling right back. As you start to center yourself and
find your inner peace, you will start to flourish and live within the
Tao.

ONLY TEACHERS

For example, when I was first starting the insurance business, I had no idea what I was getting into. None. I vowed that I would do my homework before I would get into a situation like that again where I did not know what to do. And literally I did not. I rented an office and put a sign out that said "Insurance for Sale." And lo and behold, somebody walked in and wanted to buy insurance. I had no idea what to do. So my partner and I discovered that we had to get licensed and that we needed insurance companies to represent. I reacted. I never said, "Is this what I really want? Is this what is going to make me happy?" No, no, no! All I was concerned about was the money—working for the money and getting the money. What am I going to do to get the money and what to do with the money once I got it? I was sold a bill of goods early on that money would buy me happiness. And then I discovered, as I mentioned before, that it only creates misery if you do not know what to do with it.

Money brings thieves and the thieves take it away from you. You work all your life to get the money, and once you get the money, someone takes it away from you. I forgot that I came into this world with nothing and I will leave with nothing. In other words, everything in the

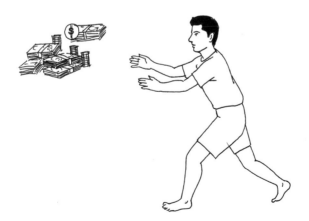

Fig. 4.27. All I was concerned about was the money—working for the money and getting the money.

Fig. 4.28. You learn from experiences. As you gain knowledge,
you learn what to do for yourself.

material realm does not belong to us. If you earn it, it does not really matter because you will not keep it in the next world, especially if you do not know what to do with it in this world.

I thought that if it belonged to me, when I left this earth plane I would take it with me. The only thing I enter this earth plane with is my consciousness or soul or spirit. That is what I leave with. So everything else is just a learning process. You learn from the experiences. As you gain the knowledge, you learn what to do for yourself. What makes you happy? What is your life about? Where are you trying to go?

In my business and social activities, I was brought up in an environment where you drank and smoked and that was considered a great time. Again I discovered "what not to do." Alcohol and drugs are destructive and abusive, although I was not aware of it at the time. Then I had a traumatic experience. I was at the bar drinking hard liquor with my friends. We were going to stop for food at a diner and it was late at night. I got lost following them. My car slid to the side. The next thing I knew I woke up in jail. I was all bent out of shape. I was going to get a DUI (driving under the influence of alcohol). So I did not drink for a month.

Fig. 4.29. The next thing I knew, I woke up in jail. I was all bent out of shape.

My trial date was set for a Saturday morning. The night before, I went out. I was drinking perfect Rob Roys. The next thing I remember I was sitting in another jail in a different state. The police picked me up going down the wrong lane of the expressway. I said, "I have a court date this morning. What am I going to do?" They told me, "Well, you can leave now or get some sleep. But you are going to have another court date in three or four weeks on this incident." I had just bought a brand-new car, a symbol of my success. I was still pretty groggy from the drinking even though I had slept three or four hours. As I was swerving on the road my car hit the ground wire of a telephone pole. I began driving up the wire toward the pole and I flipped my brand-new car. Then there I was, upside down in this car. I got out and sat in the police car, which had come shortly after the accident. From the front seat of the police car, I looked at my new car, upside down and totaled. I realized right then what not to do. What difference will it make to any kind of success if you are going to turn around and destroy it through alcohol or drugs? So I made up my mind, even though I had to go to the DUI judgment in the next state, that I was never going to drink again.

I was fortunate because that was an early experience in my life that

Fig. 4.30. From the front seat of the police car, I looked at my new car, which was upside down and totaled. I realized right then what not to do.

saved me a lot of pain later on. I lost my license and did not have a car for ninety days. So I began to explore another lifestyle. I took up biking and running. I experimented with other diets such as vegetarianism. This led me on a long journey to the Tao.

Believe it or not, twenty-six years later, after more than twenty-two years of sobriety, I was picked up for DUI again in another state. As I sat there again in jail, I realized the monkey mind had done it again. After twenty-six years, I had done a complete 360 and had ended up right where I started—sticking my hand in the fire again. I thought it wouldn't burn but, of course, it did just like before. The monkey mind is really tricky and convincing. I can drink and not get drunk; but with the new drinking and driving laws you cannot drink and drive. I am so happy I am back in sobriety again; hopefully I will be for another twenty-two years or more. One day at a time, I am learning what not to do.

As you accumulate the money, you become more attractive. You buy things with your money. These things that you buy attract other types of thieves who steal your money as well, but in a different way. Actually, you have neither friends nor enemies—only teachers. I was busy learning through the school of hard knocks, buying and accumulating many possessions. I drove around in antique cars and sports cars. I went on trips around the world. I belonged to various social clubs and associations. I attracted women, my real teachers leading me into aspects of life of which I had been unaware, coming from a male environment. I proceeded to have a relationship. She was interested in a home and I was interested in becoming married. So I said, "Why not buy her the home." So I did, in cash, and gave it to her as a gift in her name ("what not to do").

After many years, I discovered that she thought more of that home than she ever did of me. What was more traumatic than the loss of the money was the realization that I did not mean much to her as a person; I was just a means to an end. Many women I encountered, especially after I had achieved financial success, were really just looking for security. They really were not looking out for my best interests, but rather for their best interests. And you will discover that in both genders. You meet the thieves when you accumulate money, and they have their own agenda.

The thieves are really your teachers. They teach you what not to do, so you should not have any grudges against your thieves, and you will learn what not to do from them. When you accumulate too much money by manifesting it externally, then the thieves can easily steal it. You should use that energy to build yourself up internally—but once you manifest it into money, you open yourself up to all the thieves in

Fig. 4.31. Many women were really just looking for security.

Fig. 4.32. I was around their homes and all their security systems and guards, and they could not leave their compounds. It was just like they were in a prison.

this world, and then you need to protect yourself. It is funny because when I traveled around the world I saw all these wealthy people and they lived in their own prisons or well-guarded compounds, protected by guards and fences just like a prison.

I was around their homes and all their security systems and guards, and they could not leave their compounds. Their homes were no different than prisons, except the accommodations were nicer; but they had no privacy because the guards, maids, or caretakers were always present, everywhere we were going—to the toilet, eating, reading, walking, sleeping. They were always watching you. Wherever you wanted to walk or wherever you wanted to live, you had to be protected.

When people have wealth, other people, the have-nots, try to kidnap their children or their wives. It is all craziness. When you have too much wealth, you become greedy, and if you have too little, you become a thief. This is not the middle path and it causes all kinds of craziness. You need to live with not too much. Then you can live in peace with all your freedoms.

So getting back to the original statement, try not to have any grudges against the thieves, and try to not only forgive them, but forgive yourself, too. If you feel really bad about being taken advantage of, you should learn from your mistakes and next time you will know what not to do. That is how you are going to know.

TO HAVE ENOUGH

People tell me that I was not clever enough to hang on to my money. Anyone who believes that is a fool. If you hang on to your money and persist with it, you also will likely become that thief. The Tao says, "When you have too little money, you become a thief, and when you have too much money, you become greedy (legal thief), so the key is just to have enough."

To discover who you are, what makes you happy, and where you are going, just find out what makes you happy and sustain yourself on that. You need very little income if you have few needs. Then you discover how very little you need to extend yourself or to generate your energy in those areas. Need and want are like an insatiable disease and you will steal before you have earned it.

Other entities control the international currencies that create this imbalance of greed and want, and you will discover the only people who are in jail are people who cannot afford to stay out of prison. If you have enough money you can buy the attorneys to study the correct

Fig. 4.33. Only the poor end up in jail.

law to keep you out of prison. So, basically the poor and ignorant end up in jail. In America, the number of people who support the people who want to stay out of prison, who manage people in prison, and the people in prison themselves is getting larger and larger. It is over 10 percent of the population in America. This is really staggering.

Be happy with how little it takes you to sustain yourself and that is all. It is amazing. As the Taoists say, "How much a little a little will do." All you need is a little and that little will take care of you with very little effort.

You should also have just a little extra—just a little bit as in an insurance policy, which is your own personal insurance policy. You should have a little extra in case of a rainy day or put away a little reserve and always maintain that reserve with some of that stored energy, which is internal as well as external. This is very unassuming and you will always have enough.

The Tao says that to truly let go of anything, you need to become satiated with it and then you have had enough. You cannot go with it or resist it, because you only give it the power to overtake you, so you satiate yourself with it and become detached, not giving it any power or energy positively or negatively.

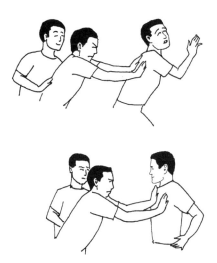

Fig. 4.34. Become satiated so you do not have to go with it or resist it.

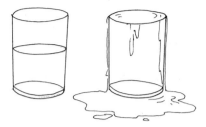

Fig. 4.35. To become satiated, you need to fill the glass until it overflows.

To become satiated is to fill a glass with water until it overflows and you cannot put any more water in it. You need to satiate every possibility until you cannot put any more in your glass. And then you fulfill yourself and become detached from it. That means you do whatever you must do to fill your glass until you cannot put any more in your glass. When you were a child you ate candy until one day you could not eat any more. You became satiated.

As adults, satisfaction comes from smoking, drinking, business, or sex instead of candy. Until we became satiated with the source of satisfaction, we will never be free of it. This is the way of the Tao. And the only way you will be free of it is when your glass overflows with it and you have just had enough.

DISCOVER WHO YOU ARE

So you do not devote your life to making money, obtaining a spouse, or obtaining possessions. What you devote your life to, your main purpose in life, is to discover who you are, not all the external things. You can only take you (consciousness) with you to the next realm anyway. And once you discover who you are, then you will realize your goal in life is to be one with your God-self living in the Tao, naturally flowing with the universe.

Who are you? Have you really asked yourself this every day? It is a good question in your meditations. As you slow your mind down in the meditation, you will discover, as I have, who you really are.

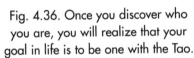

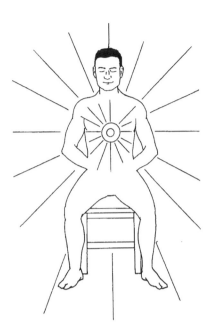

Fig. 4.36. Once you discover who you are, you will realize that your goal in life is to be one with the Tao.

Fig. 4.37. You are a light body, a beam of light.

You are a light body, a beam of light. We are all beams of light and these beams of light are all connected together in a mysterious way. We really never totally realize this in ordinary life—being, as we are, attracted by our monkey mind to the external world.

The more you become each day, the more you will start to understand who you are. It is like a tree in the woods: the more it grows, the more it becomes, and now you see how to implement this simple concept. Great sages of old saw this and lived simple lives, but we felt we should be worshipping them. Inside us life is just a reenactment of nature and all of its creation, because we can manifest everything with our own system of manifestation for obtaining possessions through telepathy and clairvoyance. We can develop these internal arts within ourselves as we are taught in the Taoist practices. We can become one with ourselves and the universe, living with the Tao.

It is all done with the power of the thought. Anything we believe

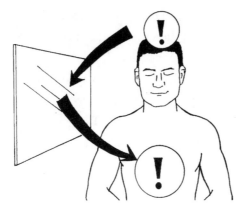

Fig. 4.38. It is all done with the power of the thought.

will be. We create every time we have a thought. How powerful thought is, but we have forgotten. We have lost the conscious connection with thought and what it can do inside and outside us.

We forgot to look inside ourselves because we have been taught always to externalize, always looking outside ourselves. We never see what really is, what the power of the thought is and our ability to create thoughts. We forget that we are divine.

Nothing ever appears to be what it actually is. You start out in life not knowing anything, and that is exactly how we end up. You start out trying something, and after a long time of trial and error, it works, but just for that moment in time. Everything changes all the time, so what once worked now does not, and what did not work does. So you just end up with what you started with: nothing. Life is just experiencing it. Life is not about obtaining things, because you have nothing to gain. You already have everything, if you slow your mind and see it. If you do not, you learn what not to do.

THE LESS YOU DO, THE BETTER

Here is another example of what not to do. At one point in my life, I was so focused on getting a certain 1953 sports car and I could not find one. I saw an ad in *USA Today* and I reacted. I called up and they said, "Yeah, we can help you out. It costs $15,000. What you should do is send us cash first. And then in another month send us the rest of the cash and in four or five weeks we will send you the kit to build it." So I said, "Great!" They said, "And just to speed things up you can mail it overnight and we will send a courier to pick it up." So in the next three days I sent them $15,000 cash. Then four and five weeks went by. I called them up and got no answer. I called the Attorney General in Florida where they were located and found out they went bankrupt and stole my money. So I just lost $15,000. This is an example of what not to do.

In life there is not a whole lot you should do. Our monkey mind keeps us chasing after things that we really have no need to do. We do so because the mind has to do something. But there is not anything really to do once you understand what you really need to make your life livable. We create all of these situations by projecting what we think we should do. In reality we do not have to do them; in fact, I discovered the less I do, the better.

We create so much pain that just feeds off itself. Once you realize you do not need all of this, you can let go of all of it. You do not need the sports cars. You do not need the security of a home, the beautiful woman in your life, the security of having a man with a home, of

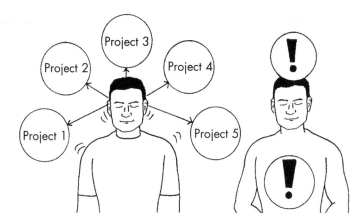

Fig. 4.39. We create all of these situations by projecting what we think we should do.

being financially set, or of working hard for financial goals. Just find your bliss and live one day at a time.

All of this is a learning process of what not to do. Once you discover who you are inside, your spirit self, then you start to feed that energy. And you start your spiritual practices. That is the way of the Tao. To do all of that, you have to discover what not to do. Because in reality, those things do not make you happy; they do not give you peace of mind. You go within yourself and make yourself happy in the glory of your God. So in my little journey I discovered what not to do.

I do not have a monkey mind like the Taoists say. I have a five-hundred-pound gorilla sitting on my shoulders, and you can believe me, I have a lot more to discover of what not to do. I am on the same journey you are, so do not think you are alone.

Here is one more example of what not to do. A fellow senior instructor advised me to invest in a turnaround money transfer that would double and triple my investment in a few months. I needed to raise money to purchase my mountain retreat, so I wired him $10,000 and was supposed to receive $60,000 in six months. I felt he was a fellow instructor and could be trusted. That was ten years ago and I have not seen a dime. He has had every excuse you can imagine, but still there is no money. I've since found out that he has initiated various tricky schemes with others who have lost large amounts of money too.

When that did not work out, I met a student and told him I still

Fig. 4.40. I do not have a monkey mind like the Taoists say. I have a five-hundred-pound gorilla sitting on my shoulders.

Fig 4.41. I wired him $50,000 and expected a return of $250,000 in six months, which would buy the land, rebuild the roads to the property, and build my dwellings. I never saw a dime.

needed to raise the money for my mountain retreat and he said he was a multimillionaire but his money was offshore in the Caribbean Islands. He also had a turnaround money transfer deal and it would return five to one. So I trusted him and thought he was sincere. I wired him $50,000 and expected a return of $250,000 in six months, which would buy the land, rebuild the roads to the property, and build my dwellings. Guess what? I never saw a dime. Funny how that works.

If you can look at life in a forgiving way, forgiving yourself for getting into real trouble in discovering what not to do, you are okay. Everything is okay. Just let go and more opportunities will flow in; but if you hang on to them, you cut the flow off and no more opportunities will come because you are blocking them off by hanging on to old situations, difficulties, or problems.

But more important, you will be happy and you will be enjoying the ride because nothing really matters. When you slow the mind down you realize everything is just an illusion and we are all actors

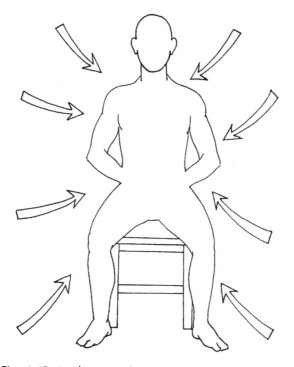

Fig. 4.42. Just let go and more opportunities will flow in.

playing out our parts and discovering what we are here to discover and what not to do.

In reality, you will discover within yourself that you are divine and everything you do is good. It is only a matter of discovering your own consciousness. Your whole purpose in being here is to discover; that is what life is all about. All your experiences and knowledge add to your understandings and your own wisdom.

Medicine Meals— Foods That Heal

OUR GREATEST APPETITES

Our two greatest appetites are sex and food, but they are also our two greatest medicines. We do not really have a true understanding of what food and sex are. We have been conditioned by our society and our upbringing to think of them in one way, but once we understand what they really are and how to utilize them, they will become our greatest medicines and we can learn to heal our bodies with them.

Fig. 5.1. Two great appetites

Fig. 5.2. Medicine meals—foods that heal

The meals we eat can actually heal our bodies when we use them as medicines. In other words, when you start to stick something in your mouth, look at it not as an enjoyment of what it tastes like, but for its healing properties. To fully grasp this, you really have to understand how your body functions.

Our health is really determined by the healing practices that we do to create an internal environment in which the body can function properly. This deals not only with the pH balance, but also our physical conditions. The Taoists have a great and vast understanding of the different body types, the different hot and cold energies in the body, and how they affect the body energy, how the energies move throughout the body. It is very important that we first start to understand how to utilize our two greatest appetites to strengthen our body instead of weaken our body. You learn to understand how your body functions and what you really need for the body and its special conditions. This takes into consideration the body types of lesser yang, greater yang, lesser yin, and greater yin; and it can be expanded to the various conditions in the body and what emphasis we should place on them to utilize these two greatest appetites. So meals can become our medicines if we first understand how the body reacts to certain internal combinations of foods, how they are assimilated, and how they are utilized in the body. We must take this into consideration as we slowly discover who we are physically and how this physical form functions and is properly put to its full use.

The Taoists are very clear on this. The internal energy of the body has to be balanced—not too much, not too little, just enough to balance every aspect of the body so the energy can flow freely. One of the problems we run into in the West is our idea that the body itself is controlled by outside influences and that the physical form actually produces the energy form. But in the Eastern and Taoist understanding, the energy itself actually manifests the physical, because in essence, we are just an electromagnetic radiation field. Once the food enters the body and is broken down and digested, we actually assimilate digested resin, not the physical food form itself but the energetic form, which gives off a positive and negative charge. How we utilize that charge is really determined by the internal environment of the body. If that environment is not balanced, this creates a reaction to the foods and their electrical charge to determine the course of the body, either the creative cycle or the destructive cycle, which is prevalent in every other aspect of nature. You see, the same energy

Fig. 5.3. Creative and destructive cycles

in a tree is in us, and that same life force is also in the mountain, the river, the sun, and the earth. All of these energy vibrations, this life force, are also within our body. We must learn to balance this energy to utilize the strengths of the food and actually determine our health and well-being.

Food's ability to satiate our appetite is really determined by our taste, which is learned from society, not from what food actually does to the body. If we can step back and take a clear understanding of how this food actually does trigger a certain response in our body, instead of being conditioned by society's taste, we can determine why we consume certain foods to feed our appetites. It is almost like a cycle we get into. In other words, once you develop a taste for something, you crave that taste. Health is a whole process of relearning this taste or changing the attitude toward the food, not as something to feed our appetite or feed this conditioning. Health is about learning what the food actually does in the body, so the foods can help balance and heal the body.

Getting back to the Tao again, the whole key is balance. When we are balanced, the energy flows evenly and fully throughout the body, and this flow determines our health and well-being. So by using these appetites and reconditioning our taste, creating a new appetite in our

Fig. 5.4. Balance is the key.

bodies for health and balance, as opposed to cravings and imbalances, we can create a whole cycle that perpetuates itself. We can learn how to utilize our taste and develop new taste habits to actually determine our health.

As infants we had totally different tastes and appetites. As the conditioning took place in our body from our environment and culture, it trained us in unhealthy eating habits. The Taoists say that you must first come to a point of being satiated to really move through these appetites, thereby creating different appetites with understanding, knowledge, and wisdom of how we can apply these in our daily lives. You first must take a hard look at yourself to see how these foods actually interact in your body, which leads us to the whole concept of creating a creative cycle in the body on the cellular level as opposed to a destructive cycle. Again this is the process found throughout nature: as the leaf falls from the tree, it goes into a destructive cycle and composts into the soil. The soil grows the seed (the creative cycle), which becomes a tree; the leaves are formed and then they fall, completing the cycle—from creation, or the creative cycle, to the controlling or destructive cycle. This is the basic concept of the whole Taoist system and the five elements.

To utilize our greatest appetites as our greatest medicines, we must realize that what we consume can really determine our health, and that diet is the basis of all health. Diet can consist of what we draw into our body through our meals, which determines the body's internal environment and our cell structure, where we live, and the environment in which we operate. This can also kick off the destructive cycle, when the environment of our home life or our work life creates pollutions that we have to deal with or eliminate. They create blockages and imbalances in the body. This can be the simple emotional stress from being in an environment that is not consistent with our internal balancing of our energy, or it could be in a job-related situation with extreme stress and pressure on your physical and emotional beings, which are really one. Once we start to utilize these appetites with a clear understanding of using them as medicines and not poisons, we will see how these foods actually interact with our body.

This takes into account the whole concept of the pH factor, which is also perpetuated by the Taoists' understanding of the balance of yin and yang, yang being the positive (alkaline) and yin being the negative (acidic). In studying the Tao, you will start to understand the different implications these have on cell structure. As we balance our body and the cellular structure in the blood, it manifests first from an energetic level and then into cell structure as bones and skin, determining our whole well-being and understanding. As we balance ourselves physically, using meals as our medicines, we start to balance ourselves emotionally, psychologically, and spiritually (all are one).

The key to this whole process is diet. What we put into the body determines our health and how well we eliminate the excess or the imbalances of the body. In the chapter "Mountain and Ocean," we will also learn how we can utilize the sexual energy, the other medicine, to balance and heal our bodies. The key is moderation, number one—and when you start to break down the intricacies of how the food is actually assimilated in the body and how it functions, then you will discover what foods can really heal you and contribute to your health and well-being. Initially you need to have a change in attitude, which is created by your intention. Why are you eating the food? Is it for enjoyment or is it for health? Once you make that distinction then you can start to work with a further breakdown of what foods are balancing energetically and healing for you as opposed to the foods that are not. Then you can start to make conscious choices and, with the Taoist meditation practices, slow down the mind. They might not always be the correct choices for you at the particular time, but at least you are aware that there is a choice. Where there is a choice, there is an opportunity for change. In this case, you are utilizing your meals as medicines. Once you can make that distinction, you are a lot further ahead. Again, the way of Tao is one of understanding, wisdom, and knowledge, so that you would have the opportunities to make these conscious choices for yourself.

Fig. 5.5. Eat simply with simple foods.

There are some simple guidelines for making meals into medicine. You should eat simply, with not too many ingredients; too many foods at once creates harder work for your spleen, which governs your digestive process. The simple foods will give you support by making your digestion easy, as well as giving you an inner sense of clarity. The simpler the food you eat, the more your food becomes medicine.

Second, eat lightly. Again, moderation is the key. When you overeat you congest the spleen function and that is a major cause of stagnation and dampness in the body. So the art is to stop eating before you are actually full, which is the 70 percent rule (only eating to 70 percent of your capacity). If you can do this, then you will find you will have much more energy, so never overdo anything because the body can only function as much as it can process at one given time. If you overload it, eating too much even when it is good balanced foods, you can cause great damage. If you drink too much water, it could kill you. As you slow the mind down, you start to tune into the body's needs and utilize your meals as medicines. You will understand what it is to overindulge (overeating or overdrinking) and that you just need a little bit of food and drink. As you use this moderation technique, you will discover your own standard of health and well-being.

Third, you should separate your foods and when you start to eat this simply, you will discover that either mono meals (one food at a time) or a little bit of food from two or three different food types is all you need. This is called food combining: how you mix your proteins and carbohydrates. The key is to eat simply; the more you eat individual foods by themselves the easier they will be to digest.

Fourth, when you drink with your meals, the water or liquid dilutes the digestive process, which impairs the spleen and its function. It is generally better to limit the intake to a cup of water or tea at meals than to dilute your digestive juices with too much water.

Fifth, avoid too many cold foods, because cold foods overwhelm the digestive fire and can slow down the digestive process.

Sixth, and most important, is how well you chew the food. As you break down the food you need to chew it slowly and well, which reduces the work for your stomach and your intestines, eliminating the fear that would lead to contraction in your liver and impatience pattern deficiency (a pattern of frequent urination) in your bladder. Saliva plays a very important part in the digestive process. So slowly chew and begin to digest the foods in the mouth. The saying in the Tao is, "You drink your foods and chew your liquids and do it separately." In other words, you chew the food to such a point where it is actually a liquid and then you swallow it. Your mouth is your first digestive process. You should wash the liquid around in your mouth to activate the saliva so it does its natural process of beginning the digestive process.

THE BODY—A CHEMICAL FACTORY

Your body is a chemical factory. The key to the Tao is to balance yourself chemically, first on an energetic level, which we try to do in the meditations of the Taoist practices. You learn to heal the body as you learn how the body functions on a chemical level, and when you get to the immortal Tao you will learn how to transform yourself in the alchemical process by alchemically balancing the body. You will actually change one substance, your physical body, into another substance, your spirit body. This is the same process you utilize when you first balance yourself chemically in the body to heal the body. When you start out, you learn to balance yourself chemically and you become aware of the alkaline and acidic substances in the body and how they balance one another, which is the positive and negative charge both in our energetic field and our body's molecular structure. What we are trying to do is balance the pH factor in the blood and ultimately in the body. As you work with the blood it manifests into the body (cells, bones, tendons, and muscles). This incorporates all the concepts that were brought out by Dr. Robert Young's books *Sick and Tired* and *The pH Miracle*, which tie into all the Taoist concepts of the creative cycle and the digestive cycle in the body's cellular structure.

You see, when we digest food, we break it down into its chemical parts, and as it is drawn into the blood and carried to the cells, the cells will absorb whatever chemicals on a molecular level there are in this digestive substance, by absorbing the electrical charge, either positive or negative, that it gives off. This in turn creates the internal terrain of the cell body. Now, if we can change the internal terrain of the body with the proper foods, we can determine the cell balance and activate the creative cycle. But we live in a very acidic environment internally and externally, and the more alkaline-charged foods need to become our medicines. This is how our meals become our medicines. As we digest the food in our digestive system

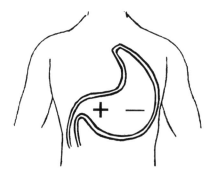

Fig. 5.6. Electrical charge, positive or negative

it becomes digested resin. The body is actually a chemical factory producing a specific electrical charge that breaks particular foods down on a molecular level into chemicals. We can learn to utilize the chemical reactions in the body to determine our health and well-being. Basically, if we can create the environment in the body of a balanced pH, positive to negative, yin to yang, we can start to utilize this whole healing process and actually transform everything in the body over a short period (two to three months, with a complete transformation in three years). This actually can take care of any of our degenerative problems that we create with the blockages caused by acids in the body.

Dr. Young proposed that every cell of the body has a life force, which he terms a microzyma. Microzymas are the cosmic dust particles—the life force that the Taoists have been talking about for centuries. Through the microzyma this life force is working in either the creative cycle or the destructive cycle, creating new cells or destroying the whole cell itself by creating a whole other organism. In the destructive cycle, this other organism starts out as a bacterium, then a yeast, then a fungus, then a mold, and ultimately a cancer. It has a life of its own and it overtakes the body. This is the whole process of the destructive cycle.

This process can be easily illustrated in a banana. If you look at

Fig. 5.7. Cosmic dust particles

a banana after you pick it from the tree it is green, or if it is ripe it is yellow. Now, as you pick it off the tree, it slowly goes to a certain point over the alkaline level and then into the acidic level, which starts the whole fermentation process. You see the spots on the banana peel, but this fermenting process is taking place inside the banana. The same would take place on a cellular level in our own human body from the inside out, appearing on our skin. Just like the banana, the body moves from yang, the creative cycle, into yin, the destructive cycle.

Now internally in the body this whole process is taking place on a chemical level in every cell. You can, with a balanced environment, maintain that young cell (banana) forever if you maintain an alkaline diet to keep the creative cycle perpetually alive. This is the theory and concept of the Tao, with the perpetual life force of the cosmic dust particles.

Once we balance ourselves by taking in the proper foods, using our meals as medicines to heal and balance the body within the blood on the cellular level, we can start to discover and experience what it is to be truly healthy and immortal. The microzyma actually determines this, working within our cell through our internal terrain. The cells are immortal. If we place our body in a natural healthy outer environment while maintaining a balanced environment internally within our cells by using food as a medicine, we create a positive creative cycle instead of a negative destructive cycle. If you learn to maintain this you can have it throughout your entire existence on the earth plane, which, in theory, could be indefinitely.

If we maintain a balanced environment internally within the cell, which is determined by the food that we take into the body, using them as medicines, you will create the positive creating cycle instead of the negative destructive cycle. You can maintain this throughout your whole existence on the earth plane if you learn to maintain the internal environment within a cell, which is determined by what we take into the body and what we place the body in, our outer environment.

Fig. 5.8. Positive creative cycle

Again, from that standpoint, we are talking about living in a natural environment, because the same energy and all the five elements in nature are inside our bodies, which is the coherent connectedness that we have within ourselves and in the environment around us. This is as opposed to living in an artificial environment, in houses and various cities made of steel and cement, which are all manmade. We are surrounded by everything from artificial light from our lamps to artificial water that is all filtered and not natural from the streams. We have artificial wood instead of sitting on and being around the trees and using natural fires, and we are not living on the earth soil and connected with the earth and the environment with greens of the trees and the foliage.

Once we separate ourselves from the five elements, we create uneasiness and an imbalance within the cells on a structural level, creating the destructive cycle. About 99 percent of our culture lives in these artificial environments—not only living in them, but also working in them. This creates added stress that kicks off this negativity or acidic buildup in the body on a cellular level, which creates a downward spiral within the body itself.

The key is to try to do a transition to utilize the chemical factory of the body to balance ourselves internally with the foods we take in. We want to maintain this balance of the acid and alkaline pH factor and keep this balance within ourselves. What we need to do is not only focus on the foods as medicine, but on the environment itself as a meal, which has a very strong influence on the body, and to utilize both internally and externally these environments as our medicines to heal and balance ourselves. Now this is a whole process, so you need to take one step at a time. Through this, you will start to learn to balance your energy within its own process of growing and reconnecting.

DIGESTION

This alkaline and acid balance is in play in all the organic material that we take in. The balance of these two gives us the key to our physical health, but first we must understand that the medium, our bloodstream, is slightly alkaline at 7.36 pH, and what we need to do is maintain this slightly alkaline balance within the blood to have a balance in our body for health and longevity.

We need to consume foods that will be slightly alkaline once we have digested them. You see, when food enters the body, it might come in as acid, but as you break it down it might give off a positive digestive resin charge (alkaline). This has all been well analyzed over many years to show us the proper foods for the balancing of our particular body. For more information on the alkaline foods, check the alkaline diet in Robert O. Young's book *Sick and Tired* or in

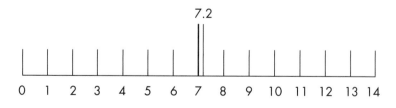

Fig. 5.9. pH balance

Fig. 5.10. Digested resin

Christopher Vasey's book *The Acid-Alkaline Diet for Optimum Health.**

Literally, we do not eat food; we digest food. What we actually assimilate is digested resin on a molecular level once it gets into the cells of our body. This digested resin has to be in the medium that is positive or alkaline. This is what we try to do to have the creative cycle. If we do not, then we enter the destructive cycle and the body breaks down by all of our modern degenerative diseases. The body destroys itself.

One of the big problems is that when we eat, we consume too many acidic foods (animal products, junk foods, and packaged foods). This creates a chemical imbalance in the body. The acidic foods in the West that create this syndrome are animal products (meats—uric acid, milk/butter—lactic acid, eggs—sulfuric acid) and a lot of foods that actually ferment in the body because of the sugar content (condiments, junk foods, candies, pastries).

*Robert O. Young, Ph.D., D.Sc., with Shelley Redford Young, L.M.T., *Sick and Tired? Reclaim Your Inner Terrain* (Pleasant Grove, Utah: Woodland Publishing, 2001) and Christopher Vasey, N.D., Jon Graham, trans., *The Acid-Alkaline Diet for Optimum Health: Restore Your Health by Creating Balance in Your Diet* (Rochester, Vt.; Healing Arts Press, 2003).

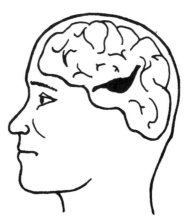

Fig. 5.11. Aneurysms kill.

Animal food products send off a negative charge that is acidic. In most animals, this means uric acid or sulfuric acid, which is neutralized with calcium. If your body did not neutralize it with calcium, you would die from internal hemorrhaging from holes burned in the arteries (aneurysm), which causes death in many people after years of consuming acidic foods with an acidic lifestyle. Finally, the acidic buildup breaks out and they die at a premature age.

Obviously, the body does not want to die, so it does what it can to preserve itself. Where does it get the calcium to neutralize the acid, which is in the body? It comes from our bones. It actually draws out the calcium, the alkaline reserve, from the bones to neutralize the uric acid in the bloodstream when it is assimilated in the cell. Over time, thirty, forty, or fifty years, what results from this is osteoporosis, which occurs in women around the age of sixty-six and in men around the age of eighty. This leads to another problem in the aging process: when the elderly fall and break bones, like hips, they never heal. The spine starts to bend down or break down, creating a hunched-over posture, and the bones become brittle and break, and then mend incorrectly.

Your body begins to disintegrate in front of your eyes and it literally shrinks because the calcium is being leached out of your bones to

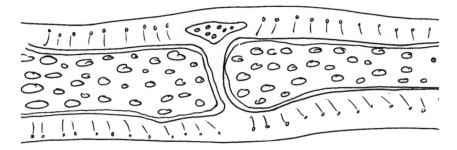

Fig. 5.12. Acids leach the body of calcium.

neutralize the uric acid from the consumption of animal food products, which we urinate out of the body. It's quite possible to urinate the bones out of the body, when all you have to do is change your diet from acid to alkaline.

Acidic foods are also concentrated sugars, honey, fruits, fruit juices, breads, and pastas, as well as all pastries, which further leach the calcium from our bones. This can also be leached out from table salt, which is chemically changed. We need a tremendous amount of sodium to maintain the body; but we need to obtain it from vegetables, sea plants, and natural mineral salts (sea salt). It is amazing what happens when you slow down the mind and make conscious choices. Number one in this process is changing your diet, which is swimming with the river instead of against it.

Once you flood yourself with uric acid from animal products, then you flood yourself with calcium, the buffer salt, from your bones to neutralize it. All the calcium is filtered from your bloodstream through your kidneys. This is how we get kidney stones, gallstones, and arthritis. You see how this is a chain reaction to all our degenerative diseases. All you have to do is change your diet and living environment.

The key to good health is creating an alkaline balance, which you can achieve through the consumption of about 80 percent alkaline foods to 20 percent acidic foods in your meals. Animal products, packaged foods, junk foods, and processed foods cause toxemia in the body, causing all the degenerative diseases like cancer, osteoporosis, heart disease, arthritis, urinary disease, diabetes, hypertension, and others. The key is to actually utilize our meals to balance and fortify our internal environment so the body can do its natural process of cleansing itself out of these built-up and stored acids.

VEGETABLE PRODUCTS

Animal food products contain no carbohydrates, fiber, or vitamin C. They are higher in uric acid and chemical sodium and lower in potassium, and they are a poorer source of calcium than plant foods. Dairy products contain pesticides and phosphates, which neutralize the benefits of the calcium and cause osteoporosis. Pure vegetarian animals (buffalos, horses, and elephants) create huge bone structures with hundreds of pounds of calcium and never drink milk or eat cheese. These vegetarian animals get all their calcium from greens, grains, nuts, and vegetables.

Most of the degenerative diseases are caused by animal food products, but not all of them. There are four other factors involved: emotional stress, concentrated sugars and salts (junk foods), continuous activity, and environmental chemical toxins. These environmental toxins are fat soluble, which means they adhere to fat. That is how we actually retain weight in the body. On average, animal food products are 30 percent fat, and chemical toxins adhere to these fats. When you consume the fats in your animal products, you consume the toxic chemicals from the pesticides, industrial waste, arsenic, aluminum, and herbicides buried in the ground and buried in the lakes, rivers, and seas. Animal flesh is further contaminated by hormone stimulants and antibiotics used in the agricultural processing industry.

Vegetable products, on the other hand, contain 1 percent or 0.5 percent fat. So if you obtain both animal and vegetable products from the same environment, which is your local area, you get the chemical toxins from the animal products but not the vegetables, because there is no real fat content in the vegetables for the toxins to adhere to.

Well how about fish? This is not an animal food product, but fish are animals and the chemical toxins are found everywhere in our environment, even the deepest seas. When a fish breathes, its gills filter the oxygen from the water and also filter the water. What do they do with the debris, poisons, and toxins they filter in the water? Those end up in the fish's body, in the fish's fat. The fish is also 30 percent fat; the toxins and chemicals, being fat soluble, adhere to this 30 percent of the fish, and that is what we end up with.

With vegetables, it is quite interesting that people do not distinguish the correct vegetables from what they actually consume. Again, with proper understanding, you will start to understand there are many vegetables that, once digested, give off a certain charge, either positive or negative, and again this has all been broken down on a molecular level in microbiology to determine this electrical charge that is sent off to neutralize and create the balance in the body and the creative cycle. The body reproduces itself over a period of months through its organs and through its breakdown of cells. The body re-creates itself again and again with the substances you put in it.

Now the body, in its struggle to survive, has various buffer states that it puts into our environment internally. The number-one buffer is fat. We actually produce our own fats to neutralize the overly acidic environment that we place ourselves in through our external environment and our internal environment. To reverse the process and create meals as medicines, we are in effect transforming the negative environment into a positive environment, from the destructive cycle to the creative cycle. On a molecular level, with the cellular structure through the blood, we can create perpetual life within our own physical body. We can refine the body and start to educate ourselves on what our body actually needs to maintain itself through this creative cycle. As we slowly determine this, we will start to discover that a whole transition will take place physically in the body. The excess fat that you have stored or created within your body to neutralize the acids that we have consumed with an improper diet and imbalance will disappear by using meals as medicine. When you are not taking in so many acids, your body will automatically and naturally eliminate the fat. This is fat buildup that has been in our bodies for years—the fat you can never lose with all of our imbalanced exercise practices and various extreme diets. Yet, it goes away naturally and quickly by changing our meals to medicines.

There is an old saying that medicines never really taste that good. Well, you can slowly learn to develop a taste that has artificially been suppressed with all the acidic condiments we put on our acid foods (meats and pastries) to make them palatable. In the same process, you can retrain yourself with the proper eating and the proper understanding of your taste for whole foods without any condiments (sugars) and again getting back to our original concept and desired manifestation. Once you understand how and why it works, you will have the desire to make it work, and then you will actually do what you need to do. That is how it is manifested (the desired objective): the mental body (concept) controls the emotional body (desire), and the emotional body controls the physical body (manifestation).

The basic theme of this chapter is that our meals are our greatest medicines, and if we understand how food functions within our body, we can create our own meals to have a balance within the cellular structure. This will create the harmony of the creative cycle and actu-

Fig. 5.13. How foods function in our body

ally give us perpetual life on a physical level. This is all in the concepts. These concepts are presented in this chapter so you can utilize them. Again, this is a transition and it takes time (years of trial and error) in this transition. But stick with it; it will happen.

Let's get back to the buffer states. First of all, the body utilizes fat to neutralize the acid, or it stores the acid so it does not burn a hole in the cellular structures or the tubing of the body. The carbonated drinks and all the junk food that we eat can burn a hole in our arteries. It is amazing when you look at what it does to your digestive system as well. You get the bloating in the upper abdominal area (beer belly), gas, diarrhea, and nausea. All these effects derive from these ill-created meals, which actually create this whole destructive cycle in the body. But utilizing the same concept and feeding the body with meals that heal, you start to create the meals as medicines within your body, which is just a basic concept shift. The body creates buffers to neutralize acids, the first buffer being the fats, which is why 80 percent of Americans and a large percentage of the whole world are overweight. Because we live in acidic environments and continue to feed ourselves acidic foods, we create a whole destructive cycle within ourselves. There is a loss of harmony and a corruption of our peace of mind in this process, which creates further ramifications to create more acidic conditions (wars, hatred, cruelty, fear, dishonesty)—all because of the acidic foods we eat within our environment.

The next buffer the body uses is cholesterol. We hear we have too much cholesterol and you have all these foods (vegetables) that have no cholesterol in them. But in fact, the body actually creates cholesterol, which is a fatty substance, and it coats the arteries with it because the acidic flow of the blood through the arteries is so strong that it will burn a hole in the artery or in the vessel itself if it is not coated with fat. That is what an aneurysm is. There is a punctured hole in the vessel and the blood seeps out into the rest of the body, which causes death at a premature age. People die every day from this, and it is simply an acidic problem. The problem for the body is that acid builds up in the body and the cholesterol gets so thick—to neutralize the acid—

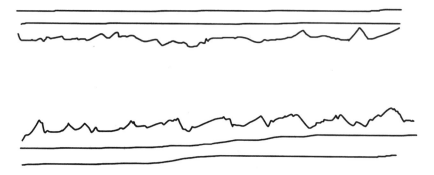

Fig. 5.14. Body buffers neutralize acids.

that it causes plugs in the arteries of the heart. This is the condition that leads to the need for open-heart surgery. During this procedure, all they are doing is opening up the chest and bypassing the blockage because the body built up the cholesterol it manufactured to neutralize the acid. But a strange thing happens. Once you eliminate the acid and flush the body out through hydrogenation, utilizing greens and neutralizing food, you can actually just take out this whole blockage and—using these medicine meals—the body will heal itself.

Medicine meals consist of vegetable products, the green products. There are various substances that you can buy (20:1 alkaline to acid) that are basically dried grasses in alkalinized water. This creates the whole pH balance to neutralize the acid and flush the acid out of the body. The more alkalinized water you put into the body, the more you flush or wash out this acidic resin, and the body will actually transform itself. Instead of being in the destructive cycle, which is ultimately death through the process of bacteria, yeast, fungus, mold, and cancer, you can reverse the process and create the whole creative cycle with young, healthy cells. This transformation, depending on your condition, can take anywhere from three months to three years. People do not realize we actually create new cells every day and we eliminate the old ones—but if you stop creating young, healthy cells, you cannot get rid of the old ones. So the old cells build up and take up their own form and life cycle (bacteria, yeast, fungus, mold, and cancer), which is totally the opposite of the actual function of the body. This is what cancer is. Cancer overruns the body on a cellular level through the blood first. As we learn to check our live blood cells and change our degenerating meals to medicine meals, we start to create a whole other cycle (creative cycle) in the body and create a whole natural environment to live within.

When you eat green vegetables, the chlorophyll (the liquid light from the sun) comes into your body and cleanses and purifies the existing cells. You see, the structure of the molecule in chlorophyll is exactly the same pattern as the cell structure in our human blood cell, with one difference. The nucleus in the chlorophyll is magnesium, which gives vegetables their green color. The nucleus in the human blood cell is iron, which gives blood its red color when it oxidizes in the exposed air. In essence, what we are doing is cleansing ourselves with the friendly green plants. The green energy cleanses the red energy of all the toxins, and that is why the strongest animals on the planet are bigger and stronger than the humans because they are in the natural flow of consuming this liquid light in the form of chlorophyll from the plants. All these animals consume a diet that's at least 95 percent leafy vegetables, leaves from the trees and grasses. The

Fig. 5.15. Green energy cleanses.

same life force of these animals is the same in the plant and is the same in us. That is why we should not consume the bodies of animals or the degenerative foods from rearranged chemicals that come out of the soil. These foods are actually oils or gas, which create plastics because they change the foods' molecular structure. This is not the same structure as our physical body, which is a big problem (the acid problem). We need to consume foods that have the same natural structure as the molecular structure of our blood.

YOU EAT IT, YOU WEAR IT

When you consume the fat from animal products—beef, chicken, pork, turkey, fowl, fish, eggs, milk, butter, cheese, and yogurt—you consume cholesterol. We manufacture all the cholesterol we need in our own body. This cholesterol is a very greasy and waxy substance, which our body cannot break down or assimilate. It is saturated fat, which is solid at room temperature. You eat it, you wear it.

The acidic foods you bring into the body neutralize into fat, so you end up wearing it all over your body, mostly in your midriff, as well as your sides and in your legs. Luckily, not too much collects around the heart or the head or you would be dead immediately. It is going to go to the areas where the body can store it, but with too much of these impure acidic foods that are not assimilated in the body, you end up wearing these foods. They are actually flushed into the body. They go through the bloodstream in the form of fat. They build up into plaque on the arteries and eventually that blocks the artery.

Then we have open-heart bypass surgery, and it costs sixty thousand dollars to open the chest up and cut the artery, bypassing the blocked artery and reconnecting it to the next artery with a tube. However, the surgeons do not remove the debris, and the procedure does nothing to stop you from having another obstruction.

This entire procedure is hideous waste of time and money when all you really need to do is stop eating the animal products and other fermenting products that caused the obstruction. Remember, plants do not contain any cholesterol at all. We produce our own cholesterol to neutralize the acids, so we need the correct environment within our body by not taking in acidic foods; and then we do need to neutralize the acid or flush it out. The less you put in, the less you have to get rid of, or the less you have to wear if you cannot get rid of it. This is the whole process of retraining yourself using medicine meals.

Many different diets have been marketed and exploited to the public. Many of them work partially for a lot of different reasons, but they never really have the true concept of how to create health. The true concept brings in the creative cycle and the destructive cycle as the pH balance of the yin and yang—the alkaline and acid—within the body. None of these other diets have the understanding of pH that Dr. Young's diet and Dr. Vasey's diet have. Their understanding coincides with this concept of the Tao.

The Taoists have always talked about the cosmic dust particles that come from the stars. These are our life force and are on the microscopic level. We cannot really see them, but they are actually particles of light. We take them into our body. No matter what we eat, 75 percent of all our nutrition comes from the air. You can live without food for sixty days or more and without water for two weeks or more, but with air you can only go without it for three or four

Fig. 5.16. Particles of light

minutes. It makes sense that what we breathe is what we actually utilize for our fuel.

As we breathe, we take in the cosmic dust particles, which Dr. Young calls the microzymas. They are actually the life force that enter and create our cells. We determine if they create a cell or destroy the cell in the creative or destructive cycle by what we eat. What we consume creates a positive or negative charge, changing the internal environment of the particular cell; and that is what determines the cycle the microzyma, or cosmic dust particle, decides to take. The microzyma has consciousness and is imperishable, so it can think and is immortal.

This coincides totally with the Taoist concept of yin and yang moving from the creative and the destructive cycles. If we can maintain balance in the internal environment of the cell and our external environment, there is no aging process, and death becomes only a memory of the past. This is what we can achieve if we realize that what we eat is what we wear. If you consume a balanced pH substance, then you do not wear any extra baggage (fat) because the body does not need to neutralize the acid with fat or cholesterol buildup. When we digest acidic foods, the acids are trapped in the body. The body has to neutralize them either by getting rid of them (urination and sweating) or storing them in the body fat.

The body creates fat to neutralize and store the acid, and that is why you have the heavy fats in your legs and around your abdominal area, which makes you immobile and is quite uncomfortable. It is very tough to get rid of it because you need to get rid of the acid, not the fat. Once you stop taking the acid into the body, the body will initially eliminate the acids naturally. As it eliminates the acids, it no longer needs the buffer state (the fats) to neutralize the acids in the body; therefore it gets rid of the fat at the same time.

That is the theory and concept. Without the theory and concept we go on in our monkey-mind way and create all these other diet variations that make no sense whatsoever and ultimately cause our own demise (more acid) instead of living within our body with medicine meals that create balance, harmony, and total longevity. You can achieve immortality on a physical level just by what you eat and do not eat.

WHOLE FOODS

A wonderful thing happens to a body when it is in an environment that is not continually plugged up: it heals itself. If we do not eat animal products and other fermenting products created from sugars, we will balance the body. This is difficult in the West because our diet is centered around these products.

You can get help, though. Five thousand years ago, meat products were not the central part of people's diets. They sustained themselves on vegetables and natural whole foods. They sustained themselves on a diet of leafy vegetables, legumes, and grasses, which are vegetables and simple carbohydrates, and they did not eat excess fruits. The best foods to eat are whole foods that are not processed or degenerated and contain all the fibers, fats, carbohydrates, proteins, minerals, vitamins, and water you need. By purchasing whole foods in bulk, they are also 40 percent cheaper than packaged processed foods, and you can get the benefit of the natural fiber.

Vegan products

Tofu

Fig. 5.17. A diet of leafy vegetables, legumes, grasses, and complex carbohydrates will balance the body.

Fiber is also very important, which is why we want to eat the foods whole, especially sprouted grains. They are water soluble, which improves the healing process of our digestive system and the elimination process through our intestines.

Eating is really a social disease where people are pressured into eating foods from family and cultural traditions that are offered at social gatherings. They are questioned and belittled if they do not comply with what others are eating. This creates a lot of ridicule and bitterness in these social gatherings.

This forces people with clear consciousness and understanding of proper eating habits to allow their body to fall into the bad eating habits shared by others. Food is meant to heal and balance our bodies, not to be used as entertainment or social acceptance. But this is what society has created for us in our conditioned communities. What creates you also created the whole foods that you are intended to eat, which are not manmade or processed foods. A lot of animal products have to be extremely processed to make them palatable for our human taste. They are not palatable because we are not supposed to take them in.

Many of your commercially processed meats are dyed red to make them more appealing to the consumer. They are red because manufacturers dye them and they make them palatable with a lot

Fig. 5.18. Whole foods have natural fiber.

of different condiments (chemical sugars and salts) so you can swallow them. In essence, what you are really tasting is the condiments. It is not the actual taste of the meat itself. No one would eat it if it wasn't processed. It does not taste like anything because it is dead. It has no life in it, no usable chi or energy. In fact, the microzyma is in the destructive cycle decomposing the meat, which is why it will rot unless it is frozen. It will break itself down, but it does not have any creative life force for our cellular structures.

The same thing is true with dairy products. They process these continually to make them palatable. If you sit back and watch the whole show it is really kind of funny what they do just to get money out of you for their products.

If you eat whole foods and you buy them bulk, you save money and get the best alkaline foods for your microzymas. The best place to purchase them is from your local farms, because then you buy it whole and consume it fresh from that local area. When possible, buy organic whole foods for their taste and nutritional value. They do not have any added chemicals in them that the body has to eliminate because the body cannot assimilate them.

Your diet should basically consist of greens, vegetables, sprouted grains, seeds, nuts, and legumes, which are easy to assimilate raw or with a small percentage of processing involved (steaming). You should learn to eat whole and fresh. There are many diet books on this that

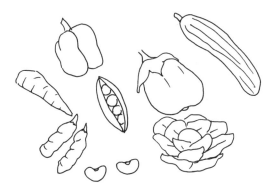

Fig. 5.19. A natural diet of whole foods will balance your pH factor.

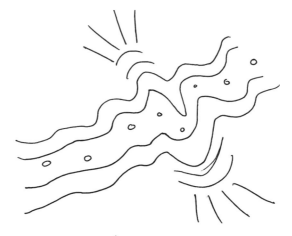

Fig. 5.20. Inflammation is caused by acid in the body.

are based on the pH balance within the blood, initiating the creative cycle controlled by the internal environment of the cell itself.

This is pretty much a mucusless diet—a diet that creates no mucus, which is a byproduct of inflammation in the body. Again, this is an inflammation that is caused by the acidic foods in the body, so you should slowly move from one point to another. You should make this transition from an acidic diet to alkaline diet, finding harmony and peace in the process.

One of the key ingredients to all of this is sodium. Sodium carbonate neutralizes the acids in the body. Many people are familiar with baking soda, which they place in the refrigerator because it eliminates the odors. Well, the odors are created by the fermenting process as the food breaks down in the destructive cycle managed by the microzymas. Many people have seen salt sticks left out for cattle and other animals so they can lick the salt. Well, sodium is very important to the body because it moves the cell structure and various liquids around in the body. Without it we cannot function properly. There are a lot of very good mineral salts; the Taoists put out an alchemical salt that heals the body. It contains the five elements and there are products like Real Salt and even nonchemical sea salt.

A lot of salts are processed with added chemicals in them that are not assimilated within the body and are just poisons to the body. What we need to do is utilize these nonchemical salts themselves to detoxify the body of any contaminations. This helps all the body fluids move in a natural way, the way of the Tao.

THE ALKALINE DIET

What people have lived on to maintain themselves for longevity is the alkaline diet. Instead of protein from meat and animal products as a major part of a meal, in the alkaline diet, greens are a large part of the meal. We take in grasses, green leafy vegetables, root vegetables, and sprouted whole grains. You get the strength of the grain itself, but in a sprouted state, which is the highest nutritional form of any plant. When a plant first sprouts, it has the highest amount of power and level of nutrition.

Green leafy vegetables would be your basic meal. This would be broccoli, collard greens, wheat greens, cucumber, lettuces (romaine and bib), pungent onions, radishes, daikons, carrots, root vegetables—

Fig. 5.21. An alkaline diet is heavily based on greens and vegetables

like turnips, sweet potatoes, yams, and beets—and kale. These are all the items in the alkaline diet; if you ate this diet, you would eliminate any allergies and skin problems and improve the digestive process. Fatigue would be a great area that you would eliminate because the body would flow naturally, balancing each cell with the chlorophyll.

Fat is not the problem. All we have is an acidic problem. With the alkaline system and diet, a person emphasizes the alkaline food, drink, and lifestyle; therefore, you maintain a basic alkaline balance of the acid/alkaline body chemistry for promoting health and vitality. It is just a matter of making a conscious choice and now you have the choice.

One big factor is the alkaline water. You need to drink water and one of the problems in our culture is that we are all dehydrated. We are all stuck (dried up) and that is what causes the problems. We need to drink more water, but it has to be alkaline. It has to give off a positive charge, which helps to neutralize and open up the body to eliminate the blockages and neutralize the acid. It also helps to flush out the waste and the buildup of the acid in the body.

The acid wastes away in our bloodstream and the kidneys pull it out as we urinate, as we breathe from the lungs, and as we sweat from the skin, which is how the acids are eliminated. So we need to move the body. This is all part of the alkaline diet and lifestyle. You can take supplements or many of the super greens, which are dried grasses and then added to water to give you a 20:1 alkaline-to-acid balance.

Fig. 5.22. Chlorophyll is the green light of the sun.

You should slowly increase your alkaline-forming foods and eat less acid-forming foods in the transition. You should also eat plenty of sprouts. One of the great ways to consume grain is just to sprout it; then you can mix, flatten, and sun dry it into a pita-like bread. It is all raw, so just put it together and let it sit and dry in the sun. Then you add a large amount of green and yellow vegetables and many of the vegetable grasses and then you just chew it well to get its full transformation.

You should avoid fungus foods such as mushrooms, algae, and truffles. These are all acidic. Obviously, avoid anything that creates sugar, which means avoiding all the alcoholic beverages (wine, beer, whiskey, brandy, gin, rum, and vodka). They are not only acid forming, but also purely microtoxic. Alcohol is a fungus-producing microtoxin made by yeast, which causes direct injury to our health.

As you learn to eat an alkaline diet, you slowly start to avoid smoking or chewing tobacco. The acid-forming substance is part of tobacco, as they actually ferment the leaves, and that is why it causes a lot of problems with the acidity in the destructive cycle. Anything that creates sugar ferments, and when it ferments it creates an acid.

What you should shop for are foods that you can utilize, which

Fig. 5.23. Mushrooms are fungus, and alcohol is formed from yeast.

are fresh tomatoes, avocados, lemons, limes, occasional grapefruit, and certain vegetables, such as kale, chard, celery, parsley, cabbage, dark leaf lettuce, spinach, romaine lettuce, peppers, broccoli, zucchini, asparagus, cucumbers, green beans, alfalfa, onions, garlic, leeks, cauliflower, fresh herbs, seaweed, eggplant, squash, and carrots. Then occasionally you can have some of the other tuber vegetables like sweet potatoes, red potatoes, and yams. You can shop for all of them in the bulk section and there are a lot of nut butters that you can get, such as raw sunflower, sesame, alfalfa, flax seed, raw almonds, and pumpkin seeds. This is all part of the transformation. Other products you can get that are somewhat processed are tofu, hummus, and other things of that nature. If you cannot get purified water the best water to actually take would be distilled or reverse osmosis purified water, and again you can use some spices with the real salt or the alchemical salts.

The most important thing if you do buy anything in the packaged area is to read the labels and watch for any acidic ingredient, such as citric acid, mushroom yeast, vinegar, corn or corn syrup, as well as peanuts. An excellent book to study on this is *Sick and Tired* by Dr. Young, which gives a breakdown of alkaline foods and of all the acidic products and what we can take to neutralize and cleanse the body. The book also explains where and how to buy the recommended foods.

THE MUCUSLESS DIET

Through the alkaline diet, you can create a mucus-free environment internally in the body. This is what we are trying to achieve. In other words, the less we build up of mucus, which inflames the body, the more the body is going to function properly. If you look at and feel your body, when you eat a lot of the animal products your body just swells up because the inflammation is taking place within the body.

In other words, the blood vessels get coated with cholesterol, which increases the size or the tightness of the body to neutralize the acid that is flowing through the blood. The beauty about the whole body is the fact that it is a continuum. It is continually working and

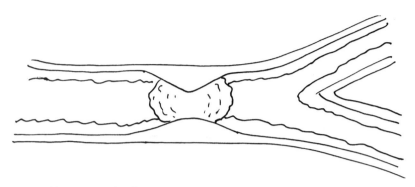

Fig. 5.24. Blood vessels are coated with cholesterol to protect
their walls from acid.

processing twenty-four hours a day, seven days a week. The body is
constantly changing according to its internal environment.

The beauty of this is that you can make a shift within a week to
two weeks to a month and more permanently work with these products and understandings for a good full year in order to do a complete
transition on your cellular level to make this transformation. This can
all be done and taken on your own with knowledge and understanding. Just then take some time for yourself and do it.

It is quite simple and easy. You just have to learn to work within
your body. This creates a mucusless state in your body. In other
words, do not add other foods that are degenerating to your body
and obstruct the energy flow of the body. With the medicine meals
you create a mucusless diet, a diet where you are not bothered with
inflammation and bloating. It is simple, clean, and easy to follow.

You can further strengthen yourself with these understandings
within yourself not only physically, but also mentally, emotionally,
and spiritually. You see, all four bodies are really one body, but the
Taoists, in their infinite wisdom, realized that because they were on
the earth plane, they need to first work with the physical body, and in
working through the physical body we can transform the other three
bodies. We can physically see, taste, and touch the physical form the
easiest because we are here consciously.

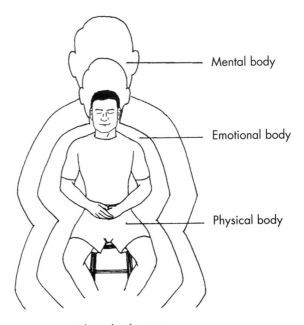

Fig. 5.25. Three bodies into one

We can make changes in the physical body, which affects all the other bodies at the same time. Why try to work with something you cannot see, smell, or touch, given that, for the time being, we are trapped in time and space with the five senses? Why not utilize those five senses to create balance and harmony within your body? Once you do that, you will find the middle point on emotional, psychological, and spiritual levels to connect with all the other aspects throughout the universe, and this is really the understanding and the key to all spiritual evolution. The key is diet. There are no two ways around it. You can think yourself out of this and think yourself out of that, but you always come back to diet. You are what you eat and if you are eating a mucusless diet you will not have any inflammation in the physical body. Without inflammation in the body, you will not have any energy blockages, and without any energy blockages you will not have any disease in the body. In other words, when the body is not at ease, it does not flow with the Tao. It does not flow effortlessly, and your life becomes a complete chore.

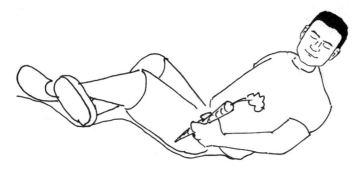

Fig. 5.26. Change your diet to the effortless path of the Tao.

When you put on an extra thirty, forty, fifty, or even one hundred pounds of fat, how do you move around? How do you defecate? How do you physically wipe yourself? How can you reach? The mucus builds up in the body because the body is inflamed and it just gets bigger and bigger. It adds fat to neutralize the acid. All we have to do is stop eating the acid-producing foods.

Understandably, we are being bombarded with acid because the other acid freaks (collective egos) in our environment just perpetuate themselves. But eventually they all disintegrate because they are all in the destructive cycle (dust to dust). When you start to practice the mucusless diet, you start to use your meals as your medicines and you create medicine meals. You use food as a medicine to create a mucusless environment internally, and gradually you will shift out of your external environment and live in the mountain or by the sea. But you have to start from the inside out; that is how you achieve health, harmony, balance, and longevity.

BREATHARIANISM

Where does all this lead? Well, as I mentioned before, we consume, no matter what we eat, 75 percent of our nutrition from the air. Once we learn how to open up the channels of the body (crown point, perineum, palms, and soles of the feet), the biggest medicine meal is fresh air. Once you open the body totally, you will start to feel and connect with your own nature (energy). From an energy standpoint, we are actually an electromagnetic radiation field.

Once you can make this bridge, you do not need to consume anything except the air by breathing through the largest organ of the body, the skin. Eventually you can breathe through your skin totally without air moving through the nostrils or mouth into the lungs. This is the Taoist practice of Bone Marrow Nei Kung.

In fact, if you cover your whole body with paint, you will suffocate, because the skin needs to breathe. This is your third and largest lung of the body. It is also the third kidney of the body. The skin is very important in this process and you should brush it every day to open its pores.

This can be done in a transitional stage. Then your body can start to function properly where you can utilize more of the air with proper breathing from the nose/belly and skin/bone breathing. Then you can move to the mountain for the good, clean open air and gradually eliminate solid foods. In other words, you will start shifting your diet

Fig. 5.27. Cosmic dust particles are the life force and they are everywhere.

to a more alkaline diet to balance and move into a mucusless body with no inflammation.

People really eat out of boredom in America, where 80 percent of the population is overweight. Americans sit on their couches and watch TV for hours at night and by suggestion, through five-minute commercial breaks in the programming, they get the advertised food and eat it while they lie on their couches. This causes many more problems of digestion and degenerative diseases. With all of the modern conveniences, people do not have to do anything to exist except earn money—and they become bored. They use food for stimulation and excitement in their boring lives. That is why TV is so popular in today's society. People use food to entertain their senses because they have lost touch with themselves and their true nature.

When you get back to your true nature and relocate to the mountain, you eat fewer and fewer physical meals. You maybe eat one meal every three days, and then you gradually build up to one meal every week and then once a month. And gradually you will learn to live just on air as you open up the orifices of the body completely as well as the crown point, the perineum, the palms, and the soles of the feet.

Fig. 5.28. The less you eat and do, the better for your well-being.

With Taoist practices, especially the simple Chi Kung practices, you will start to open up these areas with the meditations and the practice connected with the cosmos. You will start to absorb the cosmic dust particles (the microzymas) right into your body through the air. This is how you will form the pattern and lifestyle of a breatharian living at one with the universe and all living things.

BALANCE IS THE KEY

This whole concept of medicine meals is based on balance, balancing the pH factor in the blood on a molecular level with the acid and the alkaline balance of the positive and negative (yang and yin) charges. Once you have this balance within your body, you will start to flow effortlessly. There will be no aging process then, and there will be no death as we know it.

You will be totally at balance and at peace with yourself; then you can move to the next level, which is transforming this balance and harmonized body into your spirit body. This will lead to all the immortal practices, which are based on your balance on a molecular level from a physical body and then transforming it into the spiritual body.

No matter how far you take this in your understanding and in

Fig. 5.29. Taoist meditations and Chi Kung open the body
up for breatharianism.

Fig. 5.30. Balancing the yin and yang in the cellular structure

your transition, you are going to feel better, look better, live longer, and be more at peace with yourself. Again, balance is the key, not too far left and not too far right, right down the middle, and that is the way of the Tao and its mystical path.

As you make this connection with yourself in the middle path, you start to find yourself and you start to understand and connect with the true meaning for your own self. Again, the whole key to life is the discovery of who you are. Once you make that discovery, you will move on into the discovery of where you are going.

We are all going nowhere into the continuum of life. That is really our sojourning here on the planet. To connect with that balance is the key, and within the key is diet.

You can get around everything else, but what you put into your body is what you are going to wear. If you do not put any mucus in your body or mucus-forming foods, then you will have a mucus-free body. If you put all the natural air particles with the microzymas (cosmic dust particles) into the body effortlessly, you will become a breatharian; and as you become lighter and stronger within yourself, you will start to learn of the higher conscious evolution and understandings.

The key is the balance, and to find the key to balance you form your own medicine meals and you live at harmony with yourself and in your own being. The key is to understand this and to practice this

Fig. 5.31. When you are balanced, you can discover who you really are.

Fig. 5.32. As you continue through the transition stage, you become lighter and stronger.

openly within yourself and you will find yourself connecting with this balance, moving and shifting in different directions than you are presently, not only internally, but also externally. You will attract like-minded people in harmony with themselves as you are.

The ancient sages always seemed to end up or migrate to the mountains where we have the purest balance and the purest meals available from cosmic dust particles from the heavens. The sages found high on the mountain that they could breathe and understand each of these aspects within their beings.

Balance is the key, and within that balance are the alkaline and acid pH balance of the yang and yin within the cellular structure. As you connect to your center, you will start to form your own understandings and discover or rediscover who you are and where you are going.

As you balance through your diet with medicine meals, you will start to make these discoveries. As you make these discoveries, everything will be revealed to you, all that you need to know at each stage in the effortless path of the Tao.

Cosmic Purification

DISEASE

Seventy percent of all our nutrition comes from the air, so literally we are breatharians. If we wean ourselves off the other 30 percent of material food, we are actually, in all essence, breatharians. Until we get to 100 percent of being a breatharian, the key to health is how well we get rid of the debris that we take in by not totally nurturing ourselves from the air. The Taoists have a very interesting approach to this cleansing process concerning the openings of the bodies. They believe that these openings should be cleaned out and clear, not only for healing our body, but also for the alchemical process in the immortal Tao, which involves deep meditation done for many years.

With this deep meditation we need to have all the orifices of the body cleaned out and sealed, so no debris rots in the system. If there is any debris left in these openings it can cause rotting or breakdowns and disease in our entire system. These passages need to be clear so the energy can flow freely.

The key is to have a balance of proper nutrition from the air until we can literally open up the venues of the body so they can take in the other 30 percent; but in the meantime, in the transition, the key to health is to avoid disease when we are not at ease with our body. Primarily disease is caused by the backed-up debris that we take in

Fig. 6.1. Open the nine openings.

from the material foods, which causes blockages in our system. The key is keeping open the nine openings of the body.

Disease is like the swamp that forms when free-flowing water becomes blocked and stagnant. Consider the rivers or the creeks of the forest and how they flow freely until debris from the forest falls into the creek. Over time, fallen branches and leaves creates blockages, stopping the free flow of the water. When debris blocks the flow of the water, the water becomes stagnant, and as it becomes stagnant other micro-organisms start to grow in the river or the creek, creating what we call

Fig. 6.2. Blocked-up forest river

a swamp. This brings a whole different life force into the river itself by creating stagnation and feeding new organisms in the water.

To remove these other organisms or the blockages, you need to remove the fallen branches, trees, and leaves from the creek. Once these are pulled out the river will flush itself out. As the river flushes itself out, the water runs freely and gives life to the forest and the sea.

The same is true in the body but we call it disease. The body is no longer flowing easily. It is disrupted. These blockages form at an energetic level and then manifest in the physical level. When this blockage is put in place, what happens to the river or the energy rivers of the body? They become blocked. As they become blocked, another organism forms in this stagnant area, and that is what we call cancer in the body, just like the swamp forming in the blocked river in the forest.

The key is to open up these areas of the body, and how we do this is with the seven windows of the body and the front and back doors of the body. These are the openings or the orifices of the body itself, and this is how the energy flows in and out and releases the pressures and heat of the body and also eliminates any of the blockages in the body. The disease basically is a disruption in the natural flow of your internal body, and when there is a blockage this causes stagnation. With stagnation the energy is blocked, and then what happens is another organism starts to form because you have not eliminated any of this debris from the body.

You can approach it in two different ways. The first way is to not let any of the debris into the body initially. As you refine your diet and your lifestyle, you can slowly start to eliminate the source of the problem— taking debris into the body. As I said before, we are really breatharians, so until we can draw in the other 30 percent of our nourishment through the air that we take in, we will continue to take in material food. This creates a burden on our body because we need to eliminate the excess food that we take in. Obviously the key is to eat less. The less you eat, the better, and the less you will need to eliminate.

It takes a lot of energy to digest and process the food in our body. If your body needs a rest from this overactivity and to balance the

Fig. 6.3. Eat better and less, so there will be less to eliminate.

energy, the simplest thing to do is to literally stop eating for a period of time. Depending on your lifestyle and also your habits and conditionings, you can easily start to do this. As the Taoists say, "The less you do the better." When you have a crisis of disease in the body, the less you do the better, which allows the body enough time and energy to break up these blockages and it slowly removes the debris from these energy rivers. So it does not have the additional burden of digesting the food because you are not taking any more of the debris in. This allows the body to clean itself out and start to remove these blockages in the body. The body naturally heals itself. This is "the less you do the better" concept, which allows the body to rebalance itself and recondition itself in the natural flow of the universe.

As you start to discover this, you realize that the less you do the better—the less you obstruct the natural flow of your body. In other words, you do not add any more additional debris, and the body actually will balance and heal itself. This is all part of letting go and not burdening the body with any additional demands.

It was once said that if we did nothing, 85 percent of any disease internally in the body would actually balance and heal itself. Now when I say if we do nothing, I mean we literally do not have any activity at all. In other words, we do not eat, we drink a little bit, but very little, and only very pure, clear water, and the body will actually balance itself and heal itself. The whole key is we can also help clean out and open these openings so the body can release the debris. There is a whole series of cosmic purifications that we can implement in our body. With the cosmic energy that we take in and its purification, we can allow this energy to manifest, and the body to balance and heal itself. Our orientation really is the less we do the better and the body will find a healing sensation within ourselves as we start to work with the energy and allow it to move on its own and break up these blockages. Again, this is the concept, to allow the body to naturally balance itself by not interfering with the body's natural process of healing itself.

SEVEN WINDOWS

As the Taoists look at the body, the body has seven windows with a front door and a back door, like a temple or church. In the cleansing process we should keep these areas clean, open, and flowing in order to eliminate any debris or toxins that have come in or have been stored. These are the openings that we need to seal and retain the energy, too, while at the same time eliminating any toxins and poisons that the body needs to send out.

Now the front door is the genital opening and the back door is the anus, which leads out of the digestive system. The seven windows are the five sense openings in the head. These are the two openings for the eyes, the two nostril openings, the mouth opening, and the two ear openings. In advanced meditation in the Taoist practices, we actually seal these senses off by drawing in the energy to conserve it, but in the process we must make sure that they are open and clean before we can close them.

In the cleansing process through the Tao, we can use the eyewashes to wash out the eyes, purify the eyes, and rest the eyes. We rest the eyes by covering the eyes with the palms of the hands and doing the rubbing exercises of Chi Self Massage in the Taoist formulas. We also sun the eyes by closing them and looking at the sun while slowly turning your head from right to left and back several times.

For the ear openings we can use an ear-cleaning solution as drops into the ear. This will dissolve any wax or debris from the ear. It acti-

Fig. 6.4. Cleansing the eyes

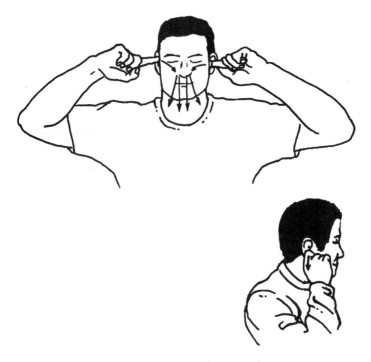

Fig. 6.5. Cleansing the ears

vates and clears out the openings while we are doing the pulling and rubbing ear exercises with the Chi Self Massage techniques. The ears are connected to the kidneys and we activate them when we do the ear exercises.

For the nostril openings we can use a solution made out of warm water and salt. We can proceed with a process called nasal douching, sending the water in through one nostril and passing it around through the other nostril. This will begin to break up any debris coming in the nostril passages and cleansing and cleaning the nose and sinus areas. To activate and stimulate these passages there are blowing and rubbing nose exercises in the Chi Self Massage.

For the debris of the mouth, we can use substances to clean the mouth out. All we do is brush our teeth in the morning, but to activate and massage the gums and tongue, use the Chi Self Massage formulas of the Tao. We can use various oils as mouthwashes, such as sunflower oil to purify the mouth opening and also we can brush with coconut oil, which is a more solid substance and it has a nice taste to it. This cleanses the gums and teeth, drawing out the impurities.

For cleaning the tongue, we can use a metal tongue scraper, scraping any extra debris off the tongue. This is how we can start to clean these seven openings of the body.

Fig. 6.6. Cleansing the nose

Fig. 6.7. Cleansing the mouth

Again, the nine openings of the body are like a temple. You have the seven windows and the front door and the back door. Now you want to make sure you retain the energy or the heat in the body and not lose it. If you leave all the windows open and all the doors open in a house, you lose a lot of energy, especially in the wintertime. So you need to seal them down and you will not lose the energy, but you want to make sure that you can open and close them freely. They have to be clean so they do not get stuck or create blockages. You need to utilize these openings and keep them open even when you want to shut them down to conserve the energy, because you want to make sure there is not any buildup of debris that would stop the energy flow itself.

There are several indirect methods of cleansing the eyes. By cleansing the liver you also relieve any blockages in the eye with a detoxifying diet as well as fasting or eating green vegetables. You can use eyebright and milk thistle eye washes and you can cover the eyes with hot and cold water therapy. You can create an eye drop by making a very dilute solution of lemon juice, apple cider, or cayenne pepper in water. There are many other natural solutions that cleanse and clean the eye. Eliminating junk foods and trans fats—which include margarine, heavy sugar, white flour, white milk, white rice, and any of the dairy products—helps tremendously to cleanse the eyes and improve vision. The nose douching by clearing out the nose with salt solutions and rubbing the insides of the nostrils with eucalyptus oil will help cleanse the sinuses, too. This opens up the eye area as well. The liver sound and the green energy, along with the balancing of the negative emotions, transforming anger into kindness with the Taoist Fusion practices, will help this whole process. Exercising overall three or four times a week would actually improve every aspect of the elimination process in detoxifying the liver, which opens and clears the eyes.

You can actually feed the eyes with the proper organic foods and

Sh-h-h-h-h-h

Fig. 6.8. Use the liver's sound to open the eyes.

super food supplements, utilizing the green foods with chlorophyll coming from green leafy vegetables. Also, you can sun the eyes, which feeds them with vitamin D. This is a simple technique of closing your eyes and then moving your head from one shoulder to the next and feeling the sun's rays coming down right on your eyes as they are closed. Also, remember to only eat when hungry and to never overeat. Drink when you are thirsty and do not overdrink any of the liquids. This adds less pressure on the liver, which actually heals the eyes. To strengthen the eye muscles, you can use various eye exercises. You can focus on something close and then slowly move your focus on objects out at farther distances and reverse, which helps the muscles of the eyes start to relax and start to reset themselves. By stretching your eyes up and down, right to left, diagonally turning the muscles and making circles with the eyes, this area opens up and the flexibility of the muscles is increased. You can strengthen the pupils by turning on and off the lights or standing in a shaded area and then in the sun.

As you squeeze the eye muscles, you tighten the muscles that close the eyes, and then you open the eyes wide and breathe out the liver's sound, "sh-h-h-h-h-h-h," opening the eyes and any blockages. You can look close and far away, which strengthens the muscles, and then you can follow a bird or watch a baseball go by. Most people lose over 50 percent of the ability to look close and look far. You should maintain the proper amount of sleep for resting the eyes. You also can do the proper eye palming, by just covering the eyes with your palms for five minutes daily to feel and rest the eyes.

The eyes are connected to the liver and they are overworked because in our society, we have too much visual attention and we really lose focus.

The ears are connected with the kidneys. If we have too much noise or sounds we lose the ability to hear and weaken the kidneys. So be careful how you play your music or the environment you place yourself in. It is best to start to feel quietness and stillness or more natural sounds of the country environment, which will help heal the

Fig. 6.9. Still the body, balancing the kidneys and opening the ears.

kidneys and the ears while maintaining the openings in your ears for perfect hearing.

In breathing with the nostrils, you need to clean out the nostrils and keep your nostrils free, which opens up the lungs as you breathe through the nostrils fully. This gives you the capacity of breath expanding all the way through the lungs. As you exhale through the nostrils, you empty out the lungs completely. This helps eliminate a lot of the debris from the lungs and helps the whole body function with more balance and harmony.

With the tongue, the less speaking you do the better, because it only weakens the heart. One of the great things you can do is utilize the saliva. Gather saliva periodically every hour and move it around in your mouth, purifying your mouth, and then swallow the saliva with gathered air in heavy gulps. This creates a capacity of pressure in the body giving you, as the Taoists say, "the tire pressure of the body," which can maintain internal strength within the body. You see, as we age, we are literally deflated. We lose the chi pressure and the body slowly shrinks, not only on a molecular level with the breaking down of calcium, which is leached out of the body with our acidic foods, but also the body starts to shrink because we lose the air pressure in the body, like a tire slowly leaking until it becomes flat. As we age, if we do not develop this pressure and maintain it by sealing the nine openings of the body, we will lose this pressure and the body will slowly shrink, which loses our buoyancy and youthfulness.

There is a whole process with your breathing techniques and you can study many of these techniques, but the primary aspect is you need to fully expand your whole lower abdomen with the air pressure coming down through the lungs. To do so, you need to consciously focus on expanding your abdominal area as you breathe. As you start to breathe into your body, you expand the lower abdominal areas, which fills in or fills up your whole lung capacity. When you exhale you press in the abdominal area, pushing the abdominal muscles up into the chest, which eliminates all the air completely that you have breathed in. This helps you in your whole process of taking in and then eliminating, getting the oxygen out of the air and then eliminating the carbon dioxide totally out of the body. If we are going to live on 70 percent of our nutrition from the air, then we must take in fully each breath so we can get all of our nutrition.

We have a problem in our society with shallow breath. We only breathe in a little bit. Then we do not exhale fully because we have not taken in enough air. You need to take whole breaths, expanding your belly, and as you exhale flattening the belly, pushing the air out. The lungs serve as a filter, which is why you need to totally clean out the passages of the nostrils and the sinuses so the air can get through into the lungs. This is important because this is the primary source of our nutrition. If we start to develop our breathing patterns more properly, we will start to increase our health. For this to function properly you need to clean out the passages.

One of the primary areas of healing is with the heart energy connecting with the tongue and how we stimulate and also release any pressure by balancing the body with a simple technique of laughter. When you create laughter it opens the body up, and by opening this area up you expand the heart energy with joy, love, and happiness. It is a simple procedure using the belly-laughing technique, in which you bounce your belly back and forth while laughing. Just by simply giggling and then building it up to a louder laughter, you actually balance the body and release any tension in the heart, creating a good harmony within the body. This also opens up the whole heart center connected to the tongue in the mouth. Either you listen to comedy that strikes your fancy, or, in conversations with people, always be aware that laughter helps balance and harmonize your body, especially in the heart center. It is always good for your health to have a good laugh. Just be sure it is not detrimental to anyone else, but in good fun. With increased laughter, you will be able to release any tension or pressure in your life. Your life will be much happier and you will be more at peace with yourself. This simple little technique of laughter using the belly-laughing technique helps you release tears to heal the eyes. Try to stretch out your laughter for at least five minutes with a good laugh and then have five minutes of silence. This helps you bring together inner harmony.

One other way to release tension in the liver is the Liver and Gallbladder Purging Technique. What you can do is eliminate a lot of the gallstones and liver stones in the body by doing a simple technique of purging the liver. As you purge the liver you will start to eliminate these blockages in your liver and open up the eye channels, clearing out this passage. It is a simple fasting technique that you can do overnight by drinking an epsom salt solution and then drinking olive oil and a grapefruit juice mixture. There is another simple technique of purging the liver with the colloidal silver process. This actually eliminates any toxins in the blood and purifies the blood. This connects with the heart and you can actually purge by drinking it. This process draws the toxins out on a molecular level by causing them to adhere to the silver itself. The colloidal silver draws toxins out like a magnet and you eliminate them through your digestive process and urination.

THE FRONT DOOR

For the genital opening we can use various herb potions to clean out the kidneys, which govern this area, breaking down any kidney stones or other blockages in the elimination passage of the genitals. For the vagina, douching and herbal cleansing solutions work well to clean out the vaginal canal. Massaging the feet and the kidney points or walking barefoot on a pebble beach works well to break up any of the crystals from the kidneys that are settling in the soles of the feet.

To activate this region there are the Taoist exercises in the Sexual Self Massage, which include the Egg Exercise for the women strengthening this area, as well as the Chi Weightlifting with the Chi Sexual Massage to strengthen and develop these muscles around the genital area and to clean out the passages. This gives a whole other dimension for activating the energy for the front door. In other words, what you want to do is keep this passage open. This is especially important for men, in order to prevent prostate cancer. There is a technique for massaging inside the rectum and massaging with castor oil the upper part of the roof of the rectum, which is the area of the prostate. As we explain in the section on the back door, you are not only cleaning out the rectum but also massaging and activating the prostate with chi pressure or acupressure. When you press an area of the body you draw blood to it, and then when you release it the blood will flush the area out, opening the passage.

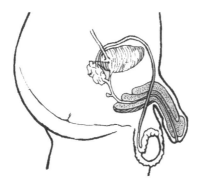

Fig. 6.10. Clean out the rectum with the finger to massage the prostate.

This is the same concept as the metaphor of branches blocking the river in the forest, so we can utilize this same concept to massage the prostate going into the rectum as well as massaging the genitals themselves and the penis shaft. For the woman, cleanse the vagina with various herbs and salt solutions and massage the ovaries with the Taoist techniques of placing the thumbs together with both hands on the outside of the pubic area locating the ovaries, the cervix, and the fallopian tubes, which will open up these channels. With the Chi Sexual Massage, what you are doing in essence is utilizing the acupressure techniques, drawing blood to the area and then releasing it by allowing the blood to flush out the area and break up any blockages.

There is a technique that is also used to purify the blood by working directly with your urine. It is called Urine Therapy. When you urinate, your urine consists of 95 percent water and 2.5 percent urea. The remaining 2.5 percent is mixed with minerals, salts, hormones, and enzymes. Only urea—the substance that gave us the term *urine*—can be poisonous when it is present in the body,

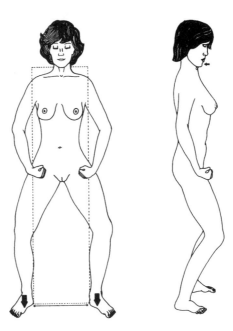

Fig. 6.11. Taoist technique for opening the ovaries, cervix, and fallopian tubes

so that is why the body eliminates it. In the practice of drinking your own urine, the urine does not immediately go back into the bloodstream.

In small amounts, the urea gets back into the body and it is purifying and cleans out any extra mucus, so the urine is entirely sterile after excretion. It has an excellent antiseptic effect on the body when you take it in. The key is to urinate in a cup and just drink the top level and not the sediment in the lower level. You just drink a few ounces of it and it helps purify and cleanse the body. Of course, the healthier you are the better it is going to work for you. If you are too toxic you could have a problem, so you have to be careful when you utilize this technique.

You can wash your ears with urine as eardrops, cleanse out the nostrils, and rub it into your hands to heal them. The smell is caused from the urea that is taken out of the blood. Actually urine is essentially purified blood. In other words, it takes the water out of the blood as the kidneys purify the blood. The urine is the product of this whole process. This therapy has been done for centuries, cleansing the openings of the body with urine as well as taking it internally. People have been known to live on it when they are deserted on the sea and they need water to drink. They drink their own urine and they survive.

Fig. 6.12. Urine drops clean out your ear openings.

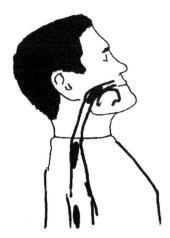

Fig. 6.13. Saliva heals your body when you swallow it.

Another point is that you can drink your own saliva. Literally, if you are cleansed at a certain level, your body will start secreting saliva in your mouth when you are thirsty and you can drink it right then. Our body actually self-preserves and recycles all of its liquids through the saliva and urine.

The Taoists always recommend you swallow your own saliva at least 15 to 30 times a day. This allows your body to heal itself. The saliva itself has a high potassium content, which really heals the body. When you were young and hurt yourself, what was the first thing your mother did? She kissed it and made it all better. The kissing transferred the saliva from her mouth, which had a healing effect on the body. This is the same for animals: as soon as they cut themselves, the first thing they do is lick the cut and that helps the body heal itself. The saliva from the tongue as they lick the wound starts to heal the wound.

THE BACK DOOR

For the anus, which includes the rectum and intestinal area, the Taoists highly recommend colonics to clear out the debris and any buildup of various toxins. There are two types of colonics. The first type is open-ended where you insert a thin tip connected to a hose into a container filled with a lukewarm water solution combined with chlorophyll, a coffee substance, or molasses, which is all inserted into the rectum.

These solutions are diluted, but the work is similar to a mouth-wash except this is in the colon, so it is a colon wash. You are washing the internal skin of the colon and releasing any blockages. With this open-ended type you can send the water into the colon and then flush the debris out as you are using the rectal muscles while on a colema board over a toilet. The closed-ended type is performed by a colon therapist with a metal insert device, which sends the water in and evacuates the debris through the other end of the tube, which is usually hooked up to a machine.

The open-ended type utilizes gravity and the actual rectal muscles to eliminate the solution and the debris. This whole process cleans out the colon and the intestines. There is a whole system of cleansing that is highly recommended for longevity through the process of colonics, and then also eating the proper diet for the best results.

Once you switch to a proper diet you will find that a lot of the gas and the smells from defecation came from eating improper foods that did not agree with the body. Defecation should not smell and you should not pass any gas, which is literally an explosion in the colon of passing bad winds due to the combinations in the digestive process.

Fig. 6.14. Gravity works for you in the open-ended colonic.

This creates a gas and a smell from the rotting food in the intestines and impurities that you are putting into the body.

If you have a cleansing diet with a lot of chlorophyll, there is no smell at all or any gas either. The smell comes from the horrible combinations of what we put into our bodies with the animal products, the acidic products, and a lot of the imbalanced combinations. These create a chemical reaction as they start to break down in the body, which causes backups in the body and blockages, which then create explosions of actual gas coming out. The body is actually telling you with the smell that you are eating improperly. There should not be any smell and you should have regular bowel movements at least one to three times per day and urination at least four or five times a day. There should not be any smell in anything that you eliminate.

The key here is to find out how your body functions, which in concept and theory is that there should not be any extra debris in the body. As you start to work for the body you will start to find the correct food combinations to take care of the body. Improper eating habits require immediate cleansing and also maintaining yourself on a healing program. Again, health is really determined by your diet. The less you eat the better, because your body gains 70 percent of its

Fig. 6.15. Your health is determined by your diet.

nutrition from the air. All you need to do is breathe properly.

As you breathe you can start to develop the conditions of the body to get your whole nutrition. You will find you need less to eat as there will be less wear and tear on your body to digest and process the foods. The key is the less you eat the better and the less you work your body the better. You just need to do enough to maintain your body so it can function by itself. Your energy should be spent on proper breathing to draw the air in properly and live in environments where you have clean open spaces to expand your energy, to heal your body, and to maintain the prominence of your health.

Again, the whole key to your health, especially for the back door, is how well you eliminate these toxins and the built-up debris you have taken in as solid foods. When you start to clean the back door out, you will improve your breathing because the lungs are connected to the colon (large intestine). As you clean out the colon you are cleaning out the lungs and helping them breathe properly. Any type of aerobic exercise—as in running or swimming—will help the elimination process by activating the lungs, which activates the colon.

Breathing is the key to health. How well you expand the lower abdominals when drawing in the air and expanding the lungs, and how well you flatten the abdominals to push the used air out of the body determines the health of your body. Any type of running or other aerobic activity like walking will help you start to develop a

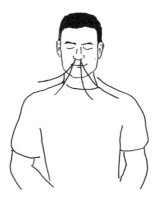

Fig. 6.16. Breathing properly is the key to your health.

clear opening through the nostrils, which affects the colon and the back door out of the body. When you eliminate any excess air, you repair and activate the colon to perform its natural process, sending the debris out of the body.

While you are doing the colonic cleanse, you can take various herbs and supplements, such as psyllium and bentonite, to activate the energy and the debris. These supplements actually loosen up any of the toxins in the body on the walls of the intestines on a cellular level, and they draw the toxins out of the colon, eliminating them through the intestinal system. This type of cleansing fast should be done periodically with colonics for health and maintenance depending on the amount of abusive eating in which you have engaged your body.

COLONICS

Colonics should be experienced every six months to cleanse out your whole system, depending on the debris you have placed in your body. The only caution is that with the colonics you can draw out a lot of the natural bacteria that you need to digest the food from the digestive wall. However, with the proper acidophilus implants, you can activate and culture the bacteria again within the colon.

The key, though, is to get the debris out of the body, allowing the body to function properly and keep this open so you do not have a blockage. The number-one cancer is colon cancer, which leads to a lot of other cancers. We should call the cancer more appropriately a swamp buildup in the body. When you get these blockages in the body, this creates another organism (swamp) that overtakes the body and is called a cancer.

With a colonic, take one or two a day for one to two weeks. With an open-ended colonic you can fill up a bucket of water, put it over the toilet to give it gravity, and sit on a colema board as you hook tubing up over the toilet. You slowly release the water from the tip of the tubing and the water squirts out into the rectum. You can massage the abdomen, moving the water up through the descending colon

Fig. 6.17. Colonics clean the colon and open the back door of the body.

Fig. 6.18. Colema boards work with the open-ended colonic.

and transverse colon, all the way to the ascending colon in a reverse process. You will feel the water start to activate the intestinal walls and start to release some of the blockages and toxins. As you start to release the blockage area, you will see this energy and feel it eliminate as you get the debris out.

With the psyllium and bentonite (bentonite is a clay), it starts to pull the debris off the cells of the colon walls, which allows you to eliminate this caked-up material. As you start to utilize this technique, the debris will come out in a kind of tubular membrane because the psyllium actually solidifies with the clay. You take both of these orally five times a day, followed by a lot of chlorophyll, so it will come out as a green membrane when you defecate it out of your body.

Again, the concept here is if you never brushed your teeth and never cleaned out your mouth, you would get this kind of mucky taste and toxic buildup in your mouth; plus you just would not feel right. Well, guess what? If you have never cleaned out your colon or rectum and you have had the buildup in there for twenty, thirty, or forty years, what do you think you have? You need to cleanse this area of the body just as you do the other end of the body (the mouth and the teeth) every day or twice a day, depending on your training. This is the best way, besides diet, to cleanse out the colon and flush out the system itself. As you start to cleanse the colon you will start to eliminate all the excess body fat and acids of the body while removing this debris and opening up this channel of the body.

You can do various exercises with this, aerobically, to activate the colon. One of the problems with the colon is that the body stands upright, which is different from other animals that are on all fours. So the whole process of bodily elimination has to move the debris up the body against gravity then across the abdomen and down through the descending colon with the topography of the large intestine. Other animals on all fours do not have to go straight up against gravity and food goes easily through the body. It is a lot easier to defecate. When we are standing on two feet we have to do the reverse process in moving the debris up the body, then down the body and that is why we need to work with the body to help the body with this process.

Number one, the most important, is the diet and what we put into the body. Again, we put far too much in the body because 70 percent of our nutrition comes from the air, which has no dealings with the debris in the body. With the whole design of the colon we have to move the debris up against gravity and then down.

First of all, we need to be aware of how the body actually functions and then to utilize our expertise to develop a way to cleanse the excess debris out of the body. Once you are processing the food you start to realize that how you defecate is so important and the best

Fig. 6.19. The bowel movement moves up against gravity to eliminate.

way is a squatting posture. In Asia, they do not have toilet seats; they squat. It is much cleaner because you do not physically sit on anything and they also use water to wash the anus instead of toilet paper. It dries pretty quickly and it is totally clean, instead of having bits of fecal matter matted up into your buttocks with paper. With this whole process we need to take the time and the energy to put it together and feel the energy move on its own.

FASTING

There are many other types of fasting, which can be done to cleanse and purify your organs individually. You can do two- or three-day fasts on certain whole foods to cleanse and flush out the vital organs such as the heart, kidneys, lungs, spleen, and liver. Generally, a water fast one day a week or one weekend a month is good to rest and rejuvenate the body. Fasting itself has been done throughout history.

On a water fast, what you are doing in essence is to allow the body to go through an autolyzation process. In other words, the body will autolyze in the physiological cleanse by breaking down the excess debris in the body, which are the blockages in the body. This allows the body to open up and free itself. The key is the less you do the better, which is the fine art of fasting. When you get a dis-ease in the body, the body is telling you to stop doing what you are doing and that means stop eating and refrain from any excess activities that you are involved in.

Fig. 6.20. Fasting is the ultimate cleanse and you do nothing.

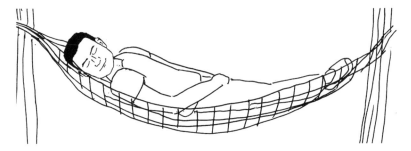

Fig. 6.21. When you fast the body automatically cleans itself.

Primarily what you do is allow the body to rest and heal itself, not adding any food to the body because this allows the energy that was expended to digest the food to be utilized to break down any of the blockages (disease) in the body and opens the body up. This is the cheapest and easiest way to approach the problem (disease).

Many in the West have said we eliminate the blockage by eliminating that part of the body, which is fine except when it is eliminated you need it to function and live on. So that does not make any sense— that is using the monkey mind to do your thinking. It costs very little to sit and do nothing; but the medical system does not promote it. They have not figured out a way to charge anybody to do nothing yet, so they do not waste their time because they cannot make any money. They would rather take out your colon or another part of your body than tell you to stop eating because it means more money in their pocket and that makes more sense to them. But you are the victim.

I would not operate on anybody if I did not make any money and doctors do not do it for free. But surgery does not really solve the problem. The problem is there is a blockage in the body and the easiest way to solve the problem is to allow the body to eliminate the blockage itself. To get the added energy it needs to do this, you simply take away that energy from the digesting and thinking process, which takes a huge amount of energy, and apply it to eliminating the blockage. You are in an inactive state when you do this.

In other words, you lie down and relax, doing nothing, which is the hardest thing for our monkey minds to do. You probably do a little bit of reading, but mostly you just observe and drink water, which flushes out the body allowing your urine to take out the debris. You literally urinate yourself back to health. There are other liquids you can take with this such as the pH balancer with the 20:1 alkaline to acid green drink, which tastes basically like water but it is a liquid form of dried grasses. This is a green powder, which liquefies when you add water to it. Use just a little teaspoon for a thirty-two-ounce bottle of purified water. This helps the whole flushing and hybridization of the body, cleansing out the built-up toxins. Primarily you urinate them out of your body. Initially there will be foul odor from the urine, but after a while there will be no smell at all.

The key here is the less you do the better, so when the body is in trouble you do not feed it. You allow the body to balance itself by resting with no activity, especially eating. In this physiological rest what you are doing is allowing the body to eliminate the built-up toxins in the body itself. These are eliminated through urinating, so you urinate yourself to health. Again, it costs very little, or no money at all, to sit or lie down and just relax without any surgeries, emotional outbursts, or consultations. You just lie there and drink the water. Your body will slowly balance itself and heal itself.

In the book *Foods that Heal*, by Dr. Beale, who practiced holistic medicine for over fifty years and studied thousands of case studies, the author realized this process of harmonization—that 85 percent of degenerative diseases inherent to the body are diet related and they healed themselves by doing absolutely nothing. Again from the professor and master of nothingness, the less you do the better. It is amazing what you can do in thirty days of cleansing just focusing on your food intake with fasting or eating only whole raw foods. You will lose twenty to thirty pounds, depending on your weight and body condition, open your body up (joints, skin, and movement), improve your sight, hearing, and thinking, and clean and brighten your skin and hair while removing wrinkles and blemishes. Just try it; it is only thirty days.

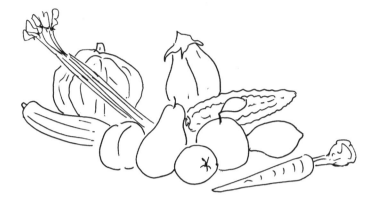

Fig. 6.22. Foods that heal

There are certain circumstances where the body is in a trauma or an accident and you have to do something quickly, in which case modern medicine is good. But for degenerative diseases that take a long period of time to manifest from improper eating and living habits, the way to balance and heal this condition is done through fasting and an alkaline diet. You actually do nothing except drink water or pH-balancing liquid to cleanse the body, allowing the body to heal itself.

It is a simple technique and costs absolutely nothing to do nothing. It is amazing that people have very little time to do nothing because they are so busy doing everything. They try to find solutions where the solution is so simple and in front of them that they cannot see it. In the Taoist meditative process and practices you allow the mind to slow down and everything becomes clear to you about what to do by nondoing. As everything becomes clear to you, you start to make some conscious choices instead of reacting and take the proper and correct action. This is called Wu Wei, the art of doing absolutely nothing.

THE THIRD LUNG

These are all important keys in cleansing through the Tao. Your skin is considered the third lung (or third kidney as the kidney is also considered the third lung) because it breathes out and eliminates the liquids from the skin by sweating. This is a very important and vital organ of the body. It should be taken care of for your protection and well-being.

By skin and hair brushing you will keep your skin pores open and clean, giving you smooth and healthy skin. By exposing the skin to the sun periodically for short periods of time, solar bathing, your skin will develop a natural glow like the sun. The skin is healed by the exposure and nourished by the sun. This feels very good, being embraced by the father energy.

By cleansing the skin with raw lemon juice through lemon baths and by nurturing your skin with natural oils, like olive oil, it will develop the suppleness and youthfulness of a child's skin. This will help keep the body balanced in the natural flow of the universe.

When you have blockages in the openings of the seven windows and front and back doors of the body, you create dis-ease and disharmony in the body. The same is true when you have blockages on the skin, the third lung and third kidney. When you block the skin you block the lungs and kidneys. Open the skin and you open the lungs and kidneys.

The natural harmony and balance with the universe from which we are created are restored through the cleansing of the Tao. The third lung is very important. The aerobic exercises will help you start to sweat or perspire and as you start to perspire you start to eliminate the built-up acids that your body is trying to eliminate to

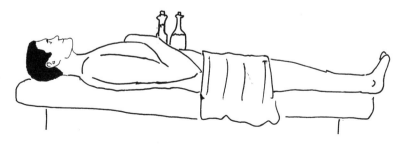

Fig. 6.23. Lemon and olive oil bathing

balance itself. A good program you should utilize is walking, running, rebounding, or hiking fifteen to thirty minutes every day where you can break a sweat. This is the key to your health and longevity. When you move your body you create an aerobic action.

As you create an aerobic action the cells bounce up and down, which allows the lymph system to be activated and start removing the toxins and debris from your cellular structures. Once it removes the toxins from the cells it has to go out of the body and that is where the sweating and the pores of the skin are very important to eliminate the built-up toxins and acids from the body.

As you start to sweat and then cleanse yourself, washing the sweat off, your body feels alive and well. Your body needs to open up these cells with aerobic activity, so you can breathe naturally and function properly with this whole healing process. Another way to open the skin pores is taking a steam bath or a dry heat sauna bath. This allows the body to sweat, opening up the pores and cleansing the body. This is very effective when done fifteen to twenty minutes daily and also very enjoyable.

Exercise is an important key to your health and longevity. To move the body, as we are all mobile units, actually helps you activate and cleanse the body by creating a balance and harmony within the

Fig. 6.24. Sweating cleanses the body.

body activating the skin pores, opening and closing them. With the Taoists' practice of the Chi Self Massage, the simple touching, rubbing, and tapping activates the skin, connecting with the energy lines of the organs. It works with the skin to move and eliminate any of the toxins when you create that moving activity.

HOW TO LIVE

The Tao teaches you how to breathe, sleep, urinate, defecate, sit, stand, walk, and exchange sexual energy in harmony with the natural flow of the universe. Every function of your life is affected, how you see, taste, hear, smell, and feel. The Tao shows you a step-by-step process through the Taoists' formulas from the nine points of your foot to drawing the sexual energy up the spine to the crown connecting the earth, cosmic, and universal energies.

The beauty of it is that if you ever have a question about the Tao, all you have to do is look out your window and the answers are all there. Watch how the tree stands rooted in the earth (Iron Shirt Chi Kung practice), how the bear walks (Pakua Palm practice), or how the river flows (Tai Chi Chi Kung practice). These are all formulas that you

Fig. 6.25. Iron Shirt Chi Kung and Tai Chi practices

will learn in the other Taoist books by Mantak Chia and in workshops offered by Universal Healing Tao teachers around the world. To access these workshops, see the resources listed at the end of this book.

The Tao teaches us how to do every aspect of living life, which is important to our living and functioning on this earth plane. It helps you in every aspect of your understanding of how to function on the earth plane. It is simple, but it is complete. All you have to do is apply yourself and utilize these techniques that make perfect sense to you. As you activate the energy you learn exactly what you need for your body and how to maintain yourself for a long, enjoyable life for hundreds of years.

You are asking yourself why would I want to live so long, 150 to 200 to 300 years? The answer is quite simple. If you feel that good, why not? The whole process is discovering how to feel good. If that means changing your lifestyle, if that means developing a new sphere of friends, well if things do not change you do not get the results. The results are pending on your activities and whom you associate with.

As you slow the mind down through the Taoist meditations, you will start to make some conscious choices. You will ask yourself, "Is this what I really want to do with my life? Is this where I really want

Fig. 6.26. When you slow down the mind you get the answers to your life.

to go? Where will I want to be ten years from now? Will I be fulfilling my life's destiny? Why am I here? What am I supposed to do with myself?" These questions will all be answered once you practice the Tao through the meditations and apply the concepts through your daily living process.

This is simply breathing, sleeping, urinating, defecating, sitting, standing, walking, and exchanging your sexual energy in harmony with the flow of the Tao or the flow of the universe. It is that simple. You do not have to do anything except apply yourself by slowing down your whole thinking process and allow yourself to make conscious choices.

As you discover these conscious choices you will find yourself in harmony with everything around you. That harmony will take you where your natural place is, connecting with all of nature's loving and giving people, aspects, and elements. This is the way of the Tao and its mystical path.

SUN AND AIR

One of the biggest aspects in our life is that we need to be exposed to the sun and to absorb the solar energy. That is the father energy itself, the universal forces above. We need to draw the cosmic dust particles into our body, which are what gives us life and what gives us our whole essence. This is why we need to be exposed to the sun.

We need it, we need to feel it, we need to feel its brilliance, and we need to connect with it every day. As we connect with it we start to understand why it is important to us. It heals us by its warmth, its energy, and its understandings. The whole concept of the son of God came from the s-u-n (*son*), from many of the chronicles throughout history. We just forgot, conditioned by our monkey mind cultures and dogmas.

We actually worship the sun in the truest sense because the sun comes up every morning and that is how we grow our food, and grow our bodies from that solar energy as we embrace the sun, our father. This along with the earth, our mother, gives us the proper knowledge

Fig. 6.27. The father energy is the universal force above.

of being the product of both the father and mother of the universe, the sun and the earth. It is with that brilliance that we should proceed in our lives with the understanding of oneness of the universe as we feel the warm energy from the sun.

As you blink your eyes into the sun you can see the violet red dots when you close them and connect with the sun rays and the cosmic dust particles. If you look at the horizon at the right time, either sunrise or sunset, you can see the cosmic dust particles coming

Fig. 6.28. The brilliance of the sun heals and warms the body.

Fig. 6.29. Solar bathing

down from the sun that feed us and give us our life force. This is what our whole energetic level is based on, the sun and its energy. With a proper connection with the sun we can start to absorb the cosmic dust particles directly into our body, giving us our life force.

To solar bathe, you should expose all of your body to the sun giving you energy where the sun does not shine or usually does not reach. We should expose our genitals and buttocks to the sun giving the body a most important healing and cleansing nutrition that we need. Sun exposure is important, but again done in moderation, not too much and not too little, just enough.

Now, you also need the proper air intake. When we live in urban environments we do not get the proper air circulation and obtain the

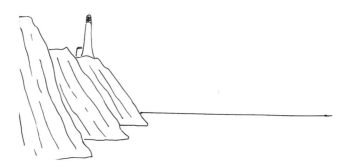

Fig. 6.30. Big openness of the mountains and the sea

proper intake of air. This is why we do a lot of shallow breathing. When we breathe in it does not feel good because there are a lot of pollutants in the congested air of these artificial environments that we inhabit. The best thing to do is to get near the big openness in the mountains or the sea and breathe in the fresh air that comes from these wide spaces.

When you confine everything into one congested area you get the stagnation of air. As it becomes stagnant your body does not pull in the air because it does not connect with you and does not feel good. That is why when you go out into the wilderness and stand on a mountain, you breathe in deeply because all that purified air makes your body feel so good. Ideally you should take a full lower abdominal belly breath and draw the air completely into your lungs, and as you exhale push it completely out.

You need to spend time in the mountains or near the ocean to breathe that clean air. Even though you are in an urban area, you will find yourself going to the mountain or the ocean to get that clean air to breathe. Your body will move you there whether you are conscious of it or not.

Fig. 6.31. We are truly breatharians.

As you slow the mind down you will discover that you are truly a breatharian. If you take the proper steps you can become united back to yourself where you are supposed to be in your life. This allows you to be at one with yourself and one with who you are.

WHERE TO LIVE

As you slow down the mind you start to discover what is important to you, who you are, and where you are going. The whole journey of life is to discover who you are and that will lead you to where you are going and then it will be revealed to you how you are going to get there. That is the Tao and its wondrous way is the path of self-discovery. As you start to discover who you are, you will discover where you are supposed to live. If you are going to be on the earth plane, you must stay connected within yourself in all the five elements or phases of the earth.

You will gradually gravitate to the openness of a natural environment where you do not live surrounded by artificial elements created by people. You are going to surround yourself with the same energy that is inside your body; the same energy that you can connect with every day to be in harmony within yourself. You see, the same energy in the tree is in the liver; the same energy in the river or creek is in your kidneys; the same energy in your heart is in the sun; the same energy in your spleen and pancreas is in the earth or the ground; and the same energy in your lungs is in the rocks or the mountains.

These are your molecular parents. These are all the elements you need to embrace to maintain your health and harmony. That is the key, to maintain yourself, and as you learn to maintain yourself you will discover that harmony inside you is being one with nature. That is why you need to be at one with yourself and in an environment where you can foster that.

When we live in artificial environments the sunshine is artificial; it is electricity in a lamp or light bulb. It is not the natural energy. When you live long enough in an artificial environment you slowly do not feel

Fig. 6.32. Our molecular parents are the five elements in the forest.

right. When you have the real thing (the sun or open campfire), it feels totally different and you have more vitality and life force inside your being and you feel more like living. It is the same thing with the water that you drink, which is filtered, pasteurized, or chemically changed. It does not taste the same. It does not feel the same because it is not the same. It is not natural; it is adulterated with no natural life.

As you take a drink of the water from a creek up in the mountains or you actually physically bathe in a creek opening up the skin pores, it is shocking at first, but when you get into it your body adjusts and relaxes, absorbing the energy. After you get out, there is a warm healing feeling that comes from inside you, giving you oneness with the environment.

It is totally refreshing and cleansing for your whole physical body. The wood energy, the energy from the liver, can't be gained from dead wood; you connect with the smells of a tree but it is different to be sitting on a wooden chair that is dead and not alive. It is inactive and nonmoving, just a corpse of itself. The feeling is not the same. They look similar, but it just is not the same. It has no energy and it does not move because it is not alive. When you walk in the forest you can smell the trees. The same when you sit next to a tree feeling that energy connection with the liver. It is totally different. This energy activates the liver to be more productive and more at harmony with itself.

When you sit on a mountain, you feel the stone (metal) and how natural it feels and how you feel connected with your lungs and your colon. Feel that energy as you embrace the mountain and massiveness of it, the strength of it, and the courage you feel when you absorb the mountain energy. It is not the same as the metal you use, which is processed, heated, reshaped, and rekindled.

Fig. 6.33. The mountain energy is powerful.

It is the same with the spleen and the pancreas. You connect with them as you walk on the bare earth with its grass, its stones, and the feel of earth itself, the dirt. You feel that connection within your body and how it feels inside you. You can smell the dirt and stick your hand in it. You can feel the cool energy of the earth and the wetness and dampness of the earth. You feel that connection with the spleen, stomach, and pancreas. It is not the same when you have artificial dirt, which is processed, reshaped, and removed. It is totally different. It does not have that life force and does not have that connection.

As you start to move your way through the five elements and their connection with your five vital organs, you slowly gravitate to an environment where these elements are natural and abundant, where the energy is strong, where your mind is clear, where your soul is at peace. This is where you will find yourself. All the sages of old always made it back up into the mountains, where you can feel and expand in yourself every aspect of these energy spheres and vortexes, rekindling with yourself and your true essence and true being.

People say, "How is everyone going to do that? We have six billion people on Earth." Well, there are six billion mountains, believe me. If you go to the Himalayas, they go on forever. The whole size of the United States could be contained within the Himalayan mountain range. Even in the United States, which only represents 8 percent of the population of the world, there is a huge mountain mass through the Rockies, the Cascades, the Appalachians, and the two coastal ranges; and there is nobody there. We could spread the whole world civilization over the mountains of North America and Asia (the Himalayas). There is plenty of space, plenty of room, once you start to connect with your true being and your true essence.

Where are you going to live? You could live in the mountains or by the openness of the sea. There are vast areas still open to everyone. You have to slow the mind down through the Taoist practices and then you will start to make these conscious choices for yourself. These conscious choices will lead you to the mountain and lead you to the sea. With the openness and vastness you will start to connect with the universe within as you expand your universe with the Tao. This is the key to the Tao and the key to life. As you reconnect yourself you will discover where you are going to be and how you are going to be. This allows you to make certain discoveries within yourself, creating the proper environment internally with cleansing, cosmic purification internally, and the cosmic purification externally in the proper environment that you are creating around yourself and within yourself; they are one and the same. Let the energy flow and flow with the energy. This is the effortless path of the Tao.

As an ancient sage once said, "As you connect with the flow, put your feet up and enjoy the ride." You do not have to do anything, except allow the energy to move you by itself. The less you do or the less you interfere with this flowing process, the more harmony and peace you will find within yourself. It is all a matter of how you want to apply yourself and how you want to work this process. It is that simple. Just enjoy yourself and for what that is worth, just enjoy where you are now and you will get to where you are supposed to go. Because you are where you are supposed to be and everywhere you have ever been is exactly where you are meant to be. It is that simple. Life is simple. We have a tendency to complicate it with our monkey mind, creating things that are not really necessary for us. All we have to do is put our feet up and enjoy the ride.

Mountain and Ocean

HOT AND COLD

The mountain and the ocean are the energy fields of the man and the woman. They are opposite but a lot alike. What we are talking about here are opposites. When the man is aroused he is hot; when the woman is aroused she is cold. When a woman is unaroused she is warm; when the man is unaroused he is cool. So, we have a real communication problem. We are talking about the aroused and unaroused stages of both men and women. If you are very hot and the person with whom you are trying to communicate is cold, the communication is difficult.

Fig. 7.1. The mountain and the ocean, the energy fields of the man and woman

Men and women have different types of energy molecularly. It is very hard to interact unless you have a clear understanding of your own energy field and how it interacts with people around you, especially the energy field of the opposite gender. But if you understand this, it opens up communication, which is the key to any type of relationship. There are the differences in the genders in the aroused state and unaroused state. When a woman is unaroused, she has warm energy, and if she gets too unaroused she gets very warm. If she is very aroused she is like ice; she gets icy cold. This icy cold is similar to someone rubbing an ice cube on your wrist and you feel a numbing sensation—it's really cold, but it is also a burning sensation. She feels as if she is hot but not like a man's hot. That is what a woman feels like when she is aroused sexually. When she is unaroused she feels kind of warm and cozy.

A man is the total opposite. When the man is aroused he is jet hot like a fire, a burning sensation. When he is unaroused he is cool and there is a cooling effect. A male's hot energy is a lot different than a woman's hot energy. And the male's cool energy is a lot different than the woman's cool energy. But the problem is that they are at the arousal and nonarousal periods at the same time when they are

Fig. 7.2. When aroused, a woman is cold and a man is hot; when unaroused, a man is cool and a woman is warm.

together, and that is where the communications breaks down. These are some of the basic differences in the energy fields. There are many that we will discuss but there are many likenesses as well.

The similarities are such that the techniques in the Taoist practices balance the energy, except that the apparatus (genders) is a little different. With the unaroused energy and the aroused energy, it is a little different when they interact. The key is to balance the energy and to connect with the inner gender within yourself, discovering the opposite gender within. And as you start to balance the energy, the hot and the cold will be balanced so that you can see the real connection within yourself for either man or woman.

In reality we are neither man nor woman. We are entrapped in the male and female body and to release this entrapment we need to marry the inner gender within ourselves. And as we marry the inner gender, we balance that energy and give birth to our own spiritual essence. That is basically the reason that you connect with the opposite gender. It is to help you discover your own opposite gender

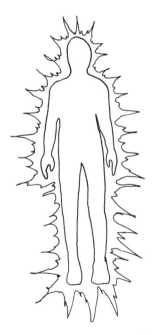

Fig. 7.3. We are neither male nor female; we are light bodies with no gender.

within. This is how it all unfolds. It takes time and understanding to start to feel this energy and to start to feel this connection. It is not impossible but you first must have the concept to achieve it. So your relationship with the other gender is the theme and driving force, as the mountain mates with the ocean.

The mountain gives the ocean structure and shape and the ocean smoothes the mountain's rough edges. The problem is the ocean tries to change the mountain, but the mountain never changes and is only smoothed at the rough edges. The truth is that what attracts the ocean (woman) to the mountain (man) is what the ocean is trying to change. Our monkey mind (ego) is getting into the act. So if the ocean does succeed she will never be happy. The mountain tries to keep the ocean from changing but she is always changing and that is what really attracts the mountain. But the mountain only gives shape and structure for the ocean, which she desires. Our monkey mind (ego) is getting into the act again. If the mountain succeeds he will never be happy. This is the same relationship we have with our inner gender and also the other genders around us.

Fig. 7.4. The ocean smoothes the mountain and the mountain gives shape to the ocean.

The woman always looks to change the man but the man never really changes. But she softens the man and smoothes the rough edges like the ocean does to the mountain or the rock. And the man never thinks that the woman will change; he thinks that the woman is like the man. But the woman is always changing, constantly in flux like the ocean. The man does give shape to the ocean and boundaries so that the woman can splash within those boundaries. That is what the woman searches for in her own nature, the structure and form that the man gives her. So the two can work together and learn from each other.

Beyond all that, within we are light bodies entrapped in the human form either as male or female. So, you should always have empathy for one another in your entrapment and the only way out is to balance the other gender within you with the help of the other gender. If you do, you will start to discover your true essence, your true being. It takes time and patience but in time you can achieve it. This is the hot and cold and when you balance it you become one with yourself and you create your own spiritual being. And in that spiritual being you can transform any aspect of yourself into the spirit right here on this earth plane. It takes time and patience, for it is a long journey.

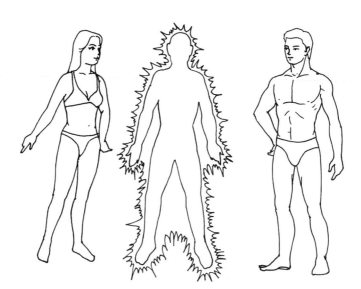

Fig. 7.5. We are light bodies entrapped in the human form as man or woman.

The Tao prepares you for this journey. But first you must understand who you are, and as you discover that, you will discover where you are going and that will be revealed to you and how you are going to get there. So, being a male or female you must know these energy fields and how they work and function—not only within yourself but also how they interact with the other gender outside yourself. And, as a Taoist would explain, there are certain energies flowing through you and what you should do is learn that energy and how it flows and flow with it.

So, if you are trying to change yourself from a man into a woman or a woman into a man you are swimming against the stream. You are causing a lot of difficulty for yourself. But no matter what you do, you are always going to be that male or female unless you transform it and marry yourself within. So, if you are really smart you put your feet up and enjoy the ride because in other journeys previously you were either a man or a woman so it really does not matter. In the end you are really just a light body within your consciousness. This is how it basically works.

The energies for the male are yang, which is positive, expansive, and generating. The energies for the woman are yin, which is absorbing and connecting. And this affects how people actually communicate with one another. A male talks in generalities, and when a woman talks, she personalizes. So if you say to a woman, "Oh, this woman over there did this wrong or she did this right," she will personalize this and identify the woman with herself. Now, if you said to the male, "You did this wrong," he thinks in generalities. He thinks you are not really talking about him personally. So the man can disconnect himself from any personal connection when somebody explains something to him, and the woman will connect herself with it. And this is a hard reality with how we run our society. In the business world, which is primarily run by men and their thinking processes, it is very impersonal, and that is how they function in it. For the woman, it is a whole different program because she personalizes and really gets too personally involved with it when it has really nothing to do with her, but because of her outlook and the way she perceives things she connects with it. By personalizing she takes on the energy and the situation for herself when the man would not normally do that, and he survives well in that world.

Now when you start to see this situation then you can apply yourself in different situations and begin to understand how the energy works. And basically it is conditioning and a lot of biological aspects within your own body that you are born into. There is a genetic code that is programmed with gender in each of us, in the genes themselves and the DNA. And this is what you must understand is working for you all the time. It has its strengths and weaknesses like everything in life. So you first must become aware of the weaknesses and then, when you become aware of the strengths, you can work with them. That is all in the understanding of the natural flow within us. Once you learn how the energy flows through you and how it interacts, then you can learn to flow with it. That is the effortless path of the Tao. So the key is to have a good understanding of what you are working with and then you can discover how that energy interacts with others and how it develops a relationship with everything around itself.

The man basically is a prisoner of the mind. If he can understand it and logically think it out, he will do it. If he cannot, he will not do it. If it is against his whole thinking process, he will not do it. He is literally a prisoner of the mind. The woman is different. She is a prisoner of the body. If she does not feel right about doing something,

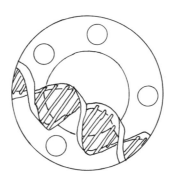

Fig. 7.6. The genetic code programs us with gender through our DNA.

she will not do it because she is attuned to her body and how it feels. And this is basically one of the major differences between the two genders. This is how they actually think and interact with one another and within themselves, and neither one clearly understands this difference. So the woman will only move if she is to do something when she feels it is correct, and that goes beyond logic sometimes. It goes beyond thinking. It is how she feels inside that is basically the way of the Tao, because the only way to understand the Tao is to feel it. The only way to feel it is to practice it. This is a problem for both genders. First of all the males cannot really feel that much inside. They have to be taught to feel internally. But, once they understand the concept (again the mind), then they can actually do the practice in a systematic way and achieve this feeling within themselves.

The women already have this practice within themselves, this feeling of understanding, but they lack the discipline to take it to the higher levels because they never really set up the understanding initially through the practices. So there is a little twist with both areas. For the woman in her feeling aspect she can get completely disenchanted or disoriented with it because it might be an imbalance in her body with her organs. I will explain that later.

We have two different thinking processes to contend with within ourselves. In terms of the opposite gender and connecting with that gender, which is the key for our evolution, we need to marry that opposite gender. Even though you might accomplish this in Single Cultivation as opposed to Dual Cultivation, you still must discover this other gender within you to do it. The easiest way to discover it is living with it outside yourself. That is what the whole purpose of relationships should be. And that really is the only reason you should be in a relationship, to discover that other gender within yourself by observing it outside yourself. For both the male and the female, this is how they discover this essence inside themselves. But you can also venture on your own and make this discovery as well. Either in the Single Cultivation or the Dual Cultivation, we are working with the hot and cold energies. This is the key to the Tao—to have a complete understanding of the hot and the cold energies, yin and yang, the female and the male. To know how the energy works by itself and how it interacts with the energy around itself is the key to your journey of self-discovery. This is the key to the Tao and your relationship with the mountain and the ocean.

THE TRACTOR AND THE LAKE

The tractor and the lake exemplify what I mean by the difference between the genders. When you drive a tractor into a lake you get stuck. And what happens when the tractor tries to fight the lake? It sinks deeper. Who is stronger, the tractor or the lake? Obviously, the lake is stronger. It not only has its own energy but it also absorbs the energy of the tractor that is exerting energy. Now, the tractor is active energy and the lake is passive energy. The lake is the yin energy or female energy, and the tractor is the yang energy or the male energy.

So the woman is far superior to the man in every aspect, physically, emotionally, psychologically, and spiritually. Physically from the waist down the woman is far superior to the man. She can outwork the man. She lives longer and has more strength physically below the waist. In the endurance of pain and physical hardships she far exceeds the man because her body can give birth to another human being. Her body is structured far better than the man's body because the genitals are inside the body protected by the body's surface. Emotionally, she

Fig. 7.7. The tractor and the lake

works more with her feelings and has more capacity with her emotional center. She can cry one minute and be smiling the next. If a man broke down and cried, which happens maybe once or twice in his life, it would take him three days to recover. He just does not have the ability to turn it on and off like the woman. Later we will get into an explanation of how that works.

Psychologically, a woman tunes in to her inner self with telepathy and clairvoyance. She opens up the crystal room and connects with that energy inside herself. The woman is more apt to make this connection than the man because of her physical structure. The woman is tuned in to herself because she is throughout her whole life internalizing and looking into herself from a very young age. A woman is more spiritually attuned than a man because of her inner connection within herself and her understanding connection with the earth energy and nature. She gives birth to another human being, which the male cannot do. Within that birth process another spirit body comes into her own body so she is obviously more connected with the spirit force or the spiritual essence of the universe. She experiences this physically, feeling and connecting with it, giving her own experience with it. Because she is yin, and yin is darkness while yang is light, she can do everything in the dark. She goes beyond the vision and light, working completely with feeling and essence and without images. Going beyond time and space, she collectively uses this superiority to her advantage because she never really informs the man that she is superior. So, the man is thinking that she is not superior and assumes that he is. When in fact he is not and she is and she never lets on to the fact that she is because being yin it is not her nature to reveal what she is. She is yin and she lives in darkness.

She feels very comfortable in darkness. You can see the man—when the sun comes up the man gets up and when the sun goes down the man goes to sleep. With the woman it is opposite because she identifies with the moon, the shadow of the sun. She gets her light from the sun, which is reflected from the moon down to the earth. That is the only reason that she gets the light, because she reflects it

Fig. 7.8. The woman lives off the reflection of the moon and
the man lives off light from the sun.

and absorbs it as the moon does to the sun. So when the moon comes
out at night that is when the woman is active. I have met many women
and have never known them to sleep. I do not understand when they
sleep or understand how they do it. It is amazing. They live their life
with a whole different vibration and connection. They live it from
inside out, not outside in as does the man. Men and women have two
differently thinking, differently functioning biological processes.
They are opposites and that is why they attract. But the real reason
that they connect and their purpose in the connection is to discover
their own opposite gender inside themselves, and as they make that
discovery they will start to connect with their own understanding.

Women dress differently than men especially in the trunk of the
body. Men's heart center is closed down and to seal it they traditionally wear a collar and tie; but a woman's heart center is open and she
wears low-cut dresses exposing her breasts. She also wears halters and
tank tops with no sleeves exposing her armpits. This area governs the
fire energy in the body, and how we use it without thinking about it.

Women wear dresses and pants that zip up the back because they urinate from the back and squat to urinate. Men wear pants with zippers in the front because they urinate from the front. So it is a practical way of having clothes designed to use in their daily functions, seeing as we all urinate three to four times per day. This area governs the water energy in the body and how we use it without thinking about it.

Women wear high-heeled shoes to raise their buttocks to unconsciously attract the males. You see the woman is the hunter and the males are the hunted, because if a woman does not want to be with a man there is nothing he can do to be with her. If a woman wants to be with a particular man it is very difficult for him to resist her advances. The women know that the men sense this and utilize this technique in the war of the sexes.

There is an old saying, "All is fair in love and war." That means there is only one war on the planet and that is between genders based on control, who is controlling whom. Men are nomads; they roam around the planet not confined to any one area, which is their nature like the sun, moving from one horizon to other. It is often said a man never has a home: he lives in his mother's and then he lives in his wife's. But a woman is territorial because by her nature she is a nester and gatherer (shopper), building her security around her house for her family. She will fight for her home and family by getting the man to build the house and defend it for her and her family, an extension of her body. So indirectly all territorial wars are caused by women, because men by their nature would never fight one another over territory. Men like to compete with one another and to them that is not fighting, it is just competing (sports and business). They just do not care about where they live, and they live at peace with one another.

When I, William Wei, rent out rooms in my rental income homes, I can have five to six men in the house and they can get along and live together without fighting. If there is a difference they will leave but they will not fight one another. But with women it is a whole different story: if you have two women in one house they will fight each other over the territory of the house. Now with one woman in a house with several men there is no problem, but if you add another woman there are big problems. It is just their nature.

I was fortunate to experience unconditional love in my life with my mother. She loved me no matter what happened or whatever I did. I had the same love for her and I would do anything for her. People tell me that this unconditional love can be achieved in a couples relationship; but I have never seen it. All the relationships that I have seen and experienced are based on conditions: you do this for me and I do that for you. And if you do not live up to our agreement I will leave and the relationship is over after you pay to end it. I guess unconditional love is a mother's love. But if you look at that love, you as a child are an appendage (extension) of your mother. You are a part of her body, so her love is for a part of her body that speaks and has its own life force, but she feels everything in that body because it is her body. This explains the unconditional love the mother has for her children and why it is unusual to find it anywhere else.

THE TAO IS FEMININE

The key message in the mountain and the ocean is the ability of the ocean to yield to the mountain. The way of the Tao is to yield because the Tao is feminine, and you find this in every aspect of life. Every time you want to overcome something, yield to its energy and use its energy for your own benefit and welfare, which is basically the message of the Tao. So the males need to discover their own yin essence and the ability to yield and absorb, and the females need to utilize this in a very instructive way. So the real power is in the yin, not the yang, as demonstrated by the tractor and the lake with the ability to absorb, not confront. Yin energy is to yield, not to bring down. It is the ability to absorb and blend in, having the ability to yield and to survive.

Seventy percent of all the wealth in the world is inherited by women. The women own everything and they are the ones in power by yielding to the male energy. They simply yield to the male energy and outlive them. The Jesuit priests revealed that to me while I was studying with them. They have a whole program devised to get donations from women for their projects and how to approach them for donations because they have all the money.

The one big thing men have to understand which helps them when dealing with women is this: the man, being yang (external), tries to master the world, but the woman, being yin (internal), does not try to master the world, she tries to master the master of the world. If she succeeds, not only does she have the man (her big prize) but also the man's world. So she is the one hunting men; men aren't hunting her. That is a big difference in how a man approaches the game of life. Once he understands what is really going on, he adjusts and then works with it. But if he does not he is in big trouble and is taken advantage of by the woman, which is basically the case in our societies.

A great example of yielding is water and the essence of water. Yielding, forgiving, understanding in letting go, and being continuous is the power of the Tao. When you start to think of the Tao, think of the yielding, feminine aspect and start to connect with it within yourself, either male or female. To resist anything, you give it the power to overtake you, so yield to it and you free yourself from it.

Fig. 7.9. Water is yielding, forgiving, understanding, and continuous.

To go with the energy, you give it the power to overcome yourself as well. So, what do you do? You do nothing and by doing nothing you yield to the energy, giving it neither positive nor negative energy, which is what it lives off, and it goes into hibernation, becoming dormant. If you give it any energy, positive or negative, you give it life again. Try this and you will be surprised by how this works.

You just let it flow and it will flow on its own course and it will eventually flow into nothingness. So the key is to let go and to let go is the yielding. As you let go, let go of every aspect of who you are and where you came from. Then you start to understand the true path within. Being male or female, just let go of your gender and, the more you let go of your gender, the more you will discover that other gender within yourself. As you discover that other gender you will discover the Tao.

It is a whole process of living life for the joy of it. Not getting anything out of life but living it for the joy of living it. We do things just for the joy of doing them. We dance to dance, sing to sing, love to love, and just be for the joy of it. It is just the joy that you experience doing it. It is just a matter of totally fulfilling yourself in this essence of who you are right now in this moment.

HOW WE URINATE AFFECTS OUR WHOLE OUTLOOK

When we are children, both genders have to urinate. The male child has all the equipment down there right in front and he can see everything. He can see the equipment and he urinates out. He does this with space repetition over the next five years before he gets trained in reading and writing. His outlook on life in this time span is already firmly established as external because he focuses externally. When the little girl urinates she looks to find where it is coming from. She looks down inside herself because she does not see anything down there. She is curious about what is inside her so she is puzzled over this issue, and she begins to look toward and feel what is inside her.

Fig. 7.10. Both genders urinate and through repetition form lifelong outlooks on life.

Her genitals are internalized and the males are externalized. Just by this practice of urinating their whole process of thinking is formed. The male generalizes and the female personalizes. The male looks outside himself and the woman looks inside herself. It is a whole different way of communicating and a whole different way of understanding and thinking, but neither one of them realizes that their thinking patterns are different, which is the reason for their communication breakdown throughout their life journey.

The man proceeds through life and looks at everything externally. It is all right there. He takes control of his genital area and he becomes master of it. He understands it and comes in contact with it every day. The woman on the other hand does not come in contact with her genitals because they are not out there. They are inside her body. Because they are inside, she is drawn to look inside her body. And as she discovers this, all kinds of aspects of her understanding change. She becomes

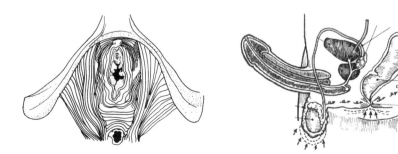

Fig. 7.11. A woman's genitals are internal and a man's are external.

connected with herself and internalizes who she is and where she is coming from.

As they communicate, there is a huge difference in what takes place between the two genders in their exchange. When you are a man explaining something to a woman and you think she has an understanding of what you are talking about, you proceed as if she thinks as you do. But she has a totally different perspective, a totally different interest, and totally different concerns. Until you make that realization that her thinking process is the opposite of yours, you will truly never be able to communicate or even understand what she is talking about and she will not be able to understand you either. This is why we have such a difference in communication between the two genders: because neither gender has a clear understanding of how the other operates and functions, and how their thinking is so much in an opposite direction. They assume it is the same.

One difference is nudity. When men drop their pants they completely reveal their genitals; there is nothing to hide; it is all out there. But for the woman, she is truly never naked. There is always something hidden because her genitals are inside her body, never to be revealed. So, she can be running around with nothing on and never

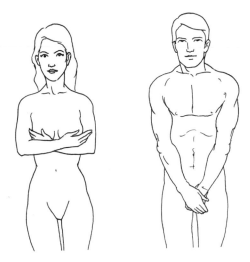

Fig. 7.12. The woman is really never completely naked or exposed, but the man is.

be naked like the man. But the man never makes this realization and she takes full advantage of the situation (pornography, strip clubs) and has for centuries received huge amounts of money but is never totally nude. If you think about it, her genitals are in her body and when she discovers that men go crazy about it, she exploits the men. She is naked but not naked, and the men chase her to see her genitals but never actually see them. Funny isn't it, what the monkey mind puts us through without us realizing it?

People make the assumption that everyone thinks as they do. But in reality, they do not. Even before the gender differences, the cultural, religious, and regional differences and genetic background create a whole variety of different understandings and different perceptions. It is surprising that the genders communicate in any way at all. That is why the statistics are very strong revealing that most relationships end in divorce because the two genders never really have an understanding of how they personally communicate and how they interact because they have no understanding of how their body functions in every aspect.

The genders are thrown into situations by reacting instead of correct action with conscious choices. They end up in relationships and the relationships either end up in divorce or they live a life of hell because they have no business being together in the first place. They were never really together for the correct reason, which is to discover their own opposite gender within. This is a different way of looking at relationships and as people make that discovery they will discover the Tao and the path within.

This is a problem that we all face but with this concept and understanding you will be farther ahead in your relationship's accomplishments. When you realize how your body flows and functions you start to understand how it interacts with everybody else. That is the key for a lasting and meaningful relationship with your opposite gender.

The male needs to discover what it is to know without knowing—in other words, using the upper mind to observe and the middle mind, the heart center, to think or to give the answers in life. Once you

Fig. 7.13. We never come together for the correct reason:
to discover the opposite gender within.

develop that understanding you can start to move into the Tao. And with the woman's aspect, she must learn to distinguish the feeling of the imbalance of the organs, which is connected in the emotional realm at the heart center, and the true feeling within herself. She will learn to connect with her male essence and develop some abilities to logically understand. This is the whole process of using logic with feeling. In other words, if you get a feeling about something and you do not really know the answer then you must verify it to some extent with your own ability to logically understand what it really means. This whole process really begins with the heart center, and you will start to move in the direction that you are supposed to by feeling the correct answer or the correct solution to any question. But you need to balance them both, the logic and the feeling. It has to make sense to a certain degree, even if you have to use different dimensions of an aspect. It has to have some logical reference to make it doable. You must truly focus within yourself and try to balance the organs, so that you do not get a mixed feeling from an imbalanced organ or imbalanced emotion about the correct answer and action.

It is an interesting area but there are several check points that you can fall back on to make sure the answer is correct. It has got to feel correct and it has got to logically make some sense in one aspect or another to make it a workable answer. You see there is a lot we do not know and even more that we do not know to know. This is the majority of our existence here. So, it is difficult to base everything on a certain logic, into which you can get trapped. You need a balance, some reference point to make your perception proper. But you really need to be connected to that feeling within. This is the whole process of learning to think with your heart and feel with your mind.

And it all started when we first urinated and our perception of how we looked at life. So, you must become aware of your own perceptions and learn to work with them as you can start to see through them for the correct action that you need to take with your life. It is all part of your own self-discovery of who you are, where you are going, and how you are going to get there. It is all part of enjoying the ride as you start to connect with yourself and everyone around you.

THE HEART CENTER

As a girl matures into an adolescent, she begins to form breasts and she begins to get in touch with her chest area, thus getting in touch with her heart center which is the center of emotion and feeling. This is the inner voice within. She starts to work directly with these emotions and feelings. This affects her gender's outlook on life. As a woman internalizes she personalizes such that she takes things personally. As a man externalizes, he generalizes or talks in generalities. You can see this has a major impact on how a man and woman live and how they communicate with each other, which leads to confusion and indifferences.

The man never touches himself in the chest area throughout his whole life. He never gets in touch literally with his heart center. He never gets in touch with his feelings and emotions. The woman becomes a master of emotions, which is the heart force, and the male becomes the master of the sexual energy (genitals), which is the kidney force with which he is in touch. Each can help the other. Once you understand the differences you can start to work with your own energy and how it interacts with the energy of other people. So, if you are a male you understand that because you are in touch with your genitals you can help the women get in touch with their genitals. In some of the Taoist practices you can start to show or utilize the ability to get in contact with the genitals for the woman by various techniques of Chi Nei Tsang massage.

For the men it is all right there so they can work the energy. With their energy if they do not get control of it or try to manage the sexual energy, it can easily control them. That is why they do a lot of crazy things when they are younger that they would never do when they are older. When they are young the sexual energy is so powerful it becomes uncontrollable or unmanageable. They get into situations that they would never get into logically or even emotionally. This energy is just overpowering. The woman on the other hand works the emotional energy because she is in touch with her heart center, literally, and to calm the male she can actually be in contact with his emotional and feeling area just by rubbing his chest. As he starts to open his heart he can start to connect with his own feelings and emotions.

The woman is really the master of this area because she has had all this experience urinating and creating this thinking process of internalizing and then carrying into her adolescence as she begins to open up her heart center literally with the forming of breasts on her chest. She starts getting in touch with feelings by caressing the breasts and starts to open up and experience all of these emotional aspects of herself, the inner voice and feeling inside herself. That is the knowing without knowing. As long as she has a clear understanding of the imbalances emotionally from the organs that can also be created in this area from this feeling inside herself that can mislead her, she will be all right.

The woman can actually help the man get in touch with his emotional feelings and the man can help the woman get in touch with her sexual energy. Literally that is what takes place initially as the woman

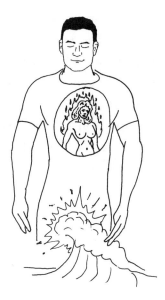

Fig. 7.14. Understand how the fire (emotional) energy and water (sexual) energy work and you discover the opposite gender within.

slowly discovers the sexual energy and how to work with it. And the woman can help him get in touch with his female energy, which is the emotional energy of the heart, and start to work with that energy. So they can help one another be in contact and balance one another from a physical aspect while working with the energy. This is how it all unfolds for the man and the woman. They start to get into contact with their essence and how that energy works and flows. As they start to make that connection, they start to see that they are really light bodies entrapped in this physical form in either gender. Once this is discovered they need to make the connection with their opposite gender within, so they can give birth to their own immortal fetus and balance the energy and move beyond gender into their spirit essence.

Let us get back to our greatest appetite—sex—and how women actually come to a climax in the arousal state of their sexual energy, which is one of our greatest feeling aspects in our lives. When a woman becomes sexually aroused, she needs to slowly get the energy aroused and then she needs to slowly come down with the energy. It takes time. This is with foreplay and staying with the other partner changing the sexual energy. The same is true for the male except instead of the water energy from the kidney, which is a sexual energy, it is in the heart, it's the yang energy, the fire energy releasing the emotions after an emotional exchange.

The woman can actually do emotional foreplay with the male to help him open up his heart center and as he starts to feel the emotions he can start to express them. He then needs to be slowly let down emotionally like a woman needs to be caressed and held after the sexual interaction. This is the same thing occurring on an emotional level for the man. The two opposites are very much a part of their whole makeup. You need to be balanced on the compatibility not only from the fire or emotional realm but also from the water and the sexual realm for a strong connection. The males primarily concern themselves with the physical or the sexual levels and the woman with the emotional realm. So, that is why they do not really become close together because they do not really understand how it works. You need to balance both, the fire and the water, for it to work correctly.

What happens when you realign the fire underneath the water? If you have the correct alignment (correct compatibility) by placing the fire underneath the water, you get steam. And that steam comes up the spine and it heals. The steam is the love that the male and female feel for one another. It is not mystical. It is really mechanical. If you have the right compatibility so that you can align the fire (emotions) of the man underneath the water (sex energy) of the woman, fire will boil the water and as the water boils the steam rises and the steam is the grace or love that they have for each other. So it is really a mechanical alignment of the proper energy compatible with their natural alignment that creates this feeling of love or the steam with which they connect. To achieve that, they must have the compatibility emotionally, which the fires blend together, but sexually the waters must blend together as well. And then they can rearrange the alignment of fire and water by realigning them with the fire beneath the water, and this is how the steam is created.

The offspring of this alignment is actually giving birth to the spiritual body within yourself and the second aspect is children that are a product of this alignment. The problem is that people have no understanding of what is taking place and that is why it usually gets all confused and screwed up. That is why, with the proper understanding of learning to work with the energy, you start to develop a clear understanding of what you are working with and the correct approach to it.

But first of all you need to understand that when you open the heart energy and the heart center, you are trying to discover within yourself your opposite gender. And through that discovery you will start to create an understanding within yourself by working with the energy, giving birth to your own spirit essence, as on the external level you give birth to a human child. You mix the two energies. One feeds the other. But your real purpose here on this earth plane is to make your own self-discovery and to begin to understand the whole essence of why you are here.

BOILING EGGS

An example of the interplay of the two genders is what I call boiling eggs. You put two eggs in a pot of hot water and you put it on the burner to boil. The male can get an erection or start the fire just like

Fig. 7.15. The correct alignment of the fire under the water will create steam, which is love.

Fig. 7.16. Boiling the woman's eggs activates a woman's orgasmic energy.

that but it takes a while for the woman to warm up sexually just as it takes a while for the water to warm up and boil. She needs some foreplay. She needs to be caressed. She needs her eggs to warm up. A woman's energy is cold by nature and you need to slowly warm up her energy. The eggs in her body, or her kidney energy, have to be activated at a slow pace and then brought to a boiling point slowly. The male sexual energy normally can turn on and off quickly but once he understands how her energy functions he can learn many other Taoist sexual techniques, such as the shallow thrusting technique, which will allow him to maintain his fire at a low temperature until she can build up her climax and boil her eggs. As her eggs are starting to boil she activates her orgasm but she also needs to come down slowly after the orgasm. That is why women like to be caressed, cuddled, and held, being with their partner many hours after the genital interaction just as you need to cool the eggs down after you boil them on the stove.

The funniest thing about this whole scenario is that the same thing is true and needed for the heart energy but in reverse. The woman can turn on and off with her emotions just as quickly as the male can turn his sexual energy or his kidney energy on and off. She has so much experience working with her feelings and her heart center that she can help the male to get in touch with his feelings and heart center. She has to caress the man with emotional foreplay and she can develop and nurture the man so that he can get in touch with his feelings.

When the man gets in touch with his feelings he needs to come down slowly just as she needs to cool the eggs down, and as the heart cools off he can get back in touch with it. So both genders, once they understand the energy fields and how they interact, can develop a nice harmony with one another by helping each other. This leads to the discovery of their own opposite gender inside themselves.

Another interesting scenario is that the man is always accused of adultery on a physical level because his genitals are external and he is in touch with them all the time, having a tendency to spread them around with more than one woman. It is interesting when you look at it because the woman is very upset that her man is having intercourse with another woman. She is not really in touch with her genitals and that is basically the understanding there. So, he commits physical adultery. The same is true with the emotional energy. A man cannot stand someone else knowing about his business and what do the women do? They turn around and commit emotional adultery with all their girlfriends or whoever will listen to them, telling everybody about all of their problems and what the man is doing. They are so free and open, because they are so in touch with their emotional realm, that they do everything in their power to explain everything to everyone else, which is just a way of expressing their emotions for emotional relief.

So the two are opposites. The females need to get in touch more with their genital energy—not that they need to be promiscuous, but they need to at least understand the difference between the genders. The males need to start to express themselves on an emotional level as the woman does. So, you need a correct balance. Right now it is one way or the other, which is a problem when you start to communicate with each other.

A woman cannot understand why the male is sleeping around and the man cannot understand why the woman is gossiping about all his activities. In the male world, you never tell anyone what you are doing or why you are doing it. It makes you lose respect and the only thing a

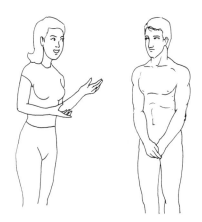

Fig. 7.17. Emotional adultery is committed by the woman and physical adultery by the man.

male can live by is respect. Usually emotional adultery is committed by the women and the men commit the physical adultery. The other interesting thing to back up this concept is what outsells all of the pornography magazines and sex films, which has to do with the kidney energy, the sexual energy. It is the emotional energy. The romance novels far outsell all of the pornography. What TV shows are on three to four times every day with five or six different shows on different channels? The emotional energy shows are the soap operas. So you can see where the male feeds his sexual energy, where he is in touch with it through pornography and sex films, and the woman feeds her emotional energy with the romance novels and the soap operas.

The difference is amazing, when you start to see the similarities from one extreme to another. They are set up anatomically different, and that is where the emphasis is. There are a lot of differences in both the male and the female; but again, we are neither male nor female, we are really just light bodies entrapped in time and space in either gender. And there are a lot of similarities. Once you discover the similarities you shall start to realize that we are really all the same in different bodies. We just have different equipment. The woman has the open, inverted version of the genitals and the male has the external, closed-in version of the genitals. The structure really determines how we communicate and how we interact not only with ourselves but everyone around us.

An interesting similarity is that the woman's vaginal canal has the same reflex points in the canal as the shaft of the penis. If the genitals of the male were pushed up into a woman's body, the testicles would be like the ovaries of the woman with the foreskin of the penis as a vaginal canal. The fallopian tubes of the female would be the vessels of the male's testicles. The G spots and arousal points on the male penis are the same as underneath the hood of the vaginal canal of the woman. One system is externalized and the other is internalized.

As the man gets the erection when the juices fill up the penis, the woman gets an erection when the juices fill up the vaginal canal. So, mechanically it is really the same except one is internal and the other

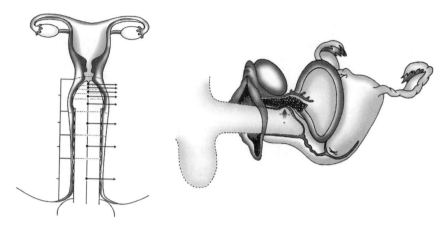

Fig. 7.18. The woman's vaginal canal has the same reflexology points as the man's penis.

Fig. 7.19. When a man gets an erection it is the same as a woman's juices that fill up the vaginal canal.

is external. But there are a lot of similarities and the arousal points of the breast are not of the same degree but they still exist. The man's nipples do get aroused and stimulated as well as they do for a woman. It is certainly a little different, but has a lot of similarities.

Once you understand the energy of the opposites, they are really similar but in different directions. When you make that connection in a relationship with your mate, you can start to feel the similarities. When you understand the blueprint of how each body is designed and how it functions in that aspect, you can get relationships to work for you. You start to feel and to see the differences but you can also see a pattern of similarities. Once you see that pattern of similarities you can start to relate on a conscious level with the other gender. As you start to relate on a conscious level with the other gender, you start to connect with the opposite gender inside yourself.

TENNIS DOUBLES MATCH

Taoists really do not look at sex and the use of sexual energy as a moral issue. To them it is more of a health issue, and if you are going to use sex you should use it properly. Once you begin to understand your energy, what it is about and what it is actually for, you can have a much healthier understanding of how to work with it and how it interacts with everyone around you, especially the opposite gender.

The best way to explain this is dual cultivation. The Taoist practices lend themselves to a monogamous relationship, similar to playing a tennis doubles match. You have a partner on your team and you learn their form and how they interact. It takes many years to develop a good rapport and good communication with each other's moves. The same thing occurs in the Taoist interaction of the sexual energy. Once you have a partner in Dual Cultivation it takes many years to perfect a

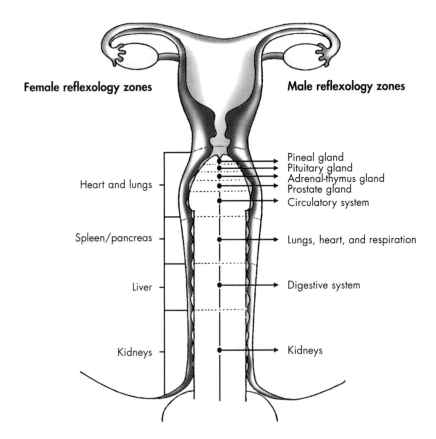

Female reflexology zones

Male reflexology zones

Heart and lungs

Spleen/pancreas

Liver

Kidneys

Pineal gland
Pituitary gland
Adrenal-thymus gland
Prostate gland
Circulatory system

Lungs, heart, and respiration

Digestive system

Kidneys

Fig. 7.20. When you understand the gender's energy blueprint,
then you will understand the genders.

Fig. 7.21. Taoist Dual Cultivation is like a tennis doubles match.

nice harmony. You do not want to switch partners just like you do not want to switch your partner in a tennis doubles match because you do not want to have to relearn all the various moves and techniques of the other partner. If you did, you would never win a match.

The same concept applies in the Tao with Dual Cultivation. As you practice tennis you serve and use your forehand and backhand as you do in singles match to help your partner in the doubles match. You start to practice Single Cultivation aspects in order to be ready for your Dual Cultivation. You need to perfect the techniques of Single Cultivation in the Taoist system with Testicle Breathing and Ovarian Breathing, genital compression for Dual Cultivation, the Big Draw, and Valley Orgasm techniques. As you work with these techniques, balancing the energy internally on a chemical level, you are going to attract a more balanced partner in your future. You should really focus on working primarily on your heart energy to balance yourself externally with love, compassion, and patience to have peace and harmony within yourself.

The key to all relationships is communication because the tongue is connected to the heart. As you move the tongue you open the heart and explain how you feel, who you are, and where you are going. As this opens up with an honest communication, you will discover if you

Fig. 7.22. You continue to use your serve, forehand, and backhand techniques in Dual Cultivation.

are compatible with each other by sharing your intent, and if your intentions are the same you succeed. If you slow your mind down the correct intention is to assist each other in your spiritual journeys.

So, the key is actually to learn to work with your partner and your own gender. As you learn to work with one another you will discover your strengths and weaknesses and you will adjust your approach around your partner. No matter who you are with, you are still going to have to serve and use your forehand and backhand, so you need your Single Cultivation techniques. As you start to develop the Dual Cultivation techniques you are always going to work with your own Single Cultivation no matter who you are with because they are always required for you to use them in a doubles match or the Dual Cultivation. You still need to perfect them and as you perfect them more and more and you are not in the Dual Cultivation situation, you will attract the right person for yourself. It just takes time but in the true reality you only have one relationship with anybody, and that is yourself. So it is time to get to know yourself and discover who are.

As you are born alone, you live alone, and you are going to ascend alone no matter who you are with and how compatible you are with them. It can be the perfect mate but the real mate is within you. Your opposite gender will be inside you. The main thing is that you should not feel that you need to be with somebody, or if you are with somebody that is all there is. In fact, you should develop the true relationship with yourself internally. As you develop that, you will discover the opposite gender within you. Once you make that discovery, you will marry that gender and then give birth to your own spiritual essence.

This is the real message in the Tao and why you interact with one another. If you get into a relationship that has needs, wants, and desires, then you will lose your center. The Taoists are funny about that. They say, "Well, it is good to experience that kind of love once in your life and then you know what not to do again and you will not fool with it again." This is all a process of your own self-discovery and understanding. As you start to work with a Dual Cultivation you will start to discover this whole aspect within yourself.

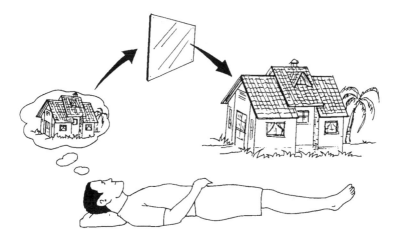

Fig. 7.23. No matter who you are with and how compatible you are with him or her, the only relationship you will ever really have is with yourself, because you are the only one who knows how you feel inside.

The Taoists highly recommend Dual Cultivation because you are working with two energy bodies as opposed to one in Single Cultivation, so the energy will be much greater. When you are working in Dual Cultivation, if you are a male, your male energy is going to be stronger than her male energy, and her female energy will be stronger than yours. It is a much more dramatic and exciting experience to be in Dual Cultivation than it is to be in Single Cultivation. You can still achieve your own spiritual evolution but it just will not be as dramatic. You do not necessarily need to be with someone to achieve this.

If you can achieve it with someone else that is the greater accomplishment and the greater experience that you will have. But if the relationship leads you away from yourself (the Tao, your self-discovery), then it is better to leave it alone and not fool with it. In other words, if you are trying to be someone else other than yourself to please another person, it will never work because you can only be yourself and eventually that is what you will be no matter what you do. Most relationships fail because over time you go back to yourself and the person you are pretending to be disappears. Then you are faced with a difficult situation which results in a divorce.

Fig. 7.24. The Tao encourages Dual Cultivation because the energy is stronger when working with two energy bodies.

SEX IS LIKE AN ITCH

The Taoist say that sex is like an itch. It feels good when you scratch it but it feels better when you do not have the itch. When you develop this balance you are going to start to attract a person who will be a person with potential spiritual energy and a life partner or spiritual helpmate. It is all part of what you are trying to achieve in your life. What takes place is that as you balance the energy you can start to connect to the energy and make conscious choices instead of being driven by your sexual desires or your sexual urges.

You will start to learn to manage and redirect the energy into a position such that you start to lose this itch or this uncontrollable sensation that has been pestering you most of your life. It is called the age of innocence when you start to move into another direction where you do not have the itch anymore. That is when you become a child again and you just do things for the enjoyment of experiencing them and for the joy of doing it. You dance to dance, sing to sing, and laugh to laugh, without trying to seek anything or any urge or desire to be someone or to accomplish something. That is the itch in life and when you realize that, you become at peace with yourself and in harmony with the world.

It takes time, but the Taoists have a couple of different approaches to this. One they call being satiated. When you are a child you search for candy, which is sweet and creates a desire, an itch to eat candy. The more you eat (you just keep eating it) the more your teeth rot and then you go to the dentist. You still go on eating all of the soda pop, candies, and cakes, until one day you become satiated. You could not eat any more candy and you could not drink any more soda. You have had enough. You outgrow that desire because you became satiated. You had enough.

It is like filling up a cup with water until you cannot put any more water into it. When you became an adult you gather all kinds of material things, until you get to a certain point when you've had enough. It is the same thing with sex and drugs. You just get to this certain point when you become satiated. You have had enough.

So, eventually with sexual energy you have had enough. Then you are looking beyond the sex into your relationship and the communication between the two genders, you and the other person. It is just a matter of having enough. It happens eventually because you can only put so much water in that cup. As you become at peace with this, you just let it run its own course. Then slowly you become satiated and you will move beyond the itch into the true understanding of yourself and the person that you are with. That is what actually happens with many couples as they start to move beyond their sexual appetites and become themselves.

Many people say that you never can become satisfied and that you cannot be satiated. You might die doing it but that is why you have the internal techniques and practices of the Tao. You slowly start to align yourself and create a whole situation where you balance the energy and the itch really starts to diminish. You start to look beyond the itch and experience the most important aspect of your relationship, which is communication. Again, the key is communication. You have to share how you feel inside and show your true intention. And when you do you can become more compatible with a person, with more understanding.

The fire and water energy will start to balance but you need to have the same intention for true communication. Why are you together? Where are you going with this relationship? What is your purpose behind this relationship? If that is not the same, then no matter what you do or how compatible you are, your energy is going to move in opposite directions and you will separate.

So, that is why you need to communicate and find out the best you can about the intentions of the other person. Why they are doing it, what they are doing, and where they want to go with it. Find out the other person's intention even if they do not verbalize it. Just watch what they do. When you see their action, it reveals to you their true intention behind what they are doing and where they are going. As an old Taoist sage once said, "Your actions speak so loudly that I can hardly hear a word you are saying."

So, watch what they do and it will show you why they are doing what they do. It will show you the intention behind what they are doing. Just wait and watch. This is especially true of women because of their yin essence. They say everything you want to hear but watch what they do and that will tell you the true meaning behind their words.

CHICKEN SOUP

The key to the Taoist sexual practices is chicken soup. When you have chicken soup or make chicken soup, you put a chicken and water in a pot and boil them. After two hours you take the chicken out of the pot and you have the broth. Now what would you rather eat, the chicken or the broth? You would rather eat the broth, because it has all of the essence of the chicken in it and the chicken tastes like rubber. It is the same with the sexual practices. The chicken is your genitals and the broth is your sexual essence, the orgasmic energy. When you cook the genitals with the Testicle and Ovarian Breathing practices, that is your chicken. And you draw its broth, the essence of the chicken or the genitals, up your spine and into the brain. Then you have a brain orgasm instead of a genital orgasm. Now what is your brain connected to? The brain is connected to all of the parts of your body, so you have a total body orgasm. What would you rather have: the chicken (genital orgasm) or the broth (brain orgasm/total body orgasm)?

Fig. 7.25. Connecting the cosmic energy with each other's eyes

Fig. 7.26. Total body orgasm

This is further developed with the Taoist formulas in the Healing Love and Dual Cultivation practices. You can develop it to such a level where you can look into each other's eyes and see the healing cosmic energy and eyes become like magnets, healing each other with love (orgasm energy). This happens as you exchange your energy between each other in heavenly bliss.

Now women already think they have a body orgasm because the genitals are internally in their body. The genital orgasm takes place inside the body but it is not the total body orgasm. The brain is connected to every part of the body and once you have an orgasm there, it sends the orgasm throughout the whole body, which is very dramatic for the male because his genitals are outside the body. The whole body orgasm feels like an electrical current going right into the body at very high voltage so if a man has a whole body orgasm he rarely goes back to the external ejaculation and losing the semen. As a male gets older he hangs on to his semen because it has all the hormones in it that he needs to grow for every cell in his body. Without these hormones he cannot create the new cells of the body. That is why it is very important for the male to hold on to his seed.

The woman on the other hand does not lose her energy through the ejaculation process with sexual interaction. She primarily loses it through the genital menstrual cycle as she discharges these fluids through her vagina. There is also a great deal of transformation in menopause. But through the Taoist techniques, the female can manage the sexual energy as well as the male. Instead of having it control her with the menstrual cycle where every month the woman is a prisoner of her body, she can take control. Every month her body shifts through this whole menstrual cycle, which is basically controlled by nature through the moon, the tide, and the sea. Every twenty-eight days women go through this cycle.

Through the Taoist practices you can actually start to manage this energy and shift from having this menstrual cycle once a month to once every two months, once every six months, or once year. And the discharge, instead of huge blood clots, can eventually be just a little spotting.

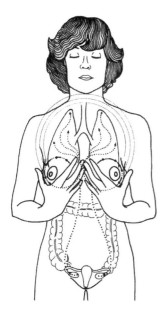 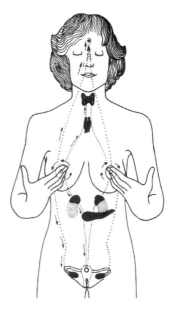

Fig. 7.27. A woman learns to manage her menstrual cycle instead of letting it control her.

Fig. 7.28. Through the Taoist practices, a woman is no longer a prisoner of her body.

The duration of the cycle itself can take, in some cases, two weeks to just an hour. Once you start to work with these techniques you start to manage the sexual energy instead of it taking control of you and your life. So it is a very liberating experience once you understand how the energy works and learn to get the energy to work for you.

These techniques are the exercises of the breast massage, ovarian compression, and breathing techniques, as well as the Big Draw and with the thrusting and shallow technique of the valley orgasm. In the orgasm, the male works up his energy sharply and then it drops when he ejaculates. If he can maintain his erection and not ejaculate he can maintain the sexual stimulus as far as the erection itself for a longer period of time to arouse the woman so that she can boil her eggs. Once arousing the energy you can create the chicken soup, to cook the genitals long enough so the essence can be drawn out and up the spine, having the orgasmic expansion in the brain and the total body orgasm through the valley orgasm technique.

How this technique works is called the valley orgasm where the male gets an erection through thrusting into the vagina. Several thrusts or too many thrusts and he will ejaculate. To stimulate his G spot underneath the shaft on the tip of the penis and the upper part of the back of the penis he thrusts it several times to maintain the erection and then he pulls out to a certain point so the head of the penis is inside the hood of the vagina where her G spot is and then he will do several shallow (circular) movements. This is circling the

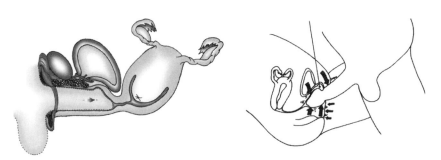

Fig. 7.29. Valley orgasm with the shallow and thrusting technique

Fig. 7.30. One thrust to three shallows and up to one thrust to nine shallows

Fig. 7.31. Perfect tennis game on the sexual courts of your bedroom

head of the penis inside the hood of the vagina, which will activate her arousal state.

And when his penis starts to shrink down, he can just simply thrust several times to maintain the erection. In other words, he can start with one thrust and three shallows and then one thrust and six shallows until he works up to one thrust and nine shallows.

This will allow her orgasmic level to work up slowly and he can maintain his erection and they can have the valley orgasm together. You can have the orgasm at the same time and heal each other by drawing the orgasmic energy up through the spine into the brain to have the full body orgasm. This can all be achieved when you are working together as tennis partners in how you make your serves, hit your backhands and forehands with the correct alignment, and position to play the perfect tennis game together on the sexual courts of your bedroom.

SPIRITUAL HELPMATES

As you can see, it is surprising with all of these communication differences that men and women ever get together at all. It is easy to understand why they have so many problems when they are together. If they are compatible, they have a great opportunity to develop divine love as spiritual helpmates to one another on their journey into nothingness.

So, our real task here is not about love or finding it, because it will find you if you do the practices. It is not about the evolution or procreation of children. The real concept of why we get together at all once you go through all of our cultural, religious, regional, and genetic differences is the attraction itself of the opposite gender. Once you connect with the understanding of the opposite gender, it really is a person who is a spiritual helpmate or energetic helpmate who will help you to make your own full self-discovery. And you will be helping your partner discover himself or herself. It is a real opening of the heart and understanding of who you are, where you are going, and how you are getting there.

Who you are is God. You are like God. You are the creator of the universe. You are the forgotten God. You have forgotten who you are. Collectively, we beautifully created the whole universe with one complete thought manifestation reflecting back into the physical realm,

Fig. 7.32. Discover your spiritual helpmate through the Taoist practices.

our physical realm, for us to experience it in the human form. We did this so perfectly that we have forgotten that we created it. We have forgotten who we are and that we are entrapped in the continuous cycle of karmic evolution. We are moving in the karmic wheel, seeming never to find our way out. But with a spiritual helpmate working with the Taoist practices we can find a way back to ourselves and our divinity.

Many of the Taoists have made this breakthrough and said that if you could break the karmic wheel then you never have to come back here and can evolve to the next level in a new life form. All this needs is a balancing of the gender within with your own external gender and once you balance this energy you give birth to your own spiritual body. Then you transform in every aspect of your physical form into the spirit body and you move out into the universe in the new spirit body with the ability to physically materialize and dematerialize at will.

To achieve this, you need to marry your opposite gender inside. As a spiritual helpmate in a relationship, your partner can help you discover the opposite gender inside you. He or she can discover the opposite gender inside him or her. So it really is important to have a helpmate to assist you in this whole process. That is the real reason you are together, just to marry yourself, not anyone else. You can truly never really marry anyone else as you never know totally how someone else feels. The only person who knows how you feel inside is yourself.

That is why all of the corporate, governmental, and the religious controls will never really control you. You are the only person who knows how you feel and think inside. You are not always that clear on this so it is your real life's journey to make that self-discovery of who you are, where you are going, and how you are going to get there. And that is the journey of the Tao, the journey into nothingness. It is all one of self-discovery, and as you slowly discover this, everything will be revealed to you on the way to that self-discovery: wherever you are going and how you are going to get there. It will all be revealed to you. The relationship that you form with yourself is the only true

Fig. 7.33. Without the sexual energy and its cultivation,
you will never evolve spiritually.

relationship you will have, but on the way you will encounter spiritual helpmates and they can spiritually (energetically) help you through this journey of self-discovery.

That is the real message of the Tao and why we are here on this planet and what the sexual energy is really for—because without the sexual energy you will never evolve spiritually. If you really look into the religions and some of their practices and how they express their goals, you will really see these techniques put into place, even if they are not totally explained by either the practitioner or by their authorities. A lot of this inner alchemy has been lost over the centuries because of massive control issues through various populations and a lot of it has been suppressed, buried, and destroyed. People have really lost the connection with themselves as they lost the connection with these techniques.

But as you watch the priests when they pray, kneeling and looking up to God, you see them breathing, continuing to look upward, then getting up from their hands and knees and you realize it is just Testicle and Ovarian Breathing. It is the expansion and contraction of the genitals moving the orgasm energy up the spine to the brain. Then all of a sudden they appear to receive heavenly bliss from the heavens when, in fact, the energy has moved up the spine into the brain where they have experienced a small orgasmic flash in the brain that revitalized their whole body. If I tried to explain that to them in that fashion they would think that I was nuts and committing blasphemy. But that is exactly what took place. It is amazing that ignorance is such bliss.

Every aspect of the inner alchemy is inculcated but not explained in all the aspects of the religions. But if you sit back and do your practice you will start to see this and experience everything in your own body. You will see it in other organizations and what they are really trying to do but they have lost the connection with themselves and these understandings. They lost connection with their Tao. As you start to see this you start to become connected with it and start to realize that all sexual energy is for our own spiritual evolution to give birth to our own spiritual body. It is the immortal fetus, which will lead us into the next realm, breaking the karmic wheel. This is what the practices are about. That is why people get inundated and caught in various levels of attraction in eros love. We lose our focus and we get caught in our own traps.

In fact, this is all a part of the whole evolution internally in our bodies to move to the next level. This is primarily why we are looking for spiritual helpmates as opposed to some type of erotic or sensational exploitation of the sexual energy and the emotional energy.

Fig. 7.34. Religious organizations have lost the connection with themselves and these inner alchemy understandings. They have lost connection with their Tao.

While there are different reasons for mating such as differences in anatomy and emphasis on different intentions, one basic reason is security. This is primarily because the female kidney energy is weaker than the male kidney energy and has a lot more stress on it through the menstrual cycle as well as childbearing. In one sense it is a lot stronger but in the same breath there are a lot of insecurities. With the kidney there is a negative emotional fear and there is also a positive emotion of gentleness, which is much finer tuned in a woman than the male.

A good example of differences in the body is that a woman is like a sports car. It is a very fine-tuned instrument that needs to be fine-tuned all of the time, and very carefully. The male is like a big old pickup truck. You can ram that big old pickup truck on a mountain road and up and off a cliff but it is still there running. So, when women try to compete with men, they try to present themselves as male. They cultivate the same habits and do the same work in the business world, competing directly with men. They smoke and drink with men but their bodies are fine-tuned instruments and they cannot really do it. They break down easily. That is why women experience so

Fig. 7.35. A woman is like a sports car: a very fine-tuned instrument that needs to be treated very carefully.

many problems with PMS and so many emotional and psychological problems in our modern world. They are experiencing a breakdown of their internal being psychologically and spiritually, as well, in the loss of the feminine art of nurturing. The woman needs to have a different direction. In times past, women did and they were more protected with the energy because theirs is a whole different energy field and it is far superior, far more refined, in order to be able to give birth to another human being. In that superiority there are certain conditions that women must respect or they will break down the machine a lot more quickly, in a mechanical sense, than men will.

When there is competition, which the woman is induced into, she actually loses her own essence and her own power, her yin power. It reminds me of something that happened when I was at a college reunion and we visited the old dorm and the college had turned coed. The girls there were college students running around as if they were very excited to be living with the men. They all dressed in male boxer shorts and T-shirts, which is very unladylike and masculine. One of them ran up to me telling me about all the courses she was taking and what she was going to do in the male business world and I looked at her straight in the eyes and I said to her, "If I was a woman I would never lower myself to compete with a man." She was dumbfounded. She did not know what to say. What you are looking for in a spiritual helpmate is to discover someone who will help you discover your own opposite gender within yourself. And the women should not lower themselves to compete with the men and the men should not compete with the women. What you should try to do is find a harmony and connect with your own inner flow inside yourself. What makes you feel good inside is what you should do and that is the direction you should take in your life. That direction will be slowly revealed to you as it is unfolding in your own life. This takes time and as you study and start to connect with it the person you are supposed to be with or not be with will be revealed. It is all a matter of connecting with your true essence and your true being.

It all follows your own self-discovery. It is all in becoming who you really are and what you were meant to be. That is the discovery of your own spiritual life and as you discover this you will start to discover your own path. And it is one of joy and happiness, understanding and wisdom. This is how the mountain and ocean get together and to find the ocean inside you or the mountain inside you is the key to the spiritual path and the path of the Tao. With this understanding you will start to move forward within yourself and see this connection being slowly revealed to you in yourself, giving birth to your immortal fetus, which is giving birth to your spiritual body. Transforming the physical body into the spiritual body is the path to yourself. Once you do this you can transform your own essence and materialize it on any level, breaking the karmic wheel for your own spiritual essence. This is your true journey, being together with one other person as a spiritual helpmate to give you help on your journey and to help that person on his or her journey. It is all part of becoming your own person with your own essence and as you become your own person you become one with the universe. You are one with the universe, you are divine, and that divinity will be revealed to you as you discover who you really are.

The Money Machine

HOW MUCH MONEY?

The Taoists have a clear understanding of reacting as opposed to acting or correct action. Much of our lives we react instead of making conscious choices, which would be acting or correct action. We never really ask ourselves, "Is it good for me if I do this or that? Why am I doing it? What am I here for? Is this benefiting me? Who am I? Is this benefiting the person I really am? Do I really need this in order to exist?"

When you start reacting, you are getting away from asking these basic questions and you are reacting because of your ego. Your ego needs to be right. When you are challenged, it is your ego that makes you do things that you do without thinking because the ego thinks it can do everything. If the ego cannot do it, then it gets upset. So the ego forgets to think, if this is what you truly, really want and if it is really beneficial for you. By being challenged and reacting to that challenge, you are acting without thinking or consciously making a choice that could be beneficial to you. But when you slow the mind down through the Taoist meditative practices, you begin to think about these questions and then you start to act, which is the correct action for you at that point in time.

In the money machine, we begin to ask ourselves if we really need

Fig. 8.1. Making conscious choices: What am I doing? Why am I here?

a money machine. What is the money machine? Obviously, the title refers to a machine that produces money. What you do in essence is create a machine mechanically that actually produces money. This is what we call getting capital (money) up to create a machine that creates money and that actually produces more money (it multiplies money). You should look at your money as employees and the employees you need to take care of because these employees actually make money for you. It can really start as small as a hundred dollars or two hundred dollars, once you have this principle in place.

Gradually, you get this money to work for you. That is the whole concept behind the machine. You create a systematic way of producing money for yourself. The easiest way is to put the least amount of effort in actually putting this together. You utilize the money itself to produce the income that you desire. This is called passive income. In other words, the income that is generated is being generated by passive activity by you or nonaction by you.

This is the money machine in its essence. This can be illustrated in rental income property. When you have rental income property, you have some capital you invest in real estate and you rent it out. Usually, the rent exceeds the note or the debts that you have in the property on a monthly basis. You constantly show a profit or you generate enough income to cover the expenses of the dwelling (utilities, mortgage, taxes, and maintenance). That is a typical way of investing your money (employees) with a positive return, or you can invest in other money-returning investments such as stocks, mutual funds, and a lot of other different entities that will help produce money. Once you produce enough money from the return in capital, then you no longer need to work because you can live off the monies generated from your capital, which exceed your monthly expenses. In this way you are using the capital or funds you set up really like employees that produce money for you.

Once you have learned to live beneath your means (the means would be the generated income) then you can focus your life on your life's purpose because you have taken care of the basics (food, shelter, travel) that you need in life to cover your expenses. You should have a little left over for an emergency so if you need the money you are in a position where you are not in jeopardy. One who is rich learns to live beneath his or her means and the means is your money machine without any of your daily effort to produce it.

Basically, you need to know and find out how much money you actually need to live. From that point, you produce or put together

Fig. 8.2. Rental income property is part of the money machine.

Fig. 8.3. Learn to live beneath your means.

a systematic way of generating money within the governmental laws and apply various aspects of how to generate the money by utilizing your capital to generate the money. It is really quite simple. Again, with simple logic, 1 + 1 is 2, not 11. You put in X amount of dollars and you get X amount of dollars out. As long as the numbers add up with a positive result you take out more money than you put in, and it makes sense to do it. It works that simply. You need to invest your time and energy to analyze what is the best action you need to take. Then instead of reacting to a situation, you do your homework, or, as they say in the business world, you do the due diligence and you do correct action. In other words, you theoretically put a plan together and then systematically piece it together in the physical realm. As you start to do that, you start to build your money machine.

But first, you need to determine how much money you need to exist. After you structure the machine, then you can gauge how much money you need to cover your expenses plus a profit to reinvest in the machine. To multiply your return you can just simply duplicate the whole operation several times and utilize the law of numbers for your wealth. It is amazing how it works and continues to work once you set it up properly and duplicate it. Where you strike gold you keep on

Fig. 8.4. The money machine provides for all your responsibilities.

digging in the same spot. This is the key to a successful business.

The money machine can continue to reproduce the monies that you need to exist. Once you get the formula in place, finding how it works and getting it to work for you, then you can duplicate it. You continually duplicate it until you are working in a situation where it can be managed by others so it manages itself and you just observe from afar. That is all you need to do. At this point the money machine has a life of its own by running and managing itself while supporting you. This allows you to do other things in life that are more to your own bliss once you have covered your basics for yourself to live your life. After you get all your basics covered, then you need to develop your own destiny again after you fulfill your responsibilities (food, shelter, travel).

If you are single or married with various responsibilities that you have assumed, then you need to adhere to these as a part of your expenses. With this, you adjust your life accordingly and you place everything in that system that you created as part of its responsibility. This removes from you the pressure of supporting your assumed responsibilities as you have created this money machine to handle it.

WHAT DO WE REALLY NEED?

Well, how much money do we really need? As you slow the mind down, you realize that you do not need a whole lot of money to exist even in our inflated economies because there are only three areas you need to consider for your existence: food to eat, shelter for your body, and a little traveling money for your mobility.

As you break this down, you would be surprised how little it costs to feed yourself, when you buy whole foods for your health in bulk without packaging. With the proper housing in rental income properties, you can actually live for free, renting out part of your home to others and using the other part of the dwelling as your own living space. You have a free place to live because all your housing expenses are paid for by the renters as a part of the rental income.

Travel is an expense depending on where you want to go and how you want to get there. Daily travel can be eliminated as an expense by using a bicycle or just walking. It is better for you and improves your health. There are a lot of different ways you can simplify your life by taking mass transit. Plus anytime you travel, you can often link it up with a business situation so that your whole trip is deductible. Mixing business and travel also justifies your travel, allowing you to mix a little bit of pleasure into the traveling because you are already there for your business.

Fig. 8.5. How much money do we really need for food, shelter, and travel?

Everything can be systematically put together and totally understandable. Once you solve what you really need to eat, the shelter you need, and if you need any traveling expenses, then you can start to map out and adjust your money machine to satisfy these needs and concerns. It is all systematic once you slow your mind down through the Taoist meditations and do your due diligence to set up your money machine.

The food cost can be controlled, again by buying bulk and simple foods that adhere to your medicine meals. You can start to see how inexpensive the food can be for you to exist. Get the true nutrition you need for your body to maintain yourself as opposed to lavishing yourself in a situation with packaged foods and dining out (conventional living) that is really degenerating to your physical body. This becomes clear once you start to move in the realm of creating this money machine, which generates the amount of money that you need to feed yourself.

For shelter, there can be an excellent business relationship for you generating enough capital to invest in rental income properties. This could house you as well as generate passive income to cover your housing expenses as well as your food and any travel expenses with other

Fig. 8.6. Adjust your money machine to your living expenses.

Fig. 8.7. Various fund generators are commodities, stocks, money trading, index, and hedge funding.

various commodities (stocks, money trading, index, and hedge funding). You could generate funds as well as fund your shelter. And for your travel expenses you can utilize the mass transit system, a simple bicycle, or many other options such as carpooling, depending on whether you have a job. But if you have the correct number of rental income properties you do not need a job.

There are a lot of little options that you should take into consideration before purchasing a car. But if you decide to buy there are many ways of buying cars that can minimize your expenses and allow you to facilitate your transportation at a very inexpensive cost to yourself. There is some cost but you can really minimize it once you do your due diligence and find out what it actually costs to generate transportation for yourself. There are a lot of little ways you can work within your own limited means or within your money machine to make the whole thing work on its own. You really need to find out the exact amount of energy (money) needed to cover your expenses, what you need to expend for your existence. Again, you can simply break your living expenses down to food, shelter, and travel, which covers any basic responsibilities for yourself. The key is to systemize your money machine so you can duplicate it again and again.

If you have other dependents and are married with a family, you have to make considerations for them and their needs as well. They can also help you in securing the necessary funds through jobs, tax advantages, or helping at home and participating as a family in the income and the preservation of your family itself. There are a lot of options in the family situation, but you need to have like-minded family members who support and participate in your intention to systematically cover the expenses with the money machine and your responsibilities along with theirs.

MEDICINE MEALS

When you start understanding the medicine meals, what food you need to eat, you will discover that whole foods are the best foods for your body. When you understand how to combine them correctly for your energy fields, internally connecting with the five phases of your body and each of the five vital organs, you will discover that whole foods can be grown at virtually no cost. Or you can buy whole food items bulk, which are not packaged and even cost less than packaged food. You can eat them raw or cook (steam) them. You only need to boil water and let them absorb the water or be cooked by the steam (soak grains and legumes overnight). For vegetables, you can simply steam them or wash them and eat them raw.

Fruits already have the water in them and if they are dried foods, you can merely soak them in water overnight and they can absorb the water, and then they are ready to eat. You will find out that foods are very inexpensive if they are not packaged, especially if they are grown locally (you can find these foods at farmers markets) or grown by yourself. Remember, when you buy them in bulk, you do not pay for all the packaging fees and taxes. When you do the pricing (due diligence) you will be surprised that you can save about 40 percent on your food bill buying in bulk. This is a dramatic savings, and if you only drink clean water as your beverage, you also save on packaged liquids such as beer, alcohol, juice, and other soft drinks. When you slow the mind down, you start to realize what you actually need for food.

When you see this cost savings and see the nutritional value of whole foods (grains, vegetables, legumes, and various fruits), you realize that when you buy them locally and buy them in bulk, you save an enormous amount of money as opposed to your packaged animal products and processed foods, which cost a lot more money

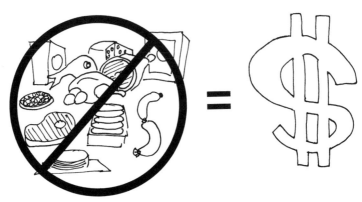

Fig. 8.8. When you do not buy packaged, processed animal products, you save money.

because you buy them packaged and processed. This creates a bodily imbalance of the internal environment, which leads to degenerative diseases. So you can learn to live with less (packaged/processed foods) while living longer and healthier.

When you stop buying processed foods and buy food in its whole state, you will discover that this cuts normal food bills by about 40 percent. This is the key concept. Once you understand that foods are your medicines and you can create medicine meals to heal your body, the whole concept starts to make sense. The cost of living and eating becomes cut by 75 percent when you eliminate all the packaged foods, restaurant costs, animal products, processed junk foods, and medical bills that cover the degenerative diseases caused by the degenerated (packaged) foods.

All these processed-food products really leach the body of its nutrition and its sodium, calcium, and other essential elements, which causes breakdowns in the body and the degenerative diseases of the body. These diseases run from colon cancer to heart disease; and you also have the expense of the insurance and medical costs needed to combat them. When you eliminate them from your diet and control your food intake to bulk whole food products, the cost savings is monumental. This is how you start to develop your own understanding of what you need for your body, and by doing due diligence you discover that medicine meals are your best way to preserve not only your body but also minimize your expense to feed and take care of your body.

When you use medicine meals, there is a huge savings in expense from medicines that are usually prescription drugs as well as the surgical operations and the medical care that you need to preserve your body when you take in all these degenerative foods, which break down the body. There is a huge cost savings in medical insurance as well as the prescription drugs that many people take because of the degenerative foods they eat and the improper lifestyles they live. So by changing their lifestyle and changing the way they approach and eat their foods by shifting to medicine meals, people not only save on the foods when they buy them whole and bulk but also save on medical insurance and the drugs that they take in association with the degenerative foods that they eat.

There is a huge, huge cost savings and relief from all the related diseases connected with smoking, alcohol, and carbonated drinks that break down the body and its system. It is all a matter of making conscious choices by slowing down the mind through the Taoist meditative practices. You start to see things clearly and you can start to make some conscious choices. Basically, that is what this is all

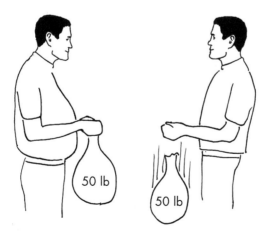

Fig. 8.9. Drop that fifty-pound sack off your back with medicine meals that heal.

about—making conscious choices—and these are the correct choices for financial and physical well-being.

As you slow the mind down, this becomes possible. It takes time and you need to do the necessary work with due diligence. But, in the long run, you will live a longer, healthier, and happier life. You live longer, you feel better, you look better, and you save a huge amount of money. What more do you want out of life? When you are at your normal weight, the aging process is slowed down enormously, but when you are twenty, thirty, forty, fifty, seventy pounds overweight, your age multiplies. It is quite easy when you just look at it. It makes sense. When you are overweight it is like carrying a fifty- or seventy-pound sack on your back. It gets tiring. It is hard to move around. It is hard to carry the extra weight. With medicine meals you take food as medicine to heal and balance the body, creating a harmony in the body. The body will eliminate the fats and the toxins if you let it do its natural process of cleansing itself by not putting any more of the toxins in the body.

So not only are you healing yourself but you are also paying yourself to do it. You have a cost savings on the processed foods (animal products and junk foods), the medical insurance (premiums and prescription drugs), the medical payments (hospital bills and operations), and dining out and fast foods (restaurant bills and snack foods). That alone will pay for your cost of living and you will learn to live for free or barely nothing at all.

SHARED LIVING SPACE

Shelter is a place to rest, which represents your other major concern for your well-being. You eat, sleep, eliminate, and do a little traveling. That is basically all the areas you need to cover for your basic functioning in life. For shelter, you usually get into real estate and find yourself in a group living situation.

Most of us were born in a family where people share living quarters. This can be extended as you become an adult. Many people share

Fig. 8.10. Many people share expenses by living in shared housing.

expenses by marrying and starting their own family or by sharing a house with like-minded people. This can cut down your expenses enormously. You will find that three to four hundred dollars a month will afford you a nice, comfortable, shared place that provides you shelter, giving you an individual room and shared living area (kitchen, bath, living room, yard, and parking).

Once you have become comfortable in this environment, you can step out on your own and buy your own rental income property, creating a positive cash flow, which produces additional income for yourself for your other expenses such as food and travel. So you can actually become autonomous without working in this whole process by living in a shared living space. To further explain this, many people get by in life and they do not even realize it when they create a family. Everyone helps out who lives in a family environment. You do not necessarily have to be married to share the same living quarters with other people, but it is very important that they are all like-minded. Not that they have to be correct or incorrect but when you are in a like-minded environment, then it is a lot easier and a more harmonious existence for yourself.

This is something you should consider because you need that harmony externally to maintain it internally in your body. This additional stress is tearing against your body, which is not exactly what you want to do, and creates problems in your life. When people smoke or drink and you do not, this creates a lot of problems. You will find yourself in a different lifestyle. This becomes uncomfortable for you in your living space and your ability to communicate or emotionally exchange with the others.

So you really need to focus on how to establish these shared living quarters and get completely familiar with doing so. You need to investigate properties doing your due diligence and selecting a property that you could rent out as a rental income property which would have housing for yourself and the other rooms to rent out to share in the expense of the home. By doing that, you also create a passive income, and if you do the numbers correctly with your due diligence, you can also create a positive cash flow generating additional income for your food and travel expenses.

In other words, the money taken in from the rental income exceeds the money expended out for the monthly expenses on the dwelling. That is a positive cash flow for your existence. You can utilize that money to repair the home and also maintain your other expenses. Then, once this process is done, you can simply duplicate it several times while keeping your personal expense the same and

Fig. 8.11. Living with like-minded people brings harmony and peace of mind to your body.

generate more income as you need in your expanded family or in expanded areas of your life. This is how it all takes place. Again, you need to slow the mind down, by first just setting this up in theory and concept in your mind, which creates the desire to manifest it in the physical world.

Again, the key to the shared housing is like-minded people so that you are comfortable with them. When you have like-minded people together, it creates a harmony that you desire in your life and it becomes an enjoyable situation for yourself. This is the key to shared housing plus the factor that you need to make sure the numbers add up so you create a passive, positive cash flow as well, which still can be done today in our society once you slow the mind down.

LIFE WITHOUT A CAR

With transportation, there are amazing ways to travel without a car. You can have a bike, you can walk, you can use public transportation such as buses and trains, or you can use a rental car if needed periodically. This becomes very inexpensive. With no car, you have no payments, no insurance, no registration, no repairs, and virtually no gas cost. It costs a lot of money to run a car, especially in the West.

With all these expenses you can easily pay—even if you bought the car outright and used, with the monthly expenses of insurance, registration, and repairs, two hundred dollars a month—a huge expense to travel around without going anywhere. So, in most situations, if you need housing in an urban area, always select an area where you can easily move around with public transportation or a bike and with all necessities within walking distance. This is the criteria by which you should consider life without a car. Life without a car is much simpler. This can be an easy transition, if you first start with a bike and everything you need is in walking distance.

A funny thing happens when you do not travel in a car for many months and years: your whole body shifts. In other words, when you are moving sixty miles an hour or ninety miles an hour in a car, your

Fig. 8.12. There are amazing ways to travel without a car:
bike, walk, bus, or train.

body molecularly is moving at that pace even though we are sitting. When you do not have to do that on a daily basis for a period of time, your whole energy shifts and it becomes more balanced, grounded, and centered. It is something to sit back and think about because when you are moving at that speed, your body does not function properly. It becomes very easy to lose your center and to lose your balance internally even though a lot of people do it. Lots of people also become very hectic in their environment and easily lose their sense of being. Welcome to our crazy society in the rat race of the West.

When you experience life without a car, you start to experience what it is to not move at fifty ort sixty or seventy miles an hour. It is a whole different lifestyle because your body is not moving molecularly at that speed. It allows you to center yourself and to have more peace

Fig. 8.13. When traveling seventy miles per hour, you are sitting
but your body is still moving.

and harmony within yourself. It becomes easier to connect with the Tao and the natural flow of the universe.

These are things you will start to consider and it will become very inexpensive to move around. You should do your local travel by bike or walking, even with bus transportation, which is not usually that fast. Again, you have to get to the bus, which is walking. The ideal situation in any local, long-distance travel is to take a bike. But for a short distance, you should actually just walk. This is a whole process of transformation and as you slow the mind down you will start to see the results.

So, life without a car saves an enormous amount of money, plus it adds to your own well-being and health while harmonizing and connecting you more strongly to your practices in the meditation postures, exercises, and techniques. This helps you in your whole well-being and saves you from a lot of the stress associated with travel at high velocity. It is all a part of what you can do as you slow the mind down to make the correct choice for you in your lifestyle, what you want in life, and how you want to obtain it.

It is really that simple. You just prepare yourself to move at your own pace without interfering in other aspects of your life. Again, slowing down the mind is the key. As you slow down the mind, you

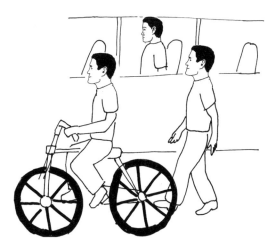

Fig. 8.14. You travel locally by bike or walking and long distances by bus.

realize there is life without a car and it is a very beautiful life. It is a wholly different existence and you are much more stable and at peace with yourself internally, freeing you up to experience the Tao.

WORK, WORK SMART, AND JUST BE SMART

If you approach life in a simpler manner, as in the Tao, you will be surprised at how little you need to generate as income to exist or to generate from your money machine. When you create your own money machine, you actually build a structure to produce energy because money is just energy. You can say you work, you work smart, and then you are just smart.

When you work, you are working for someone else, which is the training process of our institutionalized education system, making you into a product for our institutionalized economic system. When you go into an institutionalized economic system, you are supervised and controlled by someone else. Someone else is making a percentage off your work and you really are never getting fully paid for your labor and effort. You are never getting a full return on the energy that you are generating for your pay.

This is basically what most of the generations have been indoctrinateded into for the past one hundred years. Before that, 60 percent of us, especially in the West, lived off of the land (farms, forests, ranches), which meant being self-employed. Then, through the industrial age, that percentage became so small that only about 1 or 2 percent actually live on farms or ranches today, and those farms or ranches are agribusinesses operated by big industry and machinery. They have become like institutionalized factories as well and end up working for the government through our banking systems and other institutions to compete on such a large level.

So, everything has shifted in the past one hundred years. Everybody has been trained and conditioned by the institutionalized education system to work in the institutionalized economic systems. The bottom line is someone's always making a percentage off you and they are taking responsibilities for you and you are giving up your responsibility for yourself, which means you end up losing your energy to them. You are not being fully paid for your energy because they are always making a percentage off of you and your labor.

People are conditioned into thinking that someone (government or a company) will be taking care of them when they retire, but that is not the case today. You really do not have any decision or security in the outcome of your labor, especially in the later part of the twentieth century, when it became very evident that the so-called security and benefits that you would receive by working for institutions are a fallacy because a lot of them have crumbled as a result of inflation and the overburdened retirement programs that have been put in place where the company's retiree population outnumbered the actual workers 2 to 1. And business has shifted to other parts of the world, leaving the workers to pay for the retirees with half the amount of work and with half the amount of workers. This creates a situation that it is unworkable and is doomed to fail. What was once sold to the masses as security turns out to be completely insecure with no control over your own destiny and only empty promises, resulting in bankruptcy or near bankrupt institutions.

Being self-employed is just another means of employment. You are really not working for yourself. You are doing all the work yourself. You are working within a system in a quadrant explained by the rich dad, poor dad series called the E, the S, the B, and the I quadrants— four different areas of working or participating.

The E is for the employee, one who is working for someone else. The S is the self-employed. They are still working but they do everything for themselves and it is really a glorified employee, the super employee without any employee benefits. You might be working for yourself but you are always getting a percentage working for someone else. You really do not own the company that you are creating. At any point in time, the real owners will get rid of you because you have no percentage of the company and you own nothing that you have worked for, so you end up being paid a small percentage of the past.

The B is for you as the owner of the business. In other words, you get people (the employees) to work for you. You end up owning the business and the business pays you; you get to reinvest the business's profit into other businesses and you make the real money when you sell the business. You do not do the work of the company; you get others to work for you, the business. And you get 100 percent of the business because you own the business and you give out a small percentage of the business to the people working for you through the business.

Then the I is for the investor, the person who utilizes his capital and invests in other companies and other people. As people invest in other companies and other people, their money is actually their employees working for them. They take care of their employees and put them in good working situations so they can generate income from the base of their funding for them. The money invested generates income, so you generate income from your money. This is basically the ultimate position to be in as you get the money to work for you and build your money machine.

SELF-EMPLOYED

Now when you work smart, you are still working but you are working for yourself. In other words, you are getting your full pay because

Fig. 8.15. The I quadrant is for the investor, the person who utilizes his capital and invests in other companies and other people.

nobody is taking a percentage off of you. When you work for yourself, you can also cash in at the end of the duration of the work and sell your goodwill or anything you have accumulated in the process of working. But, again, this can be an illusion because you are still working. You are really never getting a percentage of the company that you are working for. You are getting a percentage of the sale. This is the misnomer, which fools many who are superstar workers, mastering and doing everything themselves but not making the big money because they do not own the company that they are building.

For many years, I was a superstar or a super worker being always self-employed and thinking that was where the ultimate position was as far as working was concerned. But I was not making the real money nor was my money machine. The problem is when you work for another company as a subcontractor or being self-employed as a subcontractor, you really own none of the business. You just make a percentage of what you sold or the percentage in which you participated. So the ideal situation is you actually become part owner of the company so you not only are getting paid for a percentage of what you generate but also a percentage of what the company actually makes. You are the owner and you have a decision on who and when people are hired or fired because you actually get involved in the hiring,

Fig. 8.16. When you work smart, you are still working, but you are working for yourself, and more importantly, no one is taking a percentage off you.

firing, and many other aspects of running the company so you have real influence on it.

By being self-employed, you are only really operating your own position for yourself and you do not really get people to work for you. *You do everything.* You set everything up. You are totally autonomous and try to do it all. From another standpoint, it's just too overwhelming. You burn yourself out and you have too many responsibilities because you are still doing all the work. The employee just does a little part of the work but you are going to do all the work. In the long term, it becomes overwhelming for any one individual.

That is why the big S stands for the super person, superman, but it is really just super employee. He does all the super jobs and gets everything done but, in reality, he is overworking himself and really never gets a piece of the bigger pie, the company he is creating and finally, in the end, after the company is built he is asked to leave and then he goes on and creates another business for someone else until he learns to own the company in the beginning and create it with the help of others.

On many occasions, I have found myself getting a small percentage of what I generated for the company that did the manufacturing or produced the product that I was selling. At the end, for whatever reason, but mostly mismanagement of funds on the part of the owners, they owned the company. They usually sold the company for a

Fig. 8.17. The ideal situation is you actually become part of the ownership in the company.

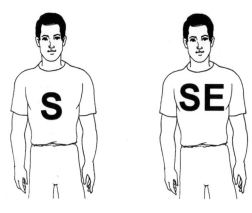

Fig. 8.18. The big S stands for the superman, but it really
just means super employee.

great deal of profit that they received and I was more or less pushed
out the door. They ended up getting compensated for the company
and I never got compensated for all the work I put into the company,
only a small percentage of what I sold in the past with that particular
company. My ego was challenged and I reacted, saying I could do this
and I could do that. I never asked myself why or how I could own
the company since I was building it. So that was not the correct and
ultimate way to go. In other words, you still are working for someone
else, when you should mind your own business and get people to work
for you and not work for them. In other words, run your own business
and develop it yourself and get other people to work for you and get
in a team together. You see, business is a team sport; it is like playing
basketball. The other team has five members. They are on the court
and you are only one guy on your side of the court. Who is going to
win? You need to put a team together. A team usually works with you,
orchestrating all the players on the team with the accountants, attorneys, manufacturers, and financial advisors, with everybody having
their own expertise. This is a whole team of people that you coor-
dinate to get the job done but you own the business. Then you end
up owning the company and you hire superstars to be players. They
are all a part of the team playing their particular part but you own

the company, you own the business. You are minding your own business. The key is to move away from being a superstar into someone who cannot do everything but only oversees the whole team, putting together the superstar players on each part of the team that you own, making sure it runs properly and produces the results that you have intended it to produce. This is the key to the whole process of owning your own business. It is becoming a business owner.

You own the business properties and you make all the final business decisions. There are many aspects of this, aspects that come forth when you own your own business. You start to develop expertise in managing and getting people to work for you instead of you working for people. That is a big shift in understanding from being self-employed to being a business owner. The self-employed work for themselves and the business owner gets people to work for them, a big shift in intention and a big shift in making money, creating your money machine. The key is to get other people to work for you.

Once you get people to work for you, then you can duplicate the business and increase your profits in a whole other aspect of generating your income. Once you generate the income, any capital you get

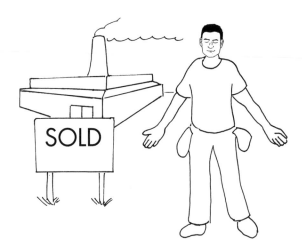

Fig. 8.19. When you do not own part of the company you built, you get nothing when it is sold.

Fig. 8.20. Owning a company, you manage people
and get them to work for you.

together you utilize and invest in real estate, because all money has
been either earned from real estate or held in real estate over the past
five hundred years. So you use your businesses (others working for
you) to generate income to invest in real estate to hold (maintain its
value) and generate more income for you.

You see, everybody needs to live someplace if they are going to be
on this planet. Either they own their own property or they are renting
from someone else but there are just so many people that can live in the
street and there are very few people that can live in the forest. So, 99
percent of them either rent or own their own property. When times are
bad, people rent. When times are good, people buy their own homes,
but no matter where they are or where the economy is at, they have to
live somewhere. Traditionally, in the last five hundred years, money has
either been made in real estate or held in real estate because of this fact,
and this will continue to happen.

The whole concept of money is to generate good debt in real
estate as opposed to bad debt. Good debt is debt that you take out
once you qualify and have someone (renters) to pay it off, creating

Fig. 8.21. The key is to get other people to work for you and
duplicate it several times.

passive income. There is a systematic way of doing things, where you
buy properties that are rented out and the renters pay off the debt. In
other words, the renters pay off the loan that you receive credit for as
a real estate investment when you put the numbers together in such a
way that it shows a passive, positive cash flow. The debt in a monthly
basis is less than the income taken in for renting it. Now, you have
good debt in rental income properties. Bad debt is you directly paying
the debt as in a car loan or your personal home (no renters).

You do enough of these with passive, positive income and the
property increases in value if they are in the correct location, but more
importantly, real estate holds the value of your investment (funds). You
can literally keep refinancing it, never selling it, and the monies that
you refinance as the value goes up keeps the interest rates down, and
then you are paying less or about the same for the same property and
you are receiving a third more or twice as much as you have invested
in it. Any of this loan money that you receive on the rental income
property is tax-free because there is no tax on loan money because you
are paying the loan back so it is not earned income. So you can feel
free to do whatever you want to do with the money, either reinvest it,
use it to live on, or whatever you need to do.

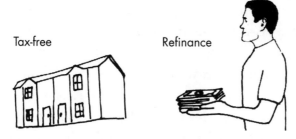

Fig. 8.22. Never sell property; always refinance and take tax-free income.

CAPITAL WORKS FOR YOU

When you are smart, you do not work at all. You have accumulated some capital and you turn the capital around to work for you. Let me illustrate again. I purchased a home and rented part of the home out. The renters paid for all of the utilities and any expenses of the home because the home was paid off. I had a free place to live. It also generated enough income to cover any food or travel expenses I had. I could save money and then reinvest the money for further needs or activities. So I had set up a money machine in real estate as part of my shelter. This is a small example, but you can magnify it into much larger areas.

So you create a business to generate capital or income by creating a team of super employees or the super self-employed and as you create that team, you have them focus on generating more and more money for you. Once you get the money, you invest it in real estate, which will produce more money for you, but more importantly it will hold the value of the money that you have put into it. That is the formula to work with and it will work for you. When you are just smart you do not work at all. You have accumulated enough capital and you can turn the capital around to work for you.

When you get capital you need to look at the capital like employees that work for you. You need to set up a factory (money machine) where they can work and generate more money or more employees (money) to go back to work for you. That is really the way that you need to look at your money—as your employees. You need to take care of these employees so you get the best return for the energy that they generate for you.

All money is just energy. You need to conserve and utilize the energy to produce more energy. This can be accomplished easily in real estate. It takes some time to develop and understand it but that also applies to any type of marketing and sales that you can generate for others and any other capital you generate to invest. Now, there are many other opportunities around the world that you can get involved with because of cyberspace (the Web). You can actually make communications and connections that moderate not only your own banking system but also pay bills and manage and get involved in all kinds of stock options in the stock houses all over the world. There are investment programs that are operated completely off the Web. You can become global with your business from your laptop on your desk. So you can have communication in almost any part of the world and still operate on a percentage and base that on the return of the investment you place into it.

Fig. 8.23. Money is just energy and you must conserve it to produce more energy (money).

Again, the formula we have is that all money is either made in real estate or held in real estate. So, any capital you generate from your monies that you already have, you invest right back into real estate, in rental income properties based on residential, commercial, or apartment complexes anywhere people need to live. That is basically the formula for capital to retain its worth. There are a lot of other areas where you can invest and get the return on your money but you need to realize that everything you invest in personally you also might lose, so only invest what you can afford to lose.

The safest investment you can make is real estate because for the last five hundred years, people need a place to live if they are going to be on the planet. If times are bad, they are going to rent. When times are good, they are going to buy the property. Either way, they are going to live somewhere. And any real estate you own is of value; that is how you retain the value of your money or your employees. There are many other options that you can get involved with—from stock to money trading, foreign currency, from mutual funds to other investments in companies, IPOs, and to regional options to purchase when a company goes public. There are many areas that you can get involved with, so there are a lot of opportunities for your employees, your capital, to earn and generate more monies for you. You literally become an investor. In other words, you learn to manage your employees. It is a slow process but it is also a very full-time job because you have this gained capital from one of your businesses. Then it is a full-time job to make sure the money is placed in the right situation.

This is how you create the money machine. The money machine is your investment machine. You become an investor. You look and review other money-making opportunities and you guard your employees and make sure they are in a situation where their efforts are returned for the maximum that you can get from them and also the security involved. So, you get the best return on your money, which is a full-time job to study every situation you need to generate that income. It is quite simple. When you slow the mind down you can start to make some conscious choices.

Fig. 8.24. The safest investment in the past five hundred years has been real estate, because people need a place to live if they are going to be on the planet.

You realize that once you get to a certain level, there is no more work involved, because with your experience building businesses in your investment realm you can invest in companies that have secured superstars in their business or company. But you want to make sure that you get the return on your investment. There is not a lot of time involved but it takes some time to investigate, to place and move the monies around, to make sure they are secured in your particular investment. It is no longer a nine-to-five job but a twenty-four-hour-a-day job as the employees (monies) are working 24/7 or being self-

Fig. 8.25. Make sure your money is well taken care of,
so it produces a good return for its efforts.

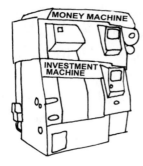

Fig. 8.26. The money machine is your investment machine.

employed, taking out all the responsibilities of the company without owning the business.

As an investor, you move into a whole other area where you are just really managing your money and you look at the money as your employees. You want to make sure that they are well taken care of and you get the most from the efforts that they have placed into whatever investment you have. You take on a whole different role and you observe things from afar, but you make conscious choices as you slow the mind down in the Taoist systematic practices of the meditations to make the correct decisions for your employees.

MEDITATION CLEARS THE MIND FOR ANSWERS

The key in this process is that through meditations, you slow the mind down and everything becomes clear regarding what you are supposed to do. You will get the answers for your life, for that stage of your life, but you need to slow the mind down for the answers to come. This is how you develop your money machine. In your first analysis you realize what you want and what you need by slowing down the mind. You discover what is really important to you and then what you have to do so you can have what you need for food, shelter, and travel. As you combine these, you will find out how simple it is to live on very, very little, so it does not take much of your effort to generate the income to sustain yourself at this level.

As I discussed in chapter 4, "What Not to Do," you begin to project, react, and accumulate things. You accumulate many responsibilities and expenses that you really do not need because they are not that important to you for your existence on the planet. So as you slow down your mind, you always understand that it is no longer a process of reacting to whether you can do this and whether you can do that. It is about what you really want to do, and what is important to you in your life.

It is good to get exposure and to experience life in every aspect but you have to make conscious decisions for yourself, which are really important in your existence. Do you really need to have ten cars to drive? Do you really need to have six houses to live in? Do you really need to travel around the world ten times? Do you really need four or five women in your life to be with? These are questions you start to ask once you slow down the mind instead of reacting to situations without asking.

It is really a process of actually asking what you need or what you can physically, emotionally, mentally, and spiritually handle. When the mind becomes clear, you start to see things as they really are and not what they are projected to be. A lot of times the monkey mind

Fig. 8.27. You will find out how simple it is to live on very, very little, so it does not take any effort to generate the income to sustain yourself.

Fig. 8.28. How many cars, houses, or partners do you need?

projects a positive or negative and gives you a false reality of what really is. As you start to look at life, while the mind is slowed down, you make conscious choices in your life. As you make conscious choices, you start to see what is really there and it allows you enough time to make the correct decision. You also have the ability as you slow the mind down to connect with the inner voice, which speaks to you nonverbally. It is a feeling and this allows you enough time to pick up a feeling to make the right decision in what you want to do.

As you study and start to develop your money machine, the money will always end up in real estate. You see with real estate, you have five sources of income. Number one, you have a place to live and it is being paid for you through the rental income. So you have a passive income and a positive cash flow. In other words, passive means you do not have to work for it; you use your capital or your credit. This is called good credit as opposed to bad credit or a good loan as opposed to a bad loan. You use your credit to purchase the property and then you have a clean place to live as you rent out the other section of the property. So you have your living space right there.

Now if the numbers are correct, the loan (monthly payment) that you take out is less than the rent that you receive. So it is a positive cash flow with a passive income. It is not negative; it is positive. That is basically what you get. You get the energy that you expended. Number

Fig. 8.29. When you own real estate, you get a free place to live that can generate income for you.

one, a free place to stay which generates income for you, number two and number three, the property increases in value so you can refinance it and when you refinance it, number four the monies you receive, especially with a lower interest rate, is a lesser payment but you make more income from the rental income. Then the monies you receive start to expand. Number five, that is all tax-free income because it is taken out of the loan and the renters are paying off the debt or paying off the mortgage on the property. This is the best scenario to be in. As you start to connect with that, you will start to see this in your life.

The sixth income you also receive is depreciation on the property, so as the property increases in value you also receive indirect income because the property is declining in physical value. You can depreciate the value it has and use that as a tax advantage to bring you more return on your investment. So any profits you make are virtually nontaxable because of the depreciation you are making. Another tax advantage you have is when you sell. You can utilize the profit on that to reinvest in more property, avoiding the taxes by turning them over into another property. So you actually have six sources of income. It really is a win, win, win, win, win, win situation, especially if you can do the numbers properly. Even if you are a little close on certain numbers, the other numbers can definitely make the investment a good investment, so you always win.

With real estate, you buy three things: location, location, location. In other words, you want the right property in the right situation where you have good access with traffic and good rentable space for

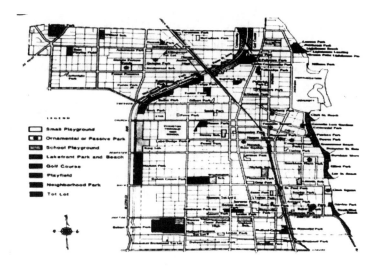

Fig. 8.30. When you look for real estate, look for three things: location, location, location.

your particular units for the people who are renting them. This will give you an advantage when you sell it, when you refinance it, and when you rent it out. So as you slow the mind down, this becomes perfectly clear to you when you start to develop this understanding with many years of practice in the meditations and connecting with the inner voice for your directions.

LEARN TO LIVE BENEATH YOUR MEANS

What you have to remember in this life is you come in with nothing and you are going to leave with nothing. So you really do not own anything except your essence or soul, which costs you nothing. So everything that you accumulate in life is really somebody else's. It is not really yours, because you cannot take it with you. You are either paying rent on it or it is drawing some form of energy from you. The less you have, the less that is drawn from you, the less with which you have to be burdened, and the freer you become. As you meditate this will make more sense to you in time and you can truly understand the meaning of Henry Thoreau's words: "A man is rich by the possessions he can afford not to own." The key is to evaluate your situation in life and realize that, no matter what you accumulate, it is really an exercise of experiencing the accumulation because you really never hold on to it in the end.

Over the course of fifty years in my own life, I have realized and seen everything that I have valued at one point disappear into nothingness. I have started my life over four different times and I have realized that each time I start it over again with accumulation of various assets and various situations to make life more effortless, in the end it has all disappeared. The only thing you really have that gives you any type of connection is your internal cultivation when you work on yourself. And that is the only thing you take with you, your consciousness. You are cultivating, becoming, and discovering its essence and its being, so you take that understanding with you and it leads you wherever it takes you.

This is the journey in life. As you head through life, you start to realize that everything that is material really is an illusion because it disappears in time. The only thing that is real is what you can consciously draw into yourself. That is why out of the first fifty-five years of my life, I have spent a good twenty years working and cultivating my internal being because that is the only real asset we have. The internal

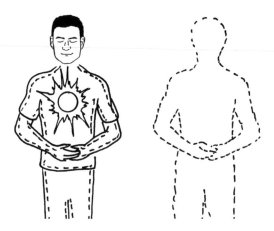

Fig. 8.31. When you cultivate your internal being, you are creating the only real asset you will ever have because it is the only tangible substance you will take with you.

being is really the only tangible substance that we can take with us wherever we go. So, when you first discover this in your journey, who you are, then you start to cultivate that essence. As you work with it over many, many years, you start to understand its importance and the benefits that you receive from it.

As you start to cultivate the energy, you will start to benefit from the rewards. Rewards are inner peace, tranquility, and harmony, not only with yourself but everything around you. This inner peace is really the serenity that you seek within yourself and is the payoff for your time and devotion to the practices, developing the stillness into nothingness. That really is the key to life.

Can you learn to live beneath your means? Do you first understand what it takes to live? Once you realize that you can live on almost nothing, you do not really need to generate a whole lot to sustain yourself. There is no real reason to generate a whole lot of income. If the income is situated in an investment, it takes very little effort on your part to maintain it or to initiate it. You are getting a better return on your time.

That is really the Taoist way, to find out how much it takes for you to expend and how much you receive in return. That is really the effortless path, but the undermining quality and understanding behind that is the less you have, the less that is required for you to utilize your energy

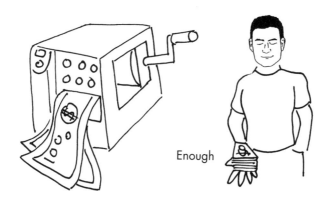

Fig. 8.32. There is no reason to generate more income when you learn to live below your means.

to maintain it. Also, too many things in life can become a burden.

I have possessed many things in my life and most of them were really just a burden. We are talking mostly about material things: clothing, jewelry, cars, houses, relationships. You find out that it just takes your time and energy, and you get very little in return. There is the initial excitement of achieving it and then the overall maintenance to maintain it over a period of time just brings your energy down and it drains you. You realize that the less you have, the better, because the less responsibility and the less burden it is on your time and energy.

So you realize that once you understand this, it takes very little to eat, very little to shelter yourself, and very little expended energy for travel. You understand your money machine can work very efficiently because you are not stressed to produce a lot of monies from it. You can create the money machine itself as a company and its employees as your dollars and you get those dollars to work for you to generate more dollars. You can set it up correctly because you have time, not being burdened with a lot of responsibilities. You can properly set it up and allow it to mature and grow on its own because you have the time for it to properly get rooted in its foundation and slowly grow. That is why real estate is a very interesting proposition, because to make transitions in acquisitions, it takes months at a time and a lot of careful planning and the situation may be involved and take time to mature. Just like growing a seed within the ground, you need to water it and give it a little bit of sunshine each day, but it really grows on its own. So the less you do with it, the better. And the funny thing about it is 99 percent of all the investments made in the world are with real estate, and they pay off wonderfully. To the majority of people, it is the biggest investment in their lives in the last fifty years. I know of many cases where the person bought the property and paid a certain amount a month over the course of thirty years, and the initial investment of $11,000 became $100,000 in the payoff. Now they have enough money to live on for the rest of their lives if invested correctly. What you end up getting is a return on the funds that you initially invested. I would say 95 percent of people who invest in a home and

Fig. 8.33. An initial home investment of $11,000 became a return of $100,000 in thirty years.

then retire have a nest egg to retire on. This has been their biggest investment, just where they live, and they do not even realize it. They did not have passive income or a positive cash flow. It was really a liability, but there was a payoff. You can take that a step further and when you purchase property, you can get passive income from the property if you work the numbers correctly.

You get the positive cash flow, the key to the whole program, by making sure that it generates enough income. It is really all about putting together the right financing by getting the alignment correct. It is just like growing a seed in the ground. In a period of time, you just relax, do your practice, and the payoff will come. It is just a matter of nurturing the property by maintaining it. That is where you are living, so create a nice environment for yourself and live in that environment and learn to cultivate your energy as you are earning money every day with the property as it increases in value. Many people have made hundreds of thousands of dollars over the past thirty years on their property and they do not see it ending at all. It is still going to accumulate especially in areas that have not had enough time to cultivate; but again, location, location, location is the key.

If you find the right location, then you will discover that the numbers start to increase. Even though I am starting over for the

Fig. 8.34. Ninety-five percent of people who invested in a home and then retired had a nest egg to retire on after selling their biggest investment.

fourth time in my life, I invested in some rental income property. I purchased it for $180,000 and in six months it was revalued at $225,000. It was a $45,000 increase in value. I refinanced and got all my money back (my down payment) and an additional $10,000 on the refinance as a result of the escalation of the property and its value.

When building this money machine, one of the big areas is to start your own business by getting a team together to run the business for you. Then you are the owner and whatever profits you generate from the business you invest in real estate to hold the money's (business profit's) value and to increase its value. The money that you generate in your businesses is reinvested in real estate and the real estate grows and holds the value of your money.

The monies really are your employees and you have to house them

Fig. 8.35. Positive cash flow is really the key to rental income properties.

and take care of them so they can produce more money for more employees to work for you. It is all capital and it is just energy, so you are utilizing energy to multiply itself and not waste itself. Anything you invest has to have a good return. That is basically how you should approach all your real estate investments. You look at them as a return on your money invested and the time it takes to get it back.

As you slowly accumulate—1, 2, 3, 10, 20, 100, or up to 1,000 units—you just duplicate what you are doing and just continue to move forward. Over time, two or three or ten years, you have accumulated enough real estate with passive income and positive cash flow—two, three, ten thousand dollars per month to sustain you and any of your other activities. Many people will have a problem with managing the property. As your real estate investment becomes a business, you hire other superstar people in the self-employed area to manage and maintain your property.

You just get a percentage of what is left after all expenses are paid. That slowly is built up, and the money is passive, a positive cash flow income. That is basically the plan for the money machine. You can do it on a small scale and then move to a larger scale. It is the same principle and the same activities. You just need to focus and it will slowly develop on its own. First, learn to live beneath your means. Then you can start to utilize the profit that is generated from the excess of your means and slowly invest it into real estate. Again, develop companies to generate income and then the profit from these companies can be invested

Fig. 8.36. I invested in rental income property for $180,000, and in six months, it was revalued at $225,000—a $45,000 increase in value. I refinanced and got all my money back plus $10,000.

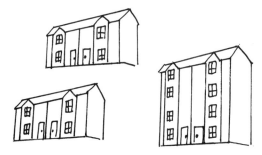

Fig. 8.37. The plan for the money machine is to start small and then move on to a larger scale.

into more real estate. That is basically how you establish your money machine, taking care of your necessities (food, shelter, and travel), and you slowly accumulate real estate to support you with positive cash flow and passive income. Again, *passive* means you do not work for it. You set it up and you keep an eye on it.

What you are actually doing is allowing the business itself to generate the income utilizing your dollars as employees to earn more dollars for you. That is the simple plan and that is the way of the Tao. Good luck with your business and creating your own money machine.

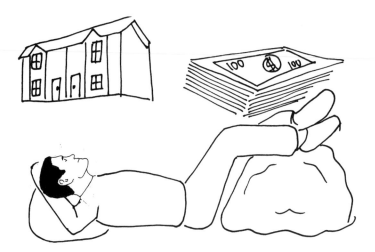

Fig. 8.38. Slowly accumulate real estate to give yourself a positive cash flow as passive income.

Beyond Death and Taxes

YOUR OVERCOAT

In the Tao, you can go beyond death and taxes. What is death? Death in all reality is like changing a coat. You have an overcoat on and you take off the overcoat. The overcoat is the physical body, and you are taking the overcoat off in death. In taking the overcoat off you have the spirit body left, so all you are doing is changing from one phase to the next.

We are all light bodies and in true reality we are consciousness, the light body. We are entrapped in the physical form within time and space. When we enter the human body, we activate the body and give it light with our consciousness. As we give it life, we are confined to the time and space with our five senses. As we start to work and cultivate the internal energy of the body, our consciousness, we discover other areas that we can connect and communicate with. This is going beyond the five senses and going beyond time and space. So the physical body is the overcoat we are wearing.

Once you develop the higher-level practices, you can move beyond the physical body while still being connected to the physical body without physically dying. This is when you do the immortal practices

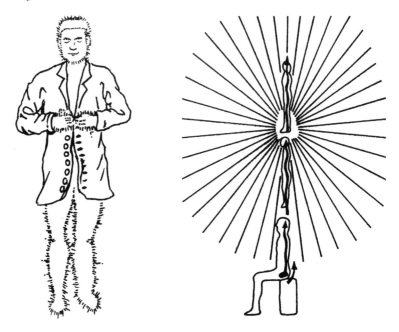

Fig. 9.1. Death is like changing a coat.   Fig. 9.2. This light body moves out of
the physical body in such a way that
nothing dies.

of the Kan and Li and you consciously leave the body. In other words, your consciousness, this light body, moves out of the physical body but you set up the physical body in such a way that it does not die. It still continues to exist in a dormant state. This is performed in the higher level in our alchemy practices of the Immortal Tao.

What takes place as you develop the energy is the consciousness moves out of the body when you seal off the physical body, sealing all the nine openings or the orifices of the body. (There are seven windows and the front door and the back door of our physical body or our temple.) Then you actually take in air through the skin with the Bone Breathing techniques and the heartbeat slows down to such a low degree where it does not appear to be running because your body is perfectly still.

You are in a meditative sitting posture where you are sitting on the sitz bones and you get a heavenly flow from the crown connecting the heavens and the earthly flow to the perineum, which is connecting with the feet. So you are really suspended in air being pulled from two different directions. The physical body becomes light and buoyant. When the body is suspended in air, light and buoyant, you can consciously leave the body with no stress on the body from the gravitational pulls. The energy can flow freely in the body because it is structurally in alignment with the heavenly and earthly forces.

The body goes into a dormant state as the bodies of many animals do. But your consciousness, as you leave the body through the crown, can start to work and gather energy on the other realm. These activities take place in the higher-level practices in the Immortal Tao system.

The physical body is really an overcoat and our real essence or the real body is our spirit body or consciousness. This goes beyond time and space, and as we work with the physical form, we start to develop our sixth and seventh senses (clairvoyance and telepathy). We start to move beyond the physical realm into the cosmic realm, going beyond time and space. These are all new and different dimensions that need to be worked with for many years to develop the techniques.

FIRE AND WATER

A strange thing happens when you learn to balance yourself alchemically. As you align the molecular structure of your physical body in tune with the natural flow of the universe, you will begin to transform yourself in the alchemical process. You will transform the physical body into the spirit body, which is covering it, and make them one. These are the immortal practices that the Taoists achieve through the fusion meditative practices, initially through energetic composting in the Taoist system. Then into the Kan and Li practices where they are mixing the fire and the water in the immortal Tao practices, achieving the ultimate communication or communion of the immortal being.

When you experience leaving the body on a conscious level through meditation, you actually experience death before dying.

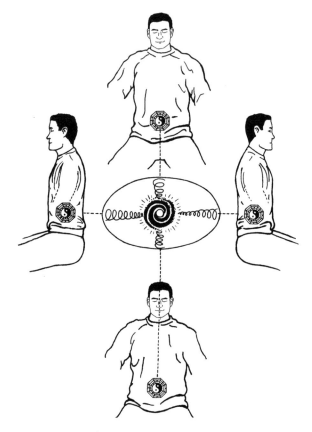

Fig. 9.3. Fusion meditative practices create energetic composting
in the Taoist system.

Once you experience this, you will never fear death, which is just
the unknown. There is nothing to fear because you have already had
that experience of death in a living state but you are still alive. When
consciousness leaves the body that is exactly what takes place in death.
So you are practicing the death experience many, many times through
the Taoist meditation practices to prepare yourself for the big event.

As you start to develop this understanding, the Taoist system
really prepares you for the whole system of life in the other realm or
life beyond this life. You do this preparation right within your life,
while still living here on Earth. It is an amazing process. In other
words, you are preparing yourself for every aspect of death in the

other realm. When you do eventually leave this body or leave the overcoat, you are ready and well prepared.

How this takes place is through meditation, when you push the energy field, your consciousness, out the crown, and you move out. It is real. You can actually feel the whole body, your conscious body, the real you. It's the person inside you, moving directly out of the body. It is an unusual experience and it is so real that it will scare you initially, and you will jump right back in the body.

With more practice, like everything else, you start to become comfortable with it and then you can literally move out of the body. This opens you up to a whole other realm and you slowly develop the senses where you actually see, hear, feel, and sense in this other realm. It is a whole different area of dimensional aspects within yourself that you will be discovering and experiencing.

Through these practices (after you leave the body many, many times, and exercise various techniques in the other realm to gather energy), you will develop your own energy field inside, and, as the Taoists say, death will have no sting when it comes. It is just a matter of practicing and working with the energy while you are still living on

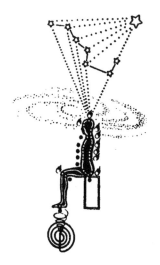

Fig. 9.4. You can actually feel your conscious body moving
directly out of the body.

Fig. 9.5. The electromagnetic radiation field of our physical body is the greatest force on the planet and is transformed into our spirit body.

Earth, utilizing the physical body to do this transformation to move into the other realm.

The purpose of the physical body actually is to be used as the primary substance to build this spirit body you are creating. As you do the practices, you start to develop an immortal fetus within the body and you give birth to this immortal fetus, similar to the physical birth you experienced as a child. When you give birth, the spirit body will grow inside your physical body as in a human pregnancy. Then you move it out of the physical body with your consciousness and start to build this spirit body in the other realm with the material of the physical body.

With enough practice and isolation, you start to build ultimately the conscious body or the spirit body from the material of the physical body. After completion, the only thing left of the physical body is the nails and hair because everything else has been transformed into the spirit body.

That is how you can utilize your physical body in the other realm. That is why they say the immortals can fly. Primarily what you are doing is materializing and dematerializing as you move from one realm (the physical realm of the five senses) to the other realm (the spirit realm). You go beyond time and space. So you can move from one realm to the other and do anything you want to do. You can com-

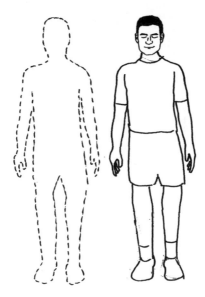

Fig. 9.6. With enough practice, you form the spirit body from the physical body, leaving only your nails and hair behind.

municate to any realm you want and go wherever you want to go. You are in a whole other dimension.

Primarily why we incarnated on this earth plane was to utilize the physical form, which is the highest force on our planet, to build our spirit body. We use the electromagnetic radiation field called the physical body to transform us into our spirit body or our consciousness. The Taoists call this building the yang spirit body. In other words, you are building a strong internal body and transforming that into this spirit body.

The astral travel a lot of people do is different from the transformation in the Taoist system to become an immortal. With astral travel, the consciousness merely leaks out or leaves the body and explores the universe. There is a golden cord that is connected to the physical body. With astral travel you are using a yin body in the other realm. This is different from what the Taoists do with the yang body. And this yin body is not as strong as the immortal body because what you are doing is building a yang body.

Fig. 9.7. With astral travel, you are using a yin body with a golden cord that is connected to the physical body.

The Taoists give the example of a child in the forest. What happens if you leave a baby in the forest or the jungle? Well, there are some big tigers and other animals in the jungle, and the child is at the mercy of all the other creatures in the jungle. The baby does not have anything to protect itself. That is the yin body, where there is astral travel. Now, the Taoists are building the yang body, so you have got that same jungle but now you are driving a big tank in the jungle. This tank is not a helpless baby and no tiger is going to put his teeth into the tank. It has guns on it, with no tires but steel track wheels. It is huge, heavy, and dense, which is what you have with a yang body when you move out of the body.

Now the weapons on the tank (yang body) are energy vortexes, which are pakuas that you develop during the Fusion practices. When you do the Fusion practice, what you are doing? In essence, you are building vortexes energetically inside the physical body. In the practice you are spinning the pakuas like a blender spins, transforming internal energy in your body into pure energy that you can utilize to

Fig. 9.8. During astral travel, the yin body is like a helpless baby
but the yang body is like an armored tank.

open the body up and to heal the body through the various channels energetically throughout the body. These vortexes also blend other energy that approaches you, either negative energy or positive energy, emotionally or mentally. You are automatically doing this transformation in the practices.

With enough practice you can actually start to witness this when you enter a room as you can feel somebody else's energy and they can feel your energy. Some people will not even get near you or they will embrace you depending on their own energy field because their energy comes next to these vortexes. These vortexes (eight sides acting as eight blades) are spinning like blenders that have the blades in them, and their energy is drawn into them and is transformed or blended into another substance. This is utilized in the energy sphere of your own body to heal the body because energy is energy and is utilized in the body.

Now, you can transform the energy or change it from one substance into another and then utilize that substance in your own physical being or your own energetic being. This is what takes place. Now, what happens when you leave the body? Well, energetically, you take these vortexes with you. Most of these are the weapons on that tank. When you complete the building of the whole tank, you transform the physical form into the spirit form and then you have the ability to materialize and dematerialize, moving from one dimension to another.

With this process the Taoists also teach a lot of moving meditations with the Tai Chi Chi Kung forms in different styles. With enough practice of many, many years, I call it the 10,000 times rule. In other words, you do the forms 10,000 times and then it becomes molecularly connected to your own energetic field. So you do the Tai Chi forms, which are standing postures in four directions, or the eight directions around, above, and below the body. You are also creating an energy field or a vortex as you do the practices. Now, after ten years of doing the practice, using the 10,000 times rule, this energy spirit that you have been building or working with through repetition has formed a pattern around the physical body. This is an energetic pattern, which is now part of your consciousness. When you leave your body consciously, what are you going to take with you? You will take the energy vortex that you have built through the Tai Chi practices with all its strike and discharge postures.

So those are all part of the weaponry of your energetic yang

Fig. 9.9. The 10,000 times rule: You do the Tai Chi forms 10,000 times and they become molecularly connected to your own energetic field and go with you.

body. You do not really utilize these weapons against any of the other energy spheres in the other realm, but they can feel the pakuas spinning. They can feel the energy discharging and transforming so they will not approach you without caution and respect. If they do, they are sure to be very friendly and hospitable to your energy field because they could easily be transformed into it. This happens through these techniques that are part of your energetic machine or your energetic spaceship, which is a tank equipped to defend you and transform anything in its path. This is where you are developing the steaming process of the fire and water practices, transforming in the internal alchemy while you are developing this spirit body.

The fire and the water are called Kan and Li. Kan is water and Li is fire. Now, when you redirect this energy and realign it, the fire is the emotional realm, the heart energy, and the water is the sexual energy, which is the kidney energy. What happens when you put the fire underneath the water? With the right alignment, you get steam, and the steam is a transforming essence in the body. You are literally steaming and purifying the internal body into its purified state. As it becomes pure and still, the energy will copulate with the light outside itself. As its copulation takes place, it gives birth to your spirit body. Then you nurture this spirit body with stillness and the connectedness within and it gradually grows the fetus into the spirit body itself. Then you move it out of the body and you start to transform the physical body into the spirit body. This has to be done in isolation and without any distractions. That is why you need to locate or connect with an area where you will not be disturbed for long periods. Once this is completed, then you move into the other dimensions.

ANOTHER DIMENSION

These practices take many years to perfect until you finally achieve them with your own immortal self. What you are doing in essence is creating an internal structure to do these transformations and experiencing them in the practice.

In other words, you are reconstructing your life internally to prepare for this transition of changing your overcoat and walking into another dimension of consciousness. Now, as you walk in this new dimension of consciousness, you are going to be taking this yang body with you. As you take the yang body with you, you start to develop deeper understandings of what is taking place around you. This is a whole other dimension that you have not really experienced on the earth plane.

When you fall asleep you are actually moving into the other realm and going through various experiences in the other realm. What you are trying to do with this practice and transformation is to become conscious of what you are actually doing in the other realm when you are asleep. In part of that consciousness, you are taking your physical body transformed into your spirit body or your consciousness. You are moving a real dense energy into the other realm and that is the objective of trying to connect with yourself and to find those other states.

Now, the other realm is the true realm. We are in the illusionary realm here. This is where all the universe is, all the galaxies and all the nothingness. So we are really in a small dimension of the whole with the earth or life on the earth. We are kind of in slow motion or stagnant in time and space, which is very limiting based on the limits of the five senses. We are utilizing our physical expression while gathering other information.

But just sit back and imagine you are in a whole other dimension, where at any time and any place you can move from one direction to another just with the power of thought. Do you want to be in Texas? Boom. Think about the state, just look and you are there. Or do you want to be anywhere on the planet or anywhere in the galaxy? Think the thought and then automatically you will be there. Your body will move beyond the physical form into the spirit form, going beyond time and space into a whole other dimension and a whole other position in the galaxy.

Now, a lot of our imagination in this area has been transcribed and documented in the movies or the medium of the day such as TV—shows like *Star Trek* or some of the other science fiction films. These are all thoughts and concepts that people wrote and actually put together with the *Star Wars* movies and any of the other movie concepts. You see, if you can think it, therefore it can be, because everything starts with a thought. It is our ability to manifest these thoughts that creates our reality. If somebody thought about transforming or materializing the physical form and dematerializing it later in another location, then that is possible. There is a lot we have not yet discovered within ourselves. The Tao is one of those discoveries and this is called transfiguration. This is all very possible if you develop enough time and energy toward this process internally with the internal alchemy practices.

What if we took all the time and energy that we use in the external realm to make our telephones, TVs, and transportation and utilized all that time, energy, and money to internally develop our own consciousness? We could do all these things. Everything that we can see in the external realm came from our energetic and mental thought forms. We have the most perfect form on the planet, our physical body, and we have not been able to duplicate it with our technology yet. Eventually, they say we will.

Fig. 9.10. We are immovable in time and space, but in the other realm there are no limits.

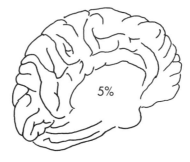

Fig. 9.11. We only use 5 to 10 percent of our brain and if we focus with the meditative practices our remaining capacity will come out.

Why waste all our time trying to develop something externally when you have the perfect vehicle to develop it internally? You know, they say we have only used 5 to 10 percent of our brain's capacity. There is a huge amount of information, data, and ability that we have not even discovered yet. The Taoists already have discovered this and by working the Taoist practices and developing the stillness, these energies or understandings will come out.

Once they come out, then you can move beyond who you are within the physical form and move into the spirit form, becoming another being, your true self. You see, we are all divine. We have just forgotten who we are. We are the forgotten gods. This is our journey, to rediscover our own divinity. As you move from this new dimension into another dimension of thinking, another dimension of manifestation, you start to develop your own spirit self, which takes place within your own being.

THE LESS YOU ACCUMULATE, THE FEWER TAXES YOU PAY

As you slow down the mind, you start to realize that the less you accumulate and consume, the fewer taxes you are obligated to pay. For example, on your food, if you grow your own food, you do not pay an excise tax or other hidden taxes that you would pay on your food consumption. This is further explained with the understanding of buying in bulk or buying locally as opposed to buying and getting something in a package.

If you buy local bulk whole foods, there are no taxes involved. And there are no hidden taxes on packaging and shipping it. This also applies to the price of clothing and other products needed for our essential existence. So, as you consume less, you are taxed less. That is why the art of doing nothing and the art of consuming nothing really eliminates any necessity for paying taxes.

So, consumption is based basically on the tax that you might pay or you might be subject to pay. There are many aspects of restructuring your life with a clear understanding that you can really go beyond any type of taxation. It just takes time. As you work within that idea, you can start to see this on a whole other dimension. Once you start to move beyond that, you can start to move in another realm beyond taxes.

As you study the tax system in whatever country you are in, there are always opportunities to have an existence that goes beyond taxes. If you do not consume anything, there is nothing you can be taxed on. If you do not need any physical transportation, you can just transfigure yourself from one position to another or from one location to another. There are no taxes on that, such as you need to be taxed on a car or plane or any other type of vehicle. As you can start to see, when you move into this new dimension of understanding, you can really move beyond consumption and beyond taxes.

With the food substance, when you go to this level, we get 70 percent of all nutrition from the air. The other 30 percent, once we learn to open up our channels, we can retain. There is no way they can tax the air. There is no taxation on air, especially if you move around in the universe going beyond time and space. There is no way to tax it. There is no way to configure it. There is no way to measure it and taxes no longer apply to you. You are materializing and dematerializing at will. You are moving all around. This is primarily a different situation all around for your own understanding and well-being.

How do you get from A to Z? Well, you start simply: the less you

Zero Tax

Fig. 9.12. Seventy percent of all nutrition comes from the air and
there is no taxation on the air.

consume, the fewer obligations you will have. So you slowly move
from taxation to using less. The only reason people consume a lot is
that they become attached to everything with advertising and gathering. You start with the internal practices and you slowly let go of your
attachments.

As you let go of the attachments, you slowly let go of your consumption. If you lose attachment, and are no longer attached to animal products, there is a huge savings on consumption there. This is
because producing these animal products costs us a lot of labor and
land involving a lot of taxation, which leads to more consumption.

Just by not eating or consuming animal products, your consumption is lessened all around and the burden of taxation is limited. The
same thing happens when you own a car. You can do this in stages
so that it all brings about its own transformation. It just takes time,
of letting go and understanding. As you slow the mind down, things
become clear to you and you start to make conscious choices. You
become at peace with yourself with a more simple existence, finding
the harmony of letting go within yourself. Once you have the stillness
and harmony within the body on a regular basis, the energy will come
within to transform you. This is the whole practice of the Tao.

Zero Tax

Fig. 9.13. By not consuming animal products, your consumption
is less and taxes are limited.

LAND PATENTS

On your shelter and real estate, you will begin to understand state and federal jurisdiction in relationship to you as a sovereign person with God-given rights as explained to you in various constitutions. You can start to set up various corporations, foreign trusts, or offshore trusts so you are not subject to their jurisdiction or taxation.

If you take title to a property, you can use an allodial title, land grant, or land patent that are not subject to government jurisdiction, property taxes, or building codes. Basically what you are doing is restructuring a completely new understanding of who you are and what you are about in relationship to local, state, and federal jurisdiction— but these understandings take much time and study.

Based on what you need to maintain yourself, when you get to this level, you discover that you need very little to maintain yourself. Basically you need to exist in an area where you can house the body, move out of the body, and do the practices in the other realm.

To optimally house the body, take a damp, cool area that is isolated. That is why the Taoists go to the mountains. To maintain a facility in the mountains, you may need some power there depending on how the facility is structured. This will solve your need to be isolated as well and to have no involvement with any type of governmental or county jurisdiction.

Fig. 9.14. If you properly take title to a property, you can use allodial titles, grants, or land patents that are not subject to government jurisdiction, property taxes, or building codes.

You can set this up by just creating a sovereign person status, which are aspects of our discussion and understanding. Once you become a sovereign person, you can utilize the allodial title or land patent on the particular property where you are housing your body. Or you can establish a nonprofit foundation.

You also can set up a simple foundation that can be run by an outside source, a nonprofit organization that actually goes beyond

NONPROFIT FOUNDATION RETREAT

Fig. 9.15. House the body in the mountains isolated in a cave under a land patent or nonprofit foundation.

the property taxes by being exempt from them; but there are some costs for administrating this type of foundation. There are other administrative activities that need to be handled, which also can be delegated to an attorney who would be in charge of the foundation itself. This will allow you space to do the transformation involved in these immortal practices. So there are many options that you can take. It is amazing: once you slow the mind down, you start to see what is available to make these conscious choices.

EXISTENCE WITHOUT MONEY

Now, taking this a step further, you can situate yourself in a position where you do not need any money to exist. Currently, you exchange your labor effort for money, but if the money is not backed by anything, you are not getting an equal exchange. This is the case relative to all the monies that are in existence today around the world in all the various countries.

To further complicate this situation, the money you receive is not debt-free. You are subject to a debt and interest, when you receive the money for your labor. This is the current monetary situation in the world, created by the IMF, International Monetary Fund. But you can create an existence without money. It is amazing but you can grow your own food and learn how to eat the wild roots (herbs) and grasses in nature, living as a bird and becoming free as a bird.

You can have a deeper understanding in an isolated area for you to do your practices. In the mountains you would be isolated where you learn to keep the energy of the body or you can develop a simple cave dwelling. You can build one yourself or find one in the mountains.

There are systematic ways of doing this and utilizing the creek (the water) for hydropower (water power) to heat the water you need to cleanse yourself and heat your dwelling (radiant floor heating). There are a lot of alternative ways you can do this without being connected to the grid. It is just applying yourself by slowing the mind down and having your intention intact. The practices of understanding health would lead you to eat what is available in the forest and the mountains.

You can easily dig up the roots from the trees, when you understand what roots are beneficial to you. You can grind them up and then eat the ground-up roots and the grasses from nature. These are the live grasses in the mountains. So you are living as a bird being as free as a bird.

People do not quite understand why anybody would want to do that when there are so many other activities, attachments, and connections with the outside world. Obviously, they would not be in the mountains to do all this. It is a theory of conscious transformation that you make in this whole process through the meditations and the practices.

You just cannot walk right into the woods from the highway with all your attachments and all your objectives from your occupation in life. You have to ask yourself what your life is about. What are you doing? How attached are you to your family, possessions, culture, or religion?

In the Tao, you become totally detached. Through your own understandings or through going to church 10,000 times or 100,000 times or being with so many different women or eating so much different food, you become satiated, you have had enough. Then you can

Fig. 9.16. As you gravitate to the mountain, your existence without money becomes a reality.

go to the mountain to do the practices in the middle of nothing. You can slow down your mind and see what you really want in life and what is really important to you.

With that understanding, you start to make some conscious choices, and then you slowly gravitate to the mountain and your existence without money becomes a reality. In essence, you become free as a bird.

FREE AS A BIRD

With study and research you can relocate possibly in this world, where there is no property tax on your property. It could be remote or under some different government regulations.

On this tax-free land, you could build an earth home and have a mountain stream running through it for your power and water, which is similar to what I have established at Wu Chi Acres in southern Oregon.

You have no need for home or automobile insurance without a conventional home or car. You can literally establish yourself on a parcel of land, checking out what regulations there are. Because it is remote and in the mountains, the only things you are concerned about are the trees and the forest fires.

There is a way to get around the forest fires by cleaning the surface of the forest floor. The big trees will not burn unless they have kindling from small, little twigs and brush to keep the fire going long enough for the big trees to catch fire. Fires can be totally eliminated by cleaning the forest floor of all debris.

The mountains always have rivers and streams in them. Why? If it rains or snows (it melts) and it runs down the crevices of the mountain into the sea, you have running water. With running water you have hydropower, which you can use to set up a nice electrical system for heating the water. When you heat your water, you can heat the dwelling with radiant heating (hot water running through the floor).

Fig. 9.17. Wu Chi Acres in southern Oregon

The most energy-efficient dwelling is the earth dwelling because once you are under five feet of earth the temperature never gets below fifty-seven degrees. You are protected and insulated by the earth.

There is no maintenance either on the earth home. Once it is in place and established, there is no cutting the grass. There is no putting the tiles or the roof siding on, or painting. It is just made out of earth and rock.

All you have to do is live there. It is like being in a cave. You can go in there and shelter your physical being, while having correct alignment, sealing off the body so no critters can come in. With the correct alignment in such a way that you can become free as a bird, your spirit leaves the body.

Now you say, "Well, if you are in the earth, how are you free as a bird?" When you consciously leave the body, you are free as a bird. Your consciousness is floating around, flying around, going wherever you want it to go, connecting with whatever you want it to connect with, like a bird or the wind.

Fig. 9.18. Running water gives you hydropower to heat your
home and for showers.

You become Jonathan Livingston Seagull, soaring to all different
parts of the planet, to all different parts of the galaxy, and to all different parts of existence. So you are free as a bird, becoming whatever
you want to become. There is no life insurance needed for this existence because you have moved beyond death. By moving beyond death
you have moved beyond taxes. There is nothing to be protected and
there is nothing to tax.

Fig. 9.19. When you consciously leave the body, you are free as a bird.

Fig. 9.20. You do not need any life insurance if you are not going to die.

You are beyond protection. You are your own protection because you have moved beyond the conventional lifestyle into a whole other realm of understanding and being. That is the realm of the Tao.

HEALING YOURSELF

Once you discover how to heal yourself and prevent disease through correct food and living, you will not need any health insurance or any doctor's care. When you have no overhead, you have no need for money.

One of the big expenses that is really crippling our society is the overhead of insurance coverage for our medical system. Once you purify the body through fasting and eating the correct diet, which is primarily greens or grasses with the alkaline balance of 20:1 alkaline to acid, you will start to discover that without the degenerative diseases there are no medical expenses.

This saves a huge amount of money because, especially in the West, health costs are driving the medical industry right out of business. To stay in a hospital room could run as high as two thousand dollars a day. Who can afford that? People are saying the insurance pays for it, but they have paid two hundred dollars a month for twenty-five years. You could retire as a multimillionaire or billionaire if you had invested that in real estate or the stock market. The whole point is you are paying for it one way or the other. More importantly, beyond the money, you are the one suffering, being victimized by the medical and insurance industries with their procedures.

In Western medicine, they primarily try to correct diseases by dismemberment. In other words, they take a part of your body off. "You have got a problem with the cancer over here. No problem, we will just take this section out, or we will burn it out, or we will just cut it open to release the pressure."

The problem when they do that is they take away essential parts of your body that you need to exist. So you end up being dismembered and totally torn apart, which means you cannot replace these missing parts or grow them back. That is not the solution because it just creates more problems and never solves the original problem, which is the imbalance of the blood in the body.

From a cost standpoint, you cannot afford to get sick using conventional medical techniques of dismemberment that only leave you dismembered, even if somebody gives you the money to pay the bill. You need all the parts of your body to live, not only for the alchemical transformation to move through the other realm, but more importantly for living and existing here in this realm.

With understanding and as you slow the mind down, things become clearer. You start to make some conscious choices and you start to heal yourself. You can make some direct decisions in your life to change your lifestyle, to change your eating habits, and have more balance and harmony in your life. Once you understand how the body functions and works, you start to live strong within your own convictions of what is really actually happening. As you start to live strong, your energy and understanding will start to shift.

This is all in the process of healing yourself physically, emotionally, psychologically, and, finally, spiritually. As you create a harmony and

Fig. 9.21. You are four bodies into one body at the same time.

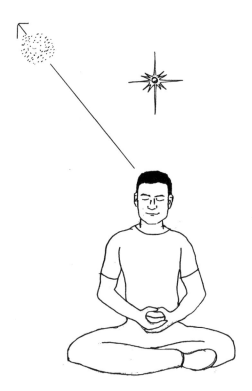

Fig. 9.22. The final part of our journey in this galaxy is to go beyond the North Star.

balance with these four bodies, within yourself, you become one. You are always four bodies. That is the understanding of the total alchemical process in the Taoist systems. In other words, you transform the physical form, which takes place in the emotional and psychological bodies, then into the spirit body or your complete energetic body. This is the ability you have to dematerialize and materialize at will.

Once you can do that, then you can move beyond time and space. As the Taoists say, "The final corner of our journey in this galaxy is to go beyond the North Star and out into the beyond," wherever that will take you.

This is all part of the discovery in healing yourself. Now, how would you start healing yourself? Well, you would just stop doing things. Again, the body will heal itself if you do absolutely nothing. In other words, you do not do any activity of any kind. You just simply rest. You can see the animals in the forest. When they get sick or ill, they cease all activity. They hardly drink and they stop eating. They do not do any activity and just rest.

They just allow the body at rest to go through the autolyzation process that the body automatically goes into to break down any toxins or poisons, eliminating them through urination, sweating, or defecation. The body is slowly eating itself back to health by eliminating all the blockages and all the excess materials it has accumulated

Fig. 9.23. When animals get sick or injured they cease all activity. They hardly drink and they stop eating.

through your improper eating habits and lifestyle. The body has to get rid of them and will heal itself as long as you are not putting any new materials into the body.

To learn to heal yourself is to learn the art of nothingness, doing nothing. In other words, do not do anything. Just relax and try to work with your internal energy through the meditations and slowly heal the body by inactivity. The art of doing nothing is the key to healing yourself.

PURE ENERGY CHI

Where is this all leading you? It is all leading to the pure essence of the Tao, which is purifying your body in the connection and the flow of the universe. As you start to purify the body, you start to become just pure energy and the body flows at a higher energetic level. You move beyond time and space into pure energy.

As you balance and harmonize the internal being, you start to feel

Fig. 9.24. Finally you become pure energy and at one with the universe.

Fig. 9.25. In purity, you have stillness. Within stillness, what you need in life will emerge for you.

and connect with this energy. As you start to feel and connect with the energy, you start to develop this pure essence inside. In purity, you have stillness. Within the stillness what you need in life will emerge to you and you flow with it in the effortless path of the Tao. Everything will be revealed to you that needs to be known at that particular time. This does take place on the physical realm first.

The Taoists work with the physical level because you can easily get in touch with it. The physical body is just a different vibration of the emotional, psychological, and spiritual bodies. It is like a fan. The fan blades, as you turn the speed up, will disappear. Now, are the blades still there? Well, it is moving so fast you cannot see the blades any more, but are the blades still there? Yes. If you slow the fan down

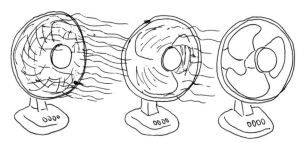

Fig. 9.26. It is the same fan, the same blades. It is just a different frequency.

or you stop the fan, you can see the blades. When you stop the fan, the blades are in the physical realm. When you speed it up, it is the emotional realm but it is still somewhat visible. When you speed it up even a little bit more, it is the mental realm. It is slightly visible. But when you put it up at full speed, the fan blades just disappear and that is the spirit realm. It is the same fan, the same blades. It is just a different frequency or your perception of the frequency, because it can go both ways. Either you can turn on the higher speeds, or it's a person looking at the fan with their perception being different.

So if you can train or utilize your abilities within yourself to perceive at a different vibration, you will be able to pick up all the other vibrations simultaneously. There are several ways of looking at it: how you perceive it, how it actually is, and with what velocity and frequency it is moving. There is always the yin and the yang, one from the outside and one from the inside.

We must pay attention to this and that is what the Tao says, that you have to pay attention. Everything is moving. Everything is continually

Fig. 9.27. You have to pay attention. Everything is moving.
Everything is continually in flux.

in flux. If you do not pay attention, you will miss what you are supposed to learn. It will come again but if you are still distracted, you are not focused, or you are not paying attention, you will miss it again.

We have been missing it many, many times throughout our many sojourns on this earth plane, until we move beyond the earth plane into the other realm and go beyond the North Star, the center of the galaxy. This is how it has unfolded. To do this, you need the pure energy, the pure chi, and to develop the pure chi, you need to first work with the physical form to balance and harmonize it.

The physical form will transform into the emotional realm, and with diet and understanding in the physical realm. In the emotional realm, this will shift the energy because you will be more alkaline, not agitated. Plus you are working with the energetic realm and you will start to feel a little more of the shift. When you start to feel a shift, you will start to see the transformation it makes. Through the fusion practices of the Taoist system, you will start to transform the emotional level and then move to the immortal practices of Kan and Li and purify the psychological and spiritual levels.

Fig. 9.28. We have been missing what we are supposed to learn many, many times throughout our many sojourns on Earth, until we move beyond the earth plane into the other realm.

TOTAL AWARENESS

In your Taoist practices, you are going to discover, as you slow the mind down, that you tune into another vibration. You begin to see things in a whole other light. You start to see the aspects of divine intervention or divine providence. What this means is that there is a direct plan for you.

You start to tune into this vibration, this understanding, and things become very clear to you. Then you begin to understand why you are here and what your life is about, where you are going and how you are going to get there.

You do not worry about freak accidents because the way of the Tao is the way of knowledge and wisdom. The way of the Tao is the way of total awareness. You will know exactly what is going on, how it will be coming, where it is coming from, and when it is coming. So you tune into a whole other dimension and you have a whole understanding of your evolution in the state of being beyond death and taxes.

Our divine intervention is our self-discovery of our own divinity. Within that discovery, you will start to see who you really are

Fig. 9.29. As you slow the mind down you tune into another vibration and see things in a whole other light.

Fig. 9.30. Divine intervention comes into play with the practice of the Tao.

and where you are going. It is all a matter of slowing down the mind, slowing it down into complete stillness. As you connect with this stillness, you will get an internal transformation within yourself that will connect with your true self.

As you connect with your true self, that true self will start to direct you in your life. You will start to develop a total awareness of everything around you and what is connecting you to the various aspects of your life, how they are connected and what things are out there. Your

Fig. 9.31. Your own energy sphere will direct you in whatever direction it will.

own energy sphere will direct you, the vibration itself will direct you in whatever direction it will. In other words, the energy that you are transforming will start to attract the same type of energy. You will not be attracted to anything that will put you in danger, anything that will put you in jeopardy, anything that will move you off your direction. This all starts within. As you start to make this transition within, you will start to feel this transformation within your body and that will move you in that same direction.

It is like momentum that takes you into a whole other dimension. The difficult things in life that people encounter happen because their inner direction is not cultivated. It is not seen, it is not worked, it is not developed—and if it is not developed, worked, and cultivated, your energy not only becomes stagnant, but it also moves in a different direction than it was originally intended.

The intention is so important but you actually have to work through every aspect within your molecular structure to maintain yourself. As you maintain yourself, you will start to see this transformation take place within your own body. As it takes place within your own body,

Fig. 9.32. The downward spiral perpetuates itself, but the upward spiral does the same. You just need to work with it long enough to get it going in the right direction.

you will start to feel the transformation within your own essence. This will attract you in other directions. It's self-perpetuating.

As this process moves through your being, you will start to discover this more and more within your own essence. As you discover this, you will start to see this transformation take place. It all leads back to your total awareness of where you are, moving you beyond time and space, and beyond death and taxes.

This total awareness will help you develop your own understanding of yourself, where you are going and how you are going to get there. It will also direct you and allow things to move in their own place and move you beyond where you think you are supposed to be and where you are supposed to go.

It almost indirectly carries you through the same aspects. You see, the downward spiral perpetuates itself, but the upward spiral does the same. You just need to work with it long enough to get it going in the right direction and you will find that you will connect with yourself and who you really are.

This is the fact of the Tao and the path that you take, moving beyond death and taxes. It is a journey and in the journey the key is to enjoy the ride. The ride becomes much more enjoyable as you start to discover it and it starts to unfold. You will start to understand your own essence, where you are going and how you are going to get there. This is the path of the Tao.

Fig. 9.33. The Tao is the path that you take to move beyond death and taxes. It is a journey and in the journey the key is enjoying the ride.

Beyond Infinity

ANOTHER MOUNTAIN

What is infinity? When we work with our internal energy, we work with infinity. We work with the continuum. In infinity, there is no beginning and no end. It just continues; it is the continuum.

That is why we say in the Tao, we have nowhere to go because we are already there. As the Taoists say, "When you climb a mountain and get to the top, you look around and there is another mountain. You climb that mountain and as you get to the top, you look around and there is another mountain." As you are becoming, there is always more to become. So, it really is not a process of getting anywhere—

Fig. 10.1. Infinity is unexplainable but it is a continuum.

Fig. 10.2. You climb a mountain and get to the top, look around, and there is another mountain.

because there is nowhere to get to, because you are always becoming something new. You always have to get to someplace else. There is no finish line. You will always continually become. You will always be continually becoming and if you are continually becoming you are already there and there is no place to go.

That is really living in the now. When you are living in the now, there is nowhere to go. Your presence is being here now. It is the key of the whole process. Just be involved, be involved with doing what you are doing now in the process of doing. You can say you have nowhere to go and all the time in the world to get there, so just enjoy the ride.

You can look at life as a circle. There is no beginning or end. There is just the continuing circle of life. The life circle is just a continuum moving from one aspect of becoming to the next. There is always something more to become. That is why there is no beginning and there is no end. It is like a circle. It just continues to continue. As you flow down the path of life, you start to see this and you start to connect with this energy, and then you realize that through this whole process, it is just the process of becoming.

As you gather information and understandings from this life's slow journey, you start to realize that there is really nowhere you are going. It is just being a part of the whole process. As you are part of the process, you start to live completely in the moment, in the presence of where you are, and you do not really focus on anything else. As you live in the present or the moment, you start to enjoy life fully.

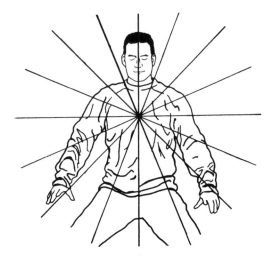

Fig. 10.3. Live in the present and you will start to enjoy life fully.

As you start to enjoy life fully, you start to experience everything that you need to experience at that moment.

As you discover another mountain to climb, there is always going to be something more to become. With this idea, the whole aging process becomes a misnomer. In other words, you do not really age. You just gain information, and you gain understandings. The whole process of aging is the process of gaining understanding and information. It is the whole process of becoming.

Once you live in the now, there is no real meaning to anything that goes away or comes in. It is really all the same. It is all the same process of becoming. It is always you, yourself, inside—if you are in the present. And you will realize that you never get old. The whole process of aging is just another process of understanding where you are, at that moment. When you live in that moment only, there is no aging process. There is no start and no end. There just is. As you start to unfold this understanding, you will start to see this clearer and clearer in your life. As you are continually becoming whatever it is you are becoming, you start to break away from the whole concept of aging, and then the whole idea of your process starts to unfold by itself. You just go from one aspect to the next.

Fig. 10.4. When you live in the moment or the present, you never age.

This also brings in the concept of the grazing principle. We have horses in a field, and they just start eating. It is living in the moment. Before long in the continuing process of eating, a horse pulls its head up and looks around and sees the other horses across the field. This is all a part of being present in the now: by just concentrating on chewing the grass, the horse ends up across the field. The same process happens in your own understanding as you take each step on your journey, climbing up that mountain, or in that process of becoming. You just focus on the step of living in the now, one step at a time.

Fig. 10.5. The grazing principle—another example of living in the now.

Then, before long, you are at the top of the mountain. And you look around and you see another mountain. As you see another mountain, you start to become what it is you are supposed to become and you just focus on the next step. As you focus on the next step, your life becomes simpler instead of worrying about where you are going and how you are going to get there. You just focus and live in that moment. That moment will take you to the next step.

That is the whole idea of the Tao and the whole process of moving beyond infinity. You move beyond time and space. You move beyond everything that is constricting you in your understandings of who you are and where you are going. So, life is just really one step at a time. If you are present and living in the present, you will start to see that within yourself. As you start to see that within yourself, you will start to connect with that energy completely within. Once you discover that, you move beyond time and space, beyond aging, and beyond every aspect of being. You just continually become what it is you are becoming. As you focus using the grazing principle in

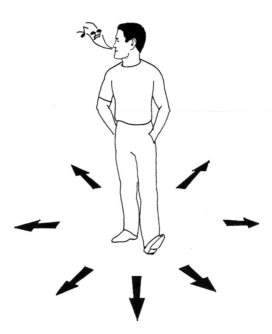

Fig. 10.6. You move beyond time and space one step at a time.

that moment, it will take you to the next moment and the next and the next. It will take you to the next mountain and to the next mountain. It is just a process of gathering information and experiences; you will start to understand and start to become. That really is the whole process of becoming who you are and what it is that you are becoming. It does not really matter *what* you are becoming. It is just a matter of focusing on the moment, and focusing on being present to whatever is happening.

As you are present, you will start to make these discoveries of what it is you are supposed to discover. It is quite simple when you take out the intention of trying to get somewhere, because there is really nowhere to go. Once you live in the now, the present, you look at the world and know where that is. It is now here. So when you are now here, there is nowhere to go or to become and you cannot come from anywhere because you are now here. If you are always here now, you will always be present in what is. Each time you look up, you will see another mountain to climb and then you will just focus on what you are doing and it will lead you to the next mountain. That is really the whole process of being present and being focused on what you are doing; and releasing any other understandings to just be present one moment at a time.

NO TIME OR SPACE

How do you get beyond infinity? There is another whole dimension within. It is like a door. In deep meditation you get to a certain point and you open a door within and you go into nothingness. This is infinity but it is beyond it. There is no measure of time or space. There is no measure or goal of becoming. It just is, which is dimensionless.

The more you meditate, the more you practice, the further and further you get into this consciousness. It is beyond words. It is beyond definition. It is beyond everything. It is going within. It is going into nothingness. It is beyond infinity. It is beyond any type of concept you can grasp.

Fig. 10.7. In deep meditation you get to a certain point and you open a door and go into nothingness.

This is the journey that you take when you focus within, moving beyond time and space, moving beyond your five senses and moving into a dimension of nothingness. It is beyond anything you can conceive. It is beyond the whole concept of infinity. You move beyond, beyond, beyond. You just are in the oneness of the universe. As you connect with that oneness, you start to feel your inner harmony and inner peace. It is just a matter of connecting and focusing, while instructing yourself to connect with it a little bit each day.

As you connect with it, a funny thing takes place. After a period of time, you start to move into this consciousness and it happens spontaneously at any time. It is this oneness and the feeling of connecting to the universe into the emptiness beyond. Spontaneously, it will start to occur in your life. All of a sudden, your body will shift and your consciousness will shift into it automatically. It will happen for five or ten minutes at a time. You will just feel suspended, like you are there but you are not there. You see everything but you are really not connected to anything. You are totally detached, totally in the feeling of this oneness, deep into the nothingness beyond infinity, fully into

Fig. 10.8. The more you practice, the further you get beyond words, beyond definition, beyond everything—going into nothingness, beyond infinity.

the molecular structure deep within your body and deep within your surroundings. Then you will just open up again and you are present to where you are at.

It will start to happen periodically many times in the course of your life. Then one day, it happens for twenty-four hours. You just feel totally at one and at peace with yourself, connected to the universe. This is how saints or sages feel. In this oneness, you move

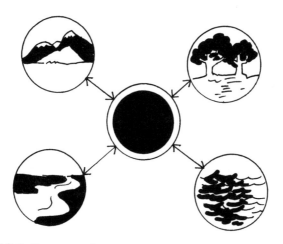

Fig. 10.9. Oneness will spontaneously start to occur in your life.

beyond infinity. You just are, beyond any measure of time or space. This feeling is one of stillness and a oneness within. This is how it takes place within your body on a molecular level, transcending your body into your emotional, psychological, and spiritual bodies, moving beyond anything that you were connected with before. This is moving beyond infinity, into the emptiness of nothingness.

Many practitioners use these meditative practices initially to get this feeling deep within. They can use their breath. As they breathe, they focus on the breath—breathing in, breathing out, breathing in, breathing out—thus relaxing and feeling the energy moving in and out of their body. They get slowly focused on every aspect of the breath. The same situation occurs as the horse chews the grass with the grazing principle. You start chewing the air, breathing in, breathing out, while taking long, deep breaths. As you start to focus on the breath filtering in your body, you become present, and all of a sudden you start to connect with that inner essence and there is a complete blank into the oneness of the void. You move beyond infinity and just go into the total emptiness of nothingness.

As you move in that direction, you start to connect with the whole universe and every aspect of it. You feel that oneness within, deep within yourself. You will be moving yourself beyond time and space. You are moving the energy beyond, beyond, beyond. This is the whole concept that you are achieving while focusing on the breath as you move through your practices, opening up the chi. You start to enter that calmness as you slow the mind down. As it speeds up in the various openings of the practice, it gets lost within you.

The whole concept of activity leads to nonactivity. Once you follow yourself in a nonactivity, you get completely absorbed. You get to a space, a gap that separates the positive and the negative. Your consciousness enters that gap, being in the presence of nothingness moving beyond infinity into a void parting from time and space where everything just is.

The whole inner space that you start to connect with feels complete within yourself. You are totally at peace and at one with the

Fig. 10.10. Activity leads to nonactivity and nonactivity leads to activity.

universe. You are totally in connection with yourself and everything around you. This is moving beyond infinity going into that empty space within.

CHRIST ON THE CROSS

When you get beyond infinity, you begin to realize that we are caught up in a struggle with good and evil—positive and negative. That struggle is really a trick. The biggest illusion within the Christian background is Christ on the cross. When Christ was on the cross there was a good thief and a bad thief on crosses next to him. The good thief was on the right-hand side and the bad thief was on the left-hand side, but they were both thieves, stealing His energy.

One was a positive energy on the right, and the other was the negative energy on the left. The positive energy is Lucifer and the

Fig. 10.11. Christ was on the cross with a good thief and a bad thief on crosses next to him.

negative energy is Satan. These are the Luciferian and satanic forces in the universe. They are both demonic. They are both the devil and they both take our energy.

In life, you have the right path and the left path. Now who was in the middle? Christ was, and His is the middle path, the path of the Tao. It is always a struggle for you to do what is right but if it goes too far and you do what is wrong, that can go too far as well. It is always pulling you away from the center, the middle path, the effortless path of the Tao.

This moves you from right to left and left to right. It is like going down a river in a canoe. If you keep hitting the bank, it is a rocky ride. But as you slow the mind down and start to focus, you keep in the middle on the center path, and then you do not rock as much or hit the shore. Finally you go in the center and you hit the center line or the point into infinity. Deep within, you go beyond infinity with the middle path. You hit the path and as you go down that path, you can interact internally with infinity, going beyond infinity into the void.

The left and right paths are continually pulling you away from

Fig. 10.12. Your Christ-self is the middle path, the path of the Tao.

your center, away from your energy that you connect with internally. As you lose your center, you get taken away from where you are trying to focus. As you start to focus there, you start to discover that everything positive or negative is really pulling you away from where you truly are going to be going. This brings you into the effortless path, while letting go of the right and left paths.

As you balance the right and the left, you start to focus on this energy in the middle and this will lead you down the inner path without any obstructions. You can see the right and the left, avoiding them. Now this is illustrated throughout the history of humanity. You have humankind, as you see, wanting to go into extremes. The extreme of Luciferian is righteousness, trying to uphold what we are trying to do. Everything is up front but it goes too far and it puts us in catastrophic situations, which brings us totally out of alignment with our inner peace and being.

This is illustrated in Catholicism and the church practices with the

Fig. 10.13. Extreme Luciferian actions are a form of righteousness
that leads to catastrophic situations.

executions in the Inquisition and the Crusades. When you kill for Christ, your action goes totally beyond the spiritual realm of Christianity to something that is not Christian. The Inquisition and the Crusades went too far right, too far into righteousness. This tendency is illustrated in

Fig. 10.14. Executions in the Inquisition and the Crusades, when they
killed for Christ, are examples of righteousness going too far.

today's society, as well, with the right-wing Christians who go for very strong extremes that eliminate many aspects of their being from the consciousness of what really is and what really works.

The left is the governments. They live in deceit or the darkness. Everything is hidden and they try to trick people into getting involved too far to the left, which is satanic. They bring us way, way to the left with deception and deceit, tricking us into thinking we are doing something good. In reality, they are taking somebody else's freedoms away. It is all part of control. Governmental control is what creates enslavement.

But the middle path is compelling. It is your Christ path. It is your path of self-discovery. That is the path connecting yourself back to yourself, discovering your own divinity and moving with that divinity into the void, going beyond infinity. The middle path connects you with your true essence, your true being and true aspect of yourself. This all takes place as you start to see the right and the left, which

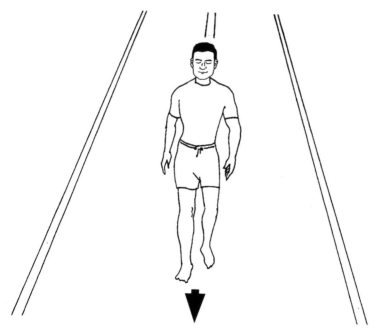

Fig. 10.15. The middle path is compelling; it is your Christ path and the path of self-discovery.

shows you the middle. When you witness this you allow yourself to accept what is there to help guide you down the middle path. This is the key to the whole process of the Tao.

Take the middle road or middle path, going not too far right nor too far left, which is further illustrated in the river as you start to see the right bank and the left bank. But your path, the path of discovery in the continuum, moves you down that river, and then you will discover who you are, where you are going, and how you are getting there. It is all done in the moment. This is the whole process of being at one with yourself in complete alignment with what is going on.

OUR GREATEST TEACHERS

This struggle of good and evil is to take your energy and attention away from the middle path. This is the struggle of duality. When you go too far right, you struggle with the Luciferian forces of righteousness and justice, but if it goes too far and becomes too extreme it causes pain and suffering to yourself and others. In the West, if you grow up in the Christian churches, you are raised Luciferian, as history shows with the Crusades and the Inquisition. As a sage once said, "The last Christian died on the cross."

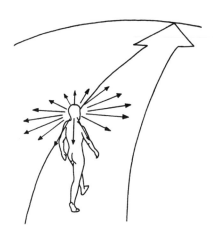

Fig. 10.16. The right and left paths are our greatest teachers; they indirectly show us the middle.

Or you go too far left with the satanic forces of darkness and deceit while essentially pulling yourself away from the Christ path or middle path. You can see this with the government intervention and manipulation by special interest groups that use the government and victimize the masses.

They are all competing for your energy, which is the struggle between good and evil. You are pulled in one direction and then you are pulled in the other direction. They are fighting one another. But that is not the real message and the real purpose in your life. Your real purpose in this life is to connect with yourself, which is connection with your godhead. This godhead is not too far right and too far left. This godhead of self-discovery is in the middle. It is a balance of right and left and that is the Tao.

When you are imbalanced you have obstructions and that is

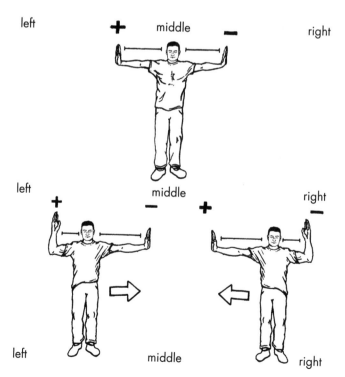

Fig. 10.17. The right and left paths are competing for your energy because they live off it.

exactly what occurs. When you balance yourself, you are not too far right and not too far left. In reality Lucifer and Satan, the right and the left paths, are not evil at all. They are really just our greatest teachers. They show us where the middle path is and teach us what not to do. They show us when you are too much to the right or too much to the left. So they can be used as guidelines to guide us through the correct path, the middle path. They help us directly down the middle path. If you look at them in this way, they will guide you. The right and left paths are a type of guidance to find the middle path.

So you should welcome them as your teacher and pay attention to whether you are too far right or too far left. Now these extremes lead us in a whole different direction. What happens is we get so caught up in the right or the left, we get stuck in a certain pattern and we stay there and our continuum does not continue. We get taken off in a whole other direction. What happens is we lose focus of our own center and who we are.

That is exactly what occurs in our societies with the influences of the right and left paths. They take us in a whole different direction and we lose sight of who we really are and where we are truly going. We get caught in this diversion of the monkey mind, tricking us with the right and left of right and wrong when nothing is right or wrong. This is what the forces of the collective evil try to do in undermining our whole process of flowing down the river. They try to pull us away from going down our true path, the middle path.

It is really only about our energy, because the Luciferian and the satanic forces are really parasites taking our energy and our force in a whole other direction to support them and what they are trying to do. You can find this in society especially with telecommunications today. Everybody's trying to convince you to go their way. Do this. Do that. It takes up all your energy and time.

Really, it is pointless until you get to the point where you want to do nothing. That is really the point where you want to be. Let the energy flow within you and your path will start to open up for you. It is very evident in our society in the West today that everybody is

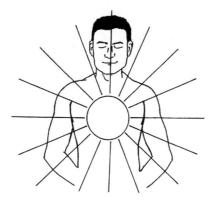

Fig. 10.18. The only peace you will find in this life is connected within yourself; it is your center.

trying to go somewhere but there is not anywhere to go. All you can be is where you are at and that is where you should be.

If you just focus on the present, living in the now, that is all you will ever really experience, and you will not torment yourself with the right and the left. You can simply look at them and see what not to do because it pulls you away from your center.

The only peace you will find in your life is connection within yourself. It is your center. This whole process continually moves you beyond time and space and beyond infinity, moving you beyond any type of measurement. That is living in the now, living in the present. As you start to connect with that energy, you will start to see where you are at and where you are going. That whole process is just slowing down the mind so it can observe what is really there. As you observe you start to feel and connect with that energy, knowing that energy will take you where you are supposed to go. It just takes time and practice, but as you slow your mind down, this becomes very clear to you and you start to experience all these aspects of life.

FULL ATTENTION

This can get pretty tricky because once you start to balance yourself and feel that you are in the middle, you can say to yourself, "I am in the middle, I am in the middle." But if you do not pay attention, all of a sudden, the right and left move or the right and left have moved. If you do not move, you are no longer in the middle. You are no longer in the center, but you think you are still in the middle because you did not move. You did not pay attention. You did not adjust yourself.

The Tao says, "You must pay attention every minute of the day all the time because everything is always moving." That is what awareness is, to be conscious means to pay attention. You have to adjust yourself by either moving to the right or to the left to keep yourself balanced, staying in your center. This connects to infinity, allowing yourself to move beyond infinity. As you practice the Taoist system, you begin to understand this and to experience this in your life.

When you look at something you presume it takes place from your perspective. You have to first of all situate yourself so you can see things as they are, and see things for what they are. As you start to look at the right and the left, you think your position is in the middle. As you gauge yourself in the middle, you start to understand that it takes time just to observe where the middle is, based on your perception of where you are looking from. So the right and the left show you where the middle is. But if you think the middle is going to stay in one position all the time, then you are in for a rude awakening, because everything is constantly changing. The right and left are always changing. What worked today might not work tomorrow or what did not work today could work tomorrow.

That is why we have a lot of these moral codes and situations with religious or governmental rules, but everything changes periodically, so the right and the left change. If you are not paying attention to the rules both of the right and the left, you lose your center and perspective. That is what happened to the religions in the Crusades and the Inquisition many centuries ago.

It seems correct one day and then several days later is not. It shifted because the right and the left shifted. They positioned themselves in situations that contradicted their whole principle of their existence. If you are stuck in dogma or in situations that are inflexible, it puts you either way right or way left, and you lose your center. That is how our collective mind, the ego, the monkey mind, tricks you.

This is a whole process of self-realization of where you are at now. You get lost in the changing evolution of where you are coming from and where you are going. It takes time to really see this in force. So if you do not pay attention, you can be way too far left or too far right because they are both changing at all times.

This happens in every aspect of your life as in your diet and how you progress in your life. What was correct today might not be correct tomorrow and you will have to change your diet. You have to change where you are at now to balance and keep your energy at a balanced state. As your body changes and various aspects of yourself change in this whole growth process, you shift to different stages, but if you are not paying attention, making certain adjustments, then you are too far left or too far right. You could be in a health situation that needs change to correct itself.

You need to change when your environment changes and you need to change yourself. There are so many different changes in life. That is why you need to pay attention. You cannot really be restricted to what was correct one day because that might not be correct today, because everything shifts and changes in every aspect. So you need to pay attention.

You need to look at things as they are, seeing the right and the

Fig. 10.19. The whole process of self-realization is where you are at now.

Fig. 10.20. When your environment changes inside and outside
you need to make adjustments.

left and realizing the right and the left do change and do shift. If they shift, you look to find the middle path. You are going to have to change your position to center yourself in that middle path and have a continual connection with yourself.

Not only do you focus within and feel the essence moving beyond time and space, but you also witness the right and left to make sure your position is in the middle. It is a whole process. But if you are aware of the concept that the right and the left do change, then they are really not our enemy but our friend and our teacher and they show us where the middle path is. Paying attention is all we need to do to see where they are at and to see where we are going.

BECOMING DETACHED

Once you find the center point in your path, you begin to connect with infinity. That infinity takes you on its own path. The key is learning to let go and become detached. We hold on to everything like squeezing our fists together. We cut off the flow of nature or the flow of the universe, but gradually, as we learn to let go, our fingers loosen and the energy starts to flow through our fingers. In Western psychology, they call it surrender. In Christianity, they call it forgiveness. In the Tao, they call it being detached.

When you start to squeeze or hang on, becoming attached to something, you have cut off that flow, that effortless flow of the universe. As you cut it off, you disconnect from the connection that you are seeking by hanging on to a situation. A lot of times, as we progress in our continuum, climbing one mountain to the next, we get attached to one particular step on the mountain.

It could be in relationships. It could be in fantasizing, having a good time, becoming stuck in our adolescence or our childhood, or in a particular location or a particular aspect of some relationship that we have. When the universe is pulling, we hold on to it and we do not connect. We disconnect from the flow by being connected to something else. By not being detached we are not letting go of the certain circumstances that we are clinging to.

Some aspects of this people call a plateau—like getting stuck on a plateau that seems so wonderful that we never want to leave it. In the whole process of being attached to it we miss out on the full continuum of our evolution. So it is a whole process of becoming but in becoming you must learn to let go of what you became. It is all a part of the process.

Not that it is right or wrong but it really impedes that connection that you really seek, which is the connection with yourself. So we are continually becoming, and if we become too attached to what we

Fig. 10.21. As you let go, your whole life will unfold.

become, we need to show a detachment to see things as they are and let go of them as they unfold.

This is quite true in relationships where we get so connected or attached to certain resentment toward others and what they did to us, what they are doing to us, or what they are attempting to do toward us. If we just forgive them and let go, then we proceed on our own continuum. But if we get stuck to certain resentments, certain hatred, or certain anger toward them, then it holds us back in that continuum.

So you must look at it from that light. But the only way to let go of it is to forgive them for what they are doing and forgive yourself for becoming attached to it. This is the whole aspect of letting go or becoming detached. That happens with many events in our lives. We are so excited and we have achieved so much or gained so many things that we want to continue to live that way. When other things change in our lives then we really cannot live that way again.

In sports, when people play so well at such a point or level, they become so attached to it they never move on in their life. They never move on into other areas of their lives where they can discover other aspects of themselves. So you need to let go or become detached in this whole process of becoming and let go of what you became so you can become something more by climbing the next mountain.

Fig. 10.22. Everything is always changing. What once was is no longer, and we must let go.

This is the whole process of letting go and becoming detached. We achieve certain things in our lives that we are quite proud of and become too attached, such that we really lose the concept of letting go. We need to let go to become. If you are always hanging on to what you became, then you never will become what you can become. It is all a part of the process of learning to let go and learning to become detached.

THE EFFORTLESS PATH

As energy continues to flow and you gain more and more confidence in letting go, a strange thing happens. You learn to flow with it and your life becomes effortless. This really is the path of the Tao, the effortless path. In other words, the universe is moving through you all the time. That is the life force and that flow is very strong; but we resist the flow or we try to hang on to it instead of letting go.

When you hang on to it you get cut off from it or you block it. When you let it go, the flow will eventually pick you up and take you where you are supposed to go, which is the direction of the flow. The flow knows where it is going. You do not really need to know where it is going because it will show you where it is going and then you will experience it spontaneously, without knowing, and experience it fully. That really is the flow of the universe, the flow of our own energy vibrating.

Fig. 10.23. As you gain more and more confidence in letting go, a strange thing happens. You learn to flow with it and your life becomes effortless.

To truly appreciate the flow, we need to be balanced and centered within ourselves to connect with it. That is the whole process of letting go and becoming detached. That will lead us to many more discoveries that we had no idea we were supposed to discover. It leads us to many more mountains to climb, many more summits to achieve and experience. It is all a part of this process of letting go. Without the letting go, you will never understand what you are supposed to become. The monkey mind tricks us into holding on because it does not want to change and have you discover who you really are. It convinces us that we have done it and we have gotten the best we can get.

In reality, there is no best. There is no worst. There is only another mountain to climb, another becoming and another understanding. It is just another aspect of becoming ourselves, but the monkey mind holds us back. It is what we talk about in a lot of other aspects of our own path. But that path is really inundated with the flow of our energy. Our path is the flow of the energy and the flow of the energy connects us back to ourselves.

Getting back to ourselves is getting to our own divinity and it is this whole path that leads us back to our true self, back to who we really are and back to our own understanding of what is. If we become too attached, life becomes an effort with too much pain, too much suffering, and too much struggle, because we are resisting the path that flows within us. It could be our natural path, what we are geared to do in life and to become. We really need to find our own bliss

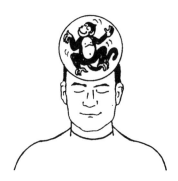

Fig. 10.24. The monkey mind tricks us into holding on.

and that is what is effortless to do, which is the nature flow moving through us. We should only do things that are really easy for us to do. Certain aspects of life are easy and certain other aspects are not easy. As you discover that, you will discover your own path and that is the effortless path, becoming who you are and what you are.

This is the effortless path. In our lives, once you are attached or detached from all the other connections in life, then you start to open yourself up to the effortless path. We really are free as a bird. We just complicate things by going out and desiring things that are not really necessary for us in our lives. It is all part of practicing and experiencing other aspects of life. When things cause pain and suffering, that means you are swimming against the river.

For the effortless path we need to see the right and the left and discover our center, which is the one that is the easiest for us to take. It is the most comfortable and there is no pain or suffering involved as we float down that river. It becomes effortless. You just put your feet up and enjoy the ride; that really is the effortless path. If we are doing something in our life that causes us pain and suffering for whatever reason, then we should change and not do it. We should see the right and the left and make the adjustments, finding our center, the center of the path, and take that path. If we could put our feet up and enjoy the ride, then that is the path we should take.

We are so conditioned by our monkey mind (collective egos) of doing this and doing that, we lose the whole concept that we are

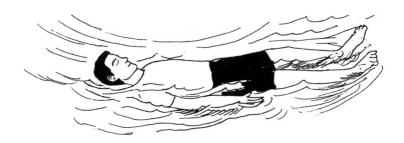

Fig. 10.25. Find your center from the right and left and follow
the effortless path.

supposed to be doing nothing, flowing down the effortless path and enjoying the ride. That is the path where there is no effort involved and it takes no strain or energy from us. We just observe what is the easiest course to achieve something and take that course, the course with the least resistance, the natural flow; but it is even beyond least resistance. It has an energy of its own and it flows. It is the natural flow like a river within us. All you have to do is just put your feet up and enjoy it. You just pay attention to the rocks and the obstacles in the way by adjusting yourself and positioning yourself to avoid them. If you hit one, then it causes pain and suffering, so you have to move out of the way of whatever obstructions are in your life. As you live this way your life becomes peaceful and you become centered and at harmony with yourself. That is what we really seek within ourselves, which is harmony. Without it, our life becomes miserable and it becomes an effort for us to do anything.

It is pretty obvious in our physical body that if we eat certain things that we think of as pleasurable, we cause an imbalance in the body, and the body puts on fat, which makes it hard to move our bodies. If somebody weighs three hundred pounds, how are you going to get out of a car or walk or do anything? That is swimming against the river. So you have got to look at the right and the left and find out what you need to do to balance your body to be a normal weight so you can move around easily and maintain without any effort on your part. When you are 300 pounds and your ideal weight is 150 pounds, it is not easy to get out of bed, walk around, or defecate.

This is just one aspect of the physical level. It's the same thing with the foods we eat. If they cause us pain and suffering with the heavy sweets, we should not eat them. If we smoke, and we are coughing and being uncomfortable, we should stop because it's causing obstructions in your body. These habits cause an effort to breathe, an effort to talk, and an effort to do anything.

These are all efforts. This is not the effortless path. With the effortless path you use no energy and everything gets done. That is the path of the Tao. So if you continue to put these obstructions in

Fig. 10.26. If you smoke, it is an effort to breathe, so let go of smoking.

your life, you really have to look at them from the right and the left. You have gone too far right or too far left. Then you just become detached, letting go of them, and they will disappear. All the obstructions cause all the effort in your life.

That is on the physical plane, but the same thing is true with the emotional level. You get involved with people who are not balanced or people who are not in concurrence with your natural flow and it causes obstructions. There are disagreements and shouting, which could lead to violence and upset your peace of mind. Many people are not of like mind and this leads to misunderstandings and confusion. There is an uncomfortable feeling and then it is an effort to be in their presence. Then you get someone who is in balance or who is connected with your energy. It becomes effortless to be around them. It is a joy. You look forward to talking with them, being with them, and being in their company. The same thing happens mentally and intellectually when you are around people who are argumentative or do not have your similar understandings, similar backgrounds, or similar concerns. It just creates an effort to be with them and to be around them. You cannot even communicate with them. It is just totally painful to be around them.

In your spiritual essence, it is also the same. If you are not connected with a deep understanding in life, there are times when you try

Fig. 10.27. With the effortless path, you do not put yourself in uncomfortable situations.

to connect with other people who are pulling you from the energy that you are trying to embrace and interact with. The path flows within you on a spiritual energetic level. Do not put yourself in certain positions where you do not feel comfortable. It is not really your essence or your real being and these situations lead you away from the effortless path of the Tao.

If you see it is not effortless, then you should not be doing it. You need to make changes and adjustments in your life. The Tao is always telling us to make adjustments. You have forces coming from all different directions. What worked today might not work tomorrow. You are getting pushed from different angles and different directions. So you have to make an adjustment in your alignment and structure to connect with the energy and send it through your body. You can realign yourself and then it becomes effortless.

This is brought out a lot in the Taoist practices when you do the Iron Shirt Practice with the Pushing techniques. People push you from the front, back, right, and left, emotionally and psychologically. You have got to make certain adjustments to align your body to connect with the energy and send it into the earth. This only requires certain slight adjustments in your structure without losing your grounding. This is the same in your life. You have to make these adjustments so you can start to reconnect yourself with the earth force. With this realignment you start to move in that effortless path again because if life is an effort then you are doing something wrong and you need to change. When you change, you align yourself so you can start to experience that effortless path again.

AMAZING GRACE

This is no longer your earthly realm. It is the heavenly realm and it will take you wherever it takes you. It first carries you with grace. The religions call it God's amazing grace, but it is your collective consciousness that moves you. That is where you connect and go beyond infinity. Once you make this connection within you start to see and experience a whole other aspect of yourself and a whole other aspect of the universe.

Grace is a beautiful experience and there is complete joy in this effortless path. When you feel this inner connection your life becomes full, and it becomes completely effortless. There is no effort to do anything. When you make this connection, grace comes over you. It is like a goodness that flows through you and adds a whole other dimension to your life.

Fig. 10.28. When you feel this inner connection, your life becomes full and completely effortless.

This is the grace of the universe. It is having your body alignment in such a way that there is a whole other energy that comes out and takes over. That energy will take you to experience even a deeper connection within yourself to where you are and where you are going. It is really effortless without explanation. It is just having the correct alignment and connection, and then just experiencing it.

As you flow down the universe and as you flow down the river of life, you will start to discover this amazing grace. You will start to experience this grace. This is the effortless existence that you will experience within yourself and around yourself. It just takes time to develop this within yourself through the practices of the Tao in aligning and refining or correcting yourself until you make the right connection within yourself and this amazing grace automatically comes out.

This is the grace of the universe. This is the effortless bliss that you experience through every aspect of your being. It gives you a graceful experience of your life, through your analogy of yourself—who you are and where you are going. It will start to make your whole essence one with the universe.

Really, it is the mixing of the steaming process in the Taoist practices of the Kan and Li when you align the fire underneath the water, the emotional energy underneath the sexual energy. As the fire heats the water, the water produces steam. This steam is the grace or love that you will experience within yourself and transform the perception of everything around you.

This is the amazing aspect of the love itself. As you move into this grace or steam within yourself, you will start to experience a purification and it will start to create an energy within itself. It is an energy that makes you move beyond what you are and you will continue to experience this throughout your life and throughout your universe. It just takes time. As this slowly unfolds, you will start to experience this in every aspect of your life.

Your life becomes a true joy and a true amazing grace comes from within yourself. You will emulate this with every person you meet and everywhere you go. This will become more prominent as you experience it more fully in your life. This amazing grace, which is achieved through the alignment of your internal structure, is created by the emotional energy underneath the sexual energy giving you the steam. This is amazing grace that comes out as a whole burst of energy in your body as you follow the effortless path of the Tao.

ENJOYING THE RIDE

Where do you go from here? You have just read a lot of interesting concepts but what do you do with them? Absolutely nothing. That is the Tao. That is confusing for you, but when you start practicing the Taoist formulas through instruction and by doing nothing, it will make sense to you.

You will discover nondoing or doing nothing, what the Tao calls Wu Wei. It is the art of doing nothing, and it is really doing correct action. Correct action is the Wu Wei. It is letting go of your will, which is the action on your part. As you let go, the energy, chi, flows through you, and eventually by practicing the Taoist formulas doing correct action you will connect with that energy and become one with it. That is the Tao.

Fig. 10.29. Wu Wei is the art of doing nothing, which is really doing correct action.

The Tao says there are three ways of enlightenment. The first one is prayer and worship, which can be achieved but you do not know when, why, or how it is done. The second way is one of good works and service. But, again, you do not know when, why, or how it is done.

The third way is the way of the Tao, which is one of knowledge and wisdom. You know when, why, and how because it is an alchemical process on the molecular level. This will become clear to you as you practice. You will know when to be hard and when to be soft. That is wisdom and that is the Tao.

To enjoy the ride is discovering the art of doing nothing. As you discover that art, you will discover that the key is not to obstruct the natural flow with your action. So it consists of learning to observe and witnessing the right and the left as they unfold. As you start to witness the right and the left, you will discover what not to do. Only observing is your action and allowing that natural flow to flow through you effortlessly without any obstructions.

To observe without any external obstructions or any obstructions

Fig. 10.30. There are three ways of enlightenment: first, prayer and worship, and second, good works and service, both of which can be achieved but you do not know when, why, or how they are done. The third way, the way of the Tao, is one of knowledge and wisdom.

that you create by your activity is really what correct action is. That is to allow the natural flow of the universe to pass through you and carry you into the next situation or the next direction in your life. It is just observing by slowing the mind down, watching the right and the left, that gives you your directions on how to find the middle path.

Once you make that alignment with the middle path, you will start to discover that with nonaction you connect yourself with the true action of the universe. It is the natural flow of the universe and it will take you wherever you are supposed to go. On that journey you will discover the third way of enlightenment, which is the Tao, and that is one of knowledge and wisdom. That is the art of knowing when to be soft and when to be hard. In other words, there are certain times when you do not want to force your own energy and your energy is just to be soft and yield to the energy around you.

Then at a certain point, now and again, you need to put your foot down and be hard. You stand for what are the important aspects of your life and the integrity that needs to be shown and that needs to be experienced by you and others around you. It is paramount to what you are trying to do or become. This is when you need to be hard and explain things very clearly and very strongly to anyone that causes resistance toward you.

This is the art of wisdom and this is the Tao. This is all explained in every aspect of your understandings, as every experience that you encounter on your journey will be revealed to you for each phase of your life. You will start to understand every aspect of your being, your life, and everything around you. Everything will become clearer to you as you practice the Tao and its understandings.

We want to thank you for your time and attention. We trust that you will see your journey's way a little clearer and begin to understand and experience the way, knowing that the key to life is to enjoy the ride. So as you enjoy the ride, put your feet up and smile to yourself, feeling the energy take you where you are supposed to go on the effortless path of the Tao. Thank you again and we are going to close this final chapter giving you the real key to everything in the Tao.

ONLY THE HUMBLE CAN PERCEIVE
THE TRUTH

No matter what you know, you know nothing, for the Tao cannot be taught. Only the humble can perceive the truth, the Tao. This is a beautiful aspect of everything in the Tao. When you think you know everything, you know nothing. When you think you know nothing, you will discover everything.

Our ego or the monkey mind resists anything new. It resists anything that it cannot understand, which is everything. So only with humility can you attempt to understand what cannot be understood with the limitations of the mind, and with the understanding that you do not know everything. When you know that you know absolutely nothing, it will lead you to discover everything.

Because of that humility, you will start to understand where you are and where you are going—but only with humility will you discover the truth about who you are and where you have been and where you will go. It is a humbling stage in the process of life when you realize that you know nothing when you use your monkey mind to think because your monkey mind is your ego.

It is the I (ego) that separates you from your real self, which is the whole of the universe. We are all one and that oneness is our real being. We separate from it when we get lost in our false self, the ego. Once we can see and experience who we really are, then we perceive the truth, and the truth is the Tao.

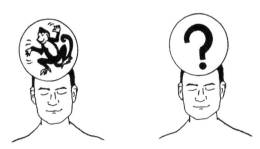

Fig. 10.31. Our ego or monkey mind resists anything new and what it cannot understand.

We step out of the illusions that we have created and become lost in. It is an amazing discovery as we realize the extent of our own self-entrapment of our collective karmic wheel and sojourn, but with that realization we also discover that we can walk out of this overwhelming entrapment because we created it.

We are the creator of what we are and we can manifest whatever we want. So we can write our own scenario for this sojourn and take it wherever we want. This is the message of the Tao. We can become an immortal and break the karmic wheel in one sojourn right now by living in the now, being in the Tao.

Life is simple and complete once you have the concept of what you are doing, which creates the desire to manifest what you want. Concept, desire, and manifestation are the whole process of becoming from the initial manifestation of the physical realm to every thought we have. It is all the same process for all of us. Just think it and you will become it. So become your own reality and this final note will help you on your journey and the realization of the Tao. But remember: only speak with simple words for the thoughts of others are slow, which allows you to disappear.

Final Note: On your journey, hold this thought and it will ease your way to the realization of the Tao: "A thousand friends are not enough, but one enemy is too many."

Fig. 10.32. We are the creator of what and who we are, and we can manifest whatever we want.

About the Authors

MANTAK CHIA

Mantak Chia has been studying the Taoist approach to life since childhood. His mastery of this ancient knowledge, enhanced by his study of other disciplines, has resulted in the development of the Universal Healing Tao system, which is now being taught throughout the world.

Mantak Chia was born in Thailand to Chinese parents in 1944. When he was six years old, he learned from Buddhist monks how to sit and "still the mind." While in grammar school he learned traditional Thai boxing, and he soon went on to acquire considerable skill in aikido, yoga, and Tai Chi. His studies of the Taoist way of life began in earnest when he was a student in Hong Kong, ultimately leading to his mastery of a wide variety of esoteric disciplines, with the guidance of several masters, including Master I Yun, Master Meugi, Master Cheng Yao Lun, and Master Pan Yu. To better understand the mechanisms behind healing energy, he also studied Western anatomy and medical sciences.

Master Chia has taught his system of healing and energizing practices to tens of thousands of students and trained more than two thousand instructors and practitioners throughout the world. He has established centers for Taoist study and training in many countries around the globe. In June of 1990, he was honored by the International Congress of Chinese Medicine and Qi Gong (Chi Kung), which named him the Qi Gong Master of the Year.

WILLIAM U. WEI

Born after World War II, growing up in the Midwest area of the United States, and trained in Catholicism, William Wei became a student of the Tao and started studying under Master Mantak Chia in the early 1980s. In the later 1980s he became a senior instructor of the Universal Healing Tao, specializing in one-on-one training. In the early 1990s William Wei moved to Tao Garden, Thailand, and assisted Master Mantak Chia in building Tao Garden Taoist Training Center. For six years William traveled to over thirty countries, teaching with Master Mantak Chia and serving as marketing and construction coordinator for the Tao Garden. Upon completion of Tao Garden in December 2000, he became project manager for all the Universal Tao Publications and products. With the purchase of a mountain with four waterfalls in southern Oregon, USA, in the late 1990s, William Wei is presently completing a Taoist Mountain Sanctuary for personal cultivation, higher-level practices, and ascension. William Wei is the coauthor with Master Chia of *Sexual Reflexology*, *Living in the Tao*, and the Taoist poetry book of 366 daily poems, *Emerald River*, which expresses the feeling, essence, and stillness of the Tao. He is also the cocreator with Master Mantak Chia of the Universal Healing Tao formula cards, Chi Cards (six sets of over 240 formulas), under the pen name The Professor—Master of Nothingness, the Myth that takes the Mystery out of Mysticism. William U. Wei, also known as Wei Tzu, is a pen name for this instructor so the instructor can remain anonymous and can continue to become a blade of grass in a field of grass.

The Universal Healing Tao System and Training Center

THE UNIVERSAL HEALING TAO SYSTEM

The ultimate goal of Taoist practice is to transcend physical boundaries through the development of the soul and the spirit within the human. That is also the guiding principle behind the Universal Healing Tao, a practical system of self-development that enables individuals to complete the harmonious evolution of their physical, mental, and spiritual bodies. Through a series of ancient Chinese meditative and internal energy exercises, the practitioner learns to increase physical energy, release tension, improve health, practice self-defense, and gain the ability to heal him- or herself and others. In the process of creating a solid foundation of health and well-being in the physical body, the practitioner also creates the basis for developing his or her spiritual potential by learning to tap into the natural energies of the sun, moon, earth, stars, and other environmental forces.

The Universal Healing Tao practices are derived from ancient techniques rooted in the processes of nature. They have been gathered and integrated into a coherent, accessible system for well-being that works directly with the life force, or chi, that flows through the meridian system of the body.

Master Chia has spent years developing and perfecting techniques for teaching these traditional practices to students around the world through ongoing classes, workshops, private instruction, and healing sessions, as well as books and video and audio products. Further information can be obtained at www.universal-tao.com.

THE UNIVERSAL HEALING TAO TRAINING CENTER

The Tao Garden Resort and Training Center in northern Thailand is the home of Master Chia and serves as the worldwide headquarters for Universal Healing Tao activities. This integrated wellness, holistic health, and training center is situated on eighty acres surrounded by the beautiful Himalayan foothills near the historic walled city of Chiang Mai. The serene setting includes flower and herb gardens ideal for meditation, open-air pavilions for practicing Chi Kung, and a health and fitness spa.

The center offers classes year round, as well as summer and winter retreats. It can accommodate two hundred students, and group leasing can be arranged. For information on courses, books, products, and other resources, see below.

RESOURCES

Universal Healing Tao Center
274 Moo 7, Luang Nua, Doi Saket, Chiang Mai, 50220 Thailand
Tel: (66)(53) 495-596 Fax: (66)(53) 495-852
E-mail: universaltao@universal-tao.com
Web site: www.universal-tao.com

For information on retreats and the health spa, contact:
Tao Garden Health Spa & Resort
E-mail: info@tao-garden.com, taogarden@hotmail.com
Web site: www.tao-garden.com

Good Chi • Good Heart • Good Intention

 Index

Italic page numbers indicate illustrations.

BOOKS OF RELATED INTEREST

The Secret Teachings of the Tao Te Ching
by Mantak Chia and Tao Huang

The Taoist Soul Body
Harnessing the Power of Kan and Li
by Mantak Chia

Healing Love through the Tao
Cultivating Female Sexual Energy
by Mantak Chia

Fusion of the Five Elements
Meditations for Transforming Negative Emotions
by Mantak Chia

Fusion of the Eight Psychic Channels
Opening and Sealing the Energy Body
by Mantak Chia

Healing Light of the Tao
Foundational Practices to Awaken Chi Energy
by Mantak Chia

Taoist Cosmic Healing
Chi Kung Color Healing Principles for
Detoxification and Rejuvenation
by Mantak Chia

Energy Balance through the Tao
Exercises for Cultivating Yin Energy
by Mantak Chia

INNER TRADITIONS • BEAR & COMPANY
P.O. Box 388
Rochester, VT 05767
1-800-246-8648
www.InnerTraditions.com

Or contact your local bookseller